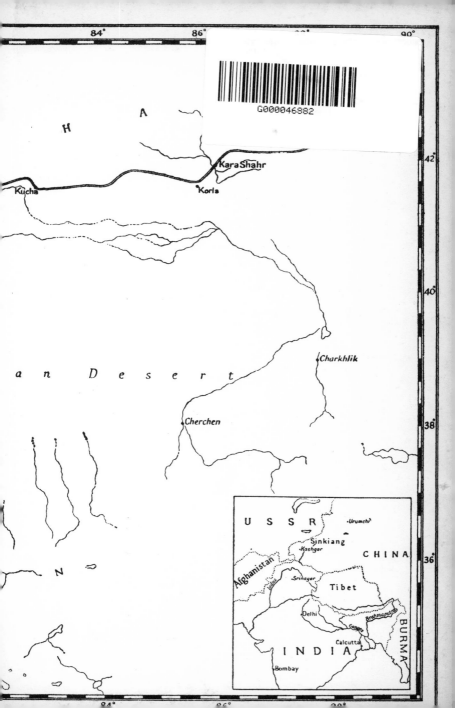

THE ANTIQUE LAND

KUNGUR, SEEN ON THE WAY TO OITAGH

The Antique Land

Diana Shipton

With a new Introduction by the Author

HONG KONG   OXFORD   NEW YORK
OXFORD UNIVERSITY PRESS
1987

Oxford University Press

Oxford New York Toronto
Petaling Jaya Singapore Hong Kong Tokyo
Delhi Bombay Calcutta Madras Karachi
Nairobi Dar es Salaam Cape Town
Melbourne Auckland

and associated companies in
Beirut Berlin Ibadan Nicosia

First published by Hodder and Stoughton 1950
This edition reprinted, with permission and with the addition
of an Introduction in Oxford Paperbacks 1987

ISBN 0 19 581588 2
OXFORD is a trade mark of Oxford University Press

Printed in Hong Kong by King's Time Printing Press Ltd.
Published by Oxford University Press, Warwick House, Hong Kong

Introduction

KASHGAR (KASHI) HAS LONG BEEN one of my dream places and from my earliest days travel has been part of my life. I was born in India in 1917, the daughter of a Forest Officer. Much of my early childhood was spent in the jungles of the United Provinces as we toured the district under my father's control. Roads were few, and we all travelled on elephants and lived in tents, our home being erected and collapsed every few days. Although it was a lonely and nomadic way of life it was some years before I realized how unusual it was to keep on the move, sleep in a tent, and never see a shop, a car, a church, or a tarmac road and passing traffic. My parents were there; dogs and elephants were there; all was familiar and secure.

When I was only five years old, my parents sent me to England where I continued my nomadic existence, living with a succession of relations; I grew up accustomed to this rootlessness. At the age of 20 I returned to India to stay with a married sister. As my brother-in-law was a Forest Officer, like my father, I was back in the northern jungles of India, and occasionally I travelled with him in the foothills, marvelling at the magnificence of the Himalayas. Beyond those great mountain barriers lay Central Asia, that vast, mysterious, and usually inaccessible land.

From childhood my heroines has been the 'lady travellers', as they were called: Isabella Bird, Mary Kingsley, and Freya Stark. Much as I loved lonely remote places, and longed to travel across deserts and explore mountain ranges, I lacked the courage and determination to pursue such dreams on my own. In India I found heroes too: the men who climbed and explored the ranges of northern India and Nepal. I read avidly about their attempts to conquer Everest and to penetrate Tibet and Afghanistan.

In 1939, while staying in Srinagar in Kashmir with friends of my parents, I met Eric Shipton, one of the heroes of my Everest reading. He was preparing for an expedition to the largely unknown Aghil Range, part of the Karakoram Range, and our hosts had invited all the members of the expedition, including their Sherpa porters, to camp in their grounds. In addition to all the bustle of their preparations, there were many social activities for the team as they made ready to leave for a winter in unexplored territory. In that magic land of lakes and mountains, romance flourished in a round of parties and picnics, and as we floated in the gondola-like boats on the Dal lake.

To my surprise, Eric invited another girl, Helen, and me to accompany his expedition for the first five days. To my even greater surprise, we were allowed to accept. This was my first experience of the tough routine of an exploratory expedition. There were none of the small luxuries of a Forest Officer's tours. Instead there were early dawn starts, long hot marches, and an evening meal of stew, prepared by the Sherpas and eaten around the fire. Eric gave me my first lessons in walking up steep hills properly, the scenery was magnificent, and the whole experience was exhilarating and exhausting. Then, with Nanga Parbat gleaming in the distance, Helen and I had to turn back.

When war was declared later that year, Eric's expedition returned to India and he joined the British army. Shortly afterwards, he was delighted to be offered the post of British Consul-General at Kashgar, in Sinkiang (Xinjiang) province in China. Its remoteness as well as its political sensitivity made it a difficult assignment. During this time, I was serving with the Auxiliary Territorial Service in England, and Eric and I did not meet again until 1942, when he had left Kashgar and had returned to England. We were married during one of my short leaves, but, apart from occasional snatched meetings, it was not until 1946 that we could enjoy married life together.

Eric was serving in Vienna when, in 1946, he was offered a second tour in Kashgar as Consul-General. With my taste for remote and mountainous country, I could not conceive of a more exciting challenge, but it involved an agonizing decision. Our son Nicolas was only nine months old — too young to face the rigours of the journey, let alone the basic lifestyle and limited medical facilities of Kashgar. After much heart-searching we left him in England in the care of someone we trusted. The remoteness of Sinkiang in 1946 may be seen in the fact that during our two years there we had no more than seven foreign visitors. (Modern tour operators now take as many as 50 visitors a day to Kashgar.)

After India became independent in 1948, the British Consulate in Kashgar was closed. Eric's next posting was to Yunnan in southwest China, where he was appointed Consul-General in Kunming. This posting brought fresh political problems. We were warned that as Mao Zedong's Communist army was marching inexorably south through China, the British Consulate might be at risk. If the Nationalist government fell and Britain refused to recognize the new regime, the Communists might in turn refuse to recognize the British representative.

However, Eric accepted the post for as long as it lasted. The lure of new and beautiful country was too strong to resist. This time we took four-year-old Nicolas with us, and our second son, John, was born in Kunming in 1950. We enjoyed our short time there and while freedom lasted we travelled as widely as we could. When life became hazardous as well as circumscribed, I decided that the time had come to leave with the children. Eric had to stay until he was officially recalled. My journey out of China, mostly by a series of steamers down the Yangtze River (Chang Jiang), was dramatic as well as difficult, and I shall never forget the kindness of the ever-increasing numbers of expelled missionaries who helped me on my way.

When Eric arrived home we had to rethink our future yet again, bearing in mind the fact that Eric was not an established member of the consular service. It was then that Everest loomed in his life again. He was asked to organize an expedition to try to approach the world's highest mountain from the south, the northern route now being closed. Although his reconnaissance was entirely successful, to his great disappointment he was not chosen to lead the assault expedition of 1953. Instead he entered a quite different world, becoming Warden of the Outward Bound Mountain School at Eskdale, Cumberland, in England.

Sadly, it was here that our paths divided. Eric writes in his autobiography, *That Untravelled World*, 'Diana and I started to form attachments more or less simultaneously, based, I suppose, upon the attractions that we found lacking in each other.' That may be true. I am glad and grateful that we remained friends until his death in 1977.

I no longer climb high passes, nor even gentle slopes, but I will always remember with nostalgia and deep gratitude my time in Sinkiang; the remote, strange magic of what was once an 'antique land'.

THE ANTIQUE LAND

by

Diana Shipton

Decorations by
JILL DAVIS

LONDON
HODDER AND STOUGHTON

Contents

Illustrations

"I met a traveller from an antique land."
Percy Bysshe Shelley

CHAPTER I

The Travels Begin

BEFORE I MARRIED ERIC, there was a time when I addressed my letters to him "British Consul-General, Kashgar". When he went there I looked up Kashgar in my atlas and found it in the remote vastness of Central Asia. But in spite of Eric's descriptions I could form no clear picture of it. I knew that Marco Polo had been there, that the Old Silk Road ran through it and that it was farther from the sea than almost any other city in the world. But this jumble of knowledge only made my idea of it more dim—a city of fantasy and old romance.

However close you are to people, however mentally in tune with them, places and experiences that you have not shared have little meaning. You listen to the stories they tell you of people and countries you do not know; you look at the photographs they show you, but however interested you would like to be, the unshared existence remains like something in a novel, shadowy and unreal. Only personal experience can be a firm reality.

Four years after Eric had left Kashgar, in 1942, he was again offered the position of Consul-General there, and this time I was able to go with him. The offer came quite unexpectedly while Eric was working in Vienna. It was from there that he telephoned to me, in England, to ask if I was ready to go. It was not difficult to make up my mind, even in the three indistinct minutes allowed to us. Mentally, I began immediately to pack and to plan. In spite of my previous link with Kashgar, only now, when I was going there myself, did the isolation of the place, the whole geography, history and significance of it begin to have a vivid meaning.

It is an ancient city, once a small kingdom in its own right. Now it is only one of the towns in the Chinese province of Sinkiang. This far western province is remote, in every sense, from Central China. Its inhabitants are a different race, speaking their own language and following customs alien to their rulers. Chinese Turkestan is another name for the province, but it is a clumsy one and throughout this book I have used the comparatively modern Chinese name of Sinkiang, meaning New Dominion. Owing, I suppose, to the restrictions of Chinese "characters", they give their own names to all the places in the province. These are not so familiar to most Europeans as the old Turki names, and so, with the exception of Sinkiang, I have not used them.

Sinkiang is a country of mighty deserts where rivers are lost, of oases and great mountains. The Tien Shan range divides it into two halves. In the northern half lies Urumchi, the capital; in the southern half lies Kashgar, and others of the old city States such as Yarkand and Khotan. These oases ring the formidable Takla Makan Desert on the west. To the north, south and west of them lie the stern and beautiful ranges of the Tien Shan, Kun Lun and Pamir mountains. The approaches to Kashgar are indeed severe and its barriers strong.

British interests have been represented there since 1890, when Mr. (later Sir George) Macartney went to Kashgar as a Trade Agent. In 1908 a Consulate was established, promoted two years later to a Consulate-General.

The normal route to Kashgar from India lies through Kashmir and Gilgit. It is a six weeks' journey on horseback across one of the highest mountain ranges in the world. By this route, in winter and summer, the mail used to go regularly once a week to the Consulate. Then in 1945, after about forty years of an almost unbroken record, the postal service was stopped because the Gilgit route was cut. Sporadic rebellions had broken out in Sinkiang and in the Sarikol area rebel forces, or bandits, had attacked the mail carriers, beaten up Chinese garrisons, and closed the road to India. In 1946, when Eric and I were planning our journey to Kashgar, this road was still unsafe and the only direct communication with the British Consulate was by radio telegram. At any time a journey to Kashgar is an adventure. Now there was an added element of excitement. How were we to get there?

We still did not know the answer when we reached Delhi in August. This was at a time when the future independence of India was harassing the British and Indian Governments. In an atmosphere of damp heat and demoralizing uncertainty, no one seemed very interested in our particular problem. Various schemes were put forward. In China a Dakota might be chartered to fly us to Kashgar; we might motor up through Central China westwards across the Gobi Desert; or perhaps we could go by the very uncertain Chinese air line from Chungking to Urumchi. But finally all these plans fell through and only one alternative remained— to follow the ancient trade route through Ladakh and over the Karakoram Pass.

It is not particularly original to write about a desire to escape from the "machine age". People are frequently making "escapes" to primitive parts of the world. Perhaps they go bicycling across America backwards or sailing down the Danube in a motor-tyre, in a search for novelty.

It is getting harder to find that novelty in a world of monotones and uniformity. Without any elaborate searching, and in the ordinary course of events, Eric and I now had the opportunity to travel as men have travelled for centuries, along one of the oldest known trade routes in the world. Not because we wanted to be unusual or to write a more effective story, but because there was no possible alternative. No aeroplane or motor-car, not even a jeep, could penetrate that forbidding country. We had to rely on animals, as men have always done on that route.

A Chinese writer in about the year 25 B.C., gives a

graphic account of the difficulties and hazards to be met with in a journey from China to Kashmir, ". . . you would have to cross over great mountains, called the Headache Mountains, as they cause headaches, fever and vomiting. Then follows a path through the gorges thirty miles long and two feet wide. A single slip means being hurled into a bottomless chasm." There is nothing to prove that this refers to the Karakoram route. But the mountain ranges do not offer many alternatives. Once the first adventurers have found a way across the lowest passes and through the easiest gorges, others must follow roughly the same path. It is probable that the writer was describing the trade route that is used to-day.| Certainly about A.D. 950 there was trade being carried on between India, Yarkand and Kashgar by way of Ladakh.

It is remarkable what men will endure and dare in order to promote trade and make money. The early explorers of this path through the mountains must have had enormous courage; their descendants still need a good share of it to brave the difficulties of the journey. But I have found no definite history of this trade route. It must be as full of adventure and romance as the story of the Old Silk Road, or the overland routes of the flourishing spice trade, before men explored the sea routes. But it has never affected European trade and so it has received less attention in the West.

I felt enormously excited at the idea of this journey—as if we were going to go back in Time, travelling in the ancient past.

We were delayed in Delhi waiting for the arrival of our Sherpa servant from Darjeeling. Gyalgen had been one of Eric's faithful porters on his Mount Everest and other expeditions. Now he was being promoted to a personal servant and had agreed to accompany us to Kashgar. The worst of the Calcutta riots were then at their height, and as days passed with no word from Gyalgen we became more and more apprehensive. But there is a solid, humorous dependability about these small men from Tibet. At last, battered and dirty, five days late, Gyalgen appeared at our Delhi hotel. In his loud, chanting voice, which rises steadily the more excited he gets, he gave us a vivid account of his adventures. He had jumped first on to one train, then another; he had hidden under carriages to avoid some small "incident"; assured everyone loudly that he was a Tibetan and had no interest in their battles; watched stalwart Mussulmans advance with sticks and swords upraised while Hindus struck neatly from below with small, sharp knives. We were very relieved to see Gyalgen and also very thankful to leave Delhi. Together with an old servant of Eric's—a Hunza man called Amir Ali, who had appeared from nowhere in a way peculiar to native servants—we left for the cool loveliness of Kashmir.

There must be more written about Kashmir than almost any other part of India. But each visitor sees it in his own way, making it alive with his own particular impressions. For us Srinagar, the capital, held a special significance. We had met there, for the first time, seven years before. So once more we floated on the wide Dal Lake in gondola-like boats; watched the busy traffic of the river and canals; absorbed the delight of tall poplars, of floating gardens and lotus leaves, of blue mountains framing the whole scene. This time we followed the custom of good tourists and hired a houseboat—with food, accommodation and service all included. The houseboat was anchored under spreading chinar trees, close to the bank, while on the other side flowed the river.

We had an active week. My small bedroom was littered with things to be packed, and it was no use packing them in ordinary trunks and suit-cases. We had to design something to withstand six weeks of rough handling by the caravan men, and the bumps and cuts of rock edges. Because they were cheap, we decided to try small, tin trunks. These survived as far as Leh, where they arrived in a pitiful state. The best solution proved to be tough, deep, leather boxes called "yakdans", and strong sacks for all unbreakable things. Even the yakdans only just reached Kashgar intact. Outside on the bank was a growing mountain of paraphernalia. Eric and I, consulting complicated lists, tried to do far too many things at once. While a shoemaker waited patiently to fit the fur-lined boots we had ordered, we interviewed the man who had promised to organize all our transport. An extremely polite gentleman followed us about, repeatedly assuring us that a wave of his hand would arrange the entire journey. After requesting him to bring us some saddles, we never saw the polite gentleman again. There was food to think about, warm clothes for Gyalgen and Amir Ali, something to prevent blisters on the feet and the safest way to pack the kerosene. In order to avoid simplifying our problems too much, Eric decided that he must have a dog, for winter shooting in Kashgar. So having bought a two-months' old golden retriever, we added a collar, lead, basket and suitable foods to our shopping list. We even risked a bottle of liquid paraffin in case the puppy fell ill.

A mild, but very persistent, undercurrent to all this activity was the insinuating call of the floating salesmen on the other side of our houseboat. Just as I was sitting hot and despairing on an overfilled box, a man would appear at the window with the very latest in carved wooden screens. In the middle of an earnest discussion about plans and dates, a smiling face would rise up, apparently from the river, waving a pair of embroidered knickers. A large section of the Srinagar population used to make a living from the visitors to Kashmir. There were men ready to arrange anything from a shooting trip in the hills to an evening with a pretty girl. And, of course, there was the multitude trying to sell things. The Kashmiri is a good craftsman; many of them, having learnt from Europeans what Europeans want, had some very attractive things to offer. Little boats, piled high with wool embroidery, silk underwear, papier mâché and wood work, floated continuously round to the houseboats. The wares were tempting but this was certainly not the time nor the place to add yet more to my litter of possessions. I began by polite refusals. "Not to-day, thank you." I said. This meant nothing to the salesmen. Their little shops continued to bob patiently outside the window. Not until I had reached the stage of shouting or had ignored them for an hour, did they give up hope.

We were anxious to start the next stage of our journey. Preparations are exciting but suddenly one gets tired of

A MIGHTY "CHORTEN" AT THE BEGINNING OF A "MANI" WALL

LAMAS FROM A MONASTERY NEAR LEH

THE PALACE AT LEH, ABOVE THE BAZAAR

A CARAVAN OF PONIES

them. Small details go on accumulating, and the more one thinks about it all the more complicated it becomes. Once the journey has started one must manage with what one has, and suffer without the things which one has forgotten. But our last evening in Srinagar was tinged with regrets for what we were leaving behind. There were so many things, such as friends, cinemas, shops, quick contact with our families, a daily paper and electric light, that we were going to miss. Some of these seem trivial, but they become important when they are quite unobtainable. However much one wants to escape into remote places, there are big and small ropes to be cut before one can float freely away. Some of the ropes are hard to cut.

We arranged with our caravan to leave on September 2nd. The start of most mountain treks is a misery of blistered feet, weak tummy and depression. So we decided to break ourselves in gradually by spending two days camping in the lovely valley of Sonamarg. Eric's idea of "gradually" did not wholly agree with mine. On our first day in the mountains we climbed beyond the bright green of the grass, the dark green of the pines, up a stony, desolate little valley to where the snow and ice began. We came to a snow bridge and Eric striding ahead was half across it when, with a dull roar, the bridge and Eric disappeared into the river below. I crept nervously to the edge and saw him standing on a small remaining island of snow in the middle of the water. I never trusted a snow bridge again. Later that day the rain came down in a fierce and unrelenting torrent. Very weary, very wet and most effectively "broken in", I limped back to our camp. But I was glad to be among the mountains. When the rain stopped and we sat warm and rested, round our first camp-fire, it felt very good. We slept out under the pine trees and the stars.

On September 2nd we met our first caravan men. Headed by a talkative man in an old R.A.F. jacket, they began by arranging our baggage into neat little loads of 80 lb., each pony to carry 40 lb. a side. We told them, quite politely, that the regulation load was at least 100 lb. a side and they agreed, equally politely. It had been worth trying to increase the number of ponies we had to hire.

Having failed the men seemed to bear us no grudge. After the first three marches, when we parted, rather stormily over the question of pay, from the R.A.F. jacket and his men, we changed carriers at every stage. By this system the men did not have to go far from their homes and life near the caravan route was not disrupted. Each day the men fought for the lightest loads, a battle in which we took no part as we always walked on ahead. Our puppy was tied into a basket and whenever the caravan passed us we could see her sitting up bravely, or peacefully asleep. Sometimes she fell off as the pony stumbled over a difficult bit of the road, but she seemed quite unconcerned and adapted herself to the curious, swaying existence. We had been assured that the journey would do her no harm if we did not let her walk too much, but sometimes it seemed to me that the riding was harder work.

The two weeks' journey to Leh began. The first of the many passes we had to cross was the Zoji La. Although only 11,500 feet high it has an evil reputation for avalanches in winter and spring. In September there was no danger but the abrupt change from the fir-covered hills and gentle green of Sonamarg to the severe, grey, desolation and bleak glaciers of the Zoji, seemed to make it an unfriendly place. The sun did not shine that morning and a cold wind added to this feeling of hostility. As we climbed slowly up I heard a pitiful bleating on the hill-side above. It was a lost lamb. Having rescued it Gyalgen tried to trade it for milk from some shepherds. But no one wanted our lamb, they had no ewes they said. I tried to feed it with milk and butter from my fingers, but it took no interest in this diet. It was not until we had crossed the Zoji La that we found two children willing to take it to a mother.

We were now in Baltistan; a dry, barren country of stony hill-sides, rocky crags and glaciers hanging high above us. In sudden and startling contrast, were the brilliant patches of cultivation below the cleverly graded irrigation canals that ran along the bare slopes. Once we followed an unused channel for twelve miles and when we inquired why it had been abandoned, we were told the sad story of the men who, long ago, had spent three years working on it only to find that they had miscalculated the gradient. In that rainless country, irrigation is essential, and where water can be brought from the glacier-fed streams, crops and orchards flourish. The fields were now golden with ripe corn and the trees laden with apricots and red apples— a cool and delicious sight against the arid hills above.

It was calm, peaceful travel and we developed a pleasant routine. Tea and biscuits at 5 a.m. and then three hours of walking before we stopped for a proper breakfast. Gyalgen would produce porridge, eggs and tea in a surprisingly short time, and we allowed ourselves a long, lazy rest while the main caravan passed slowly on. We had no need to hurry and so idled our way along in weather that was sunny but not too hot. Sometimes we stopped again, to sleep in an orchard; sometimes we would scramble about on the rocks in a foaming river; and often Eric would race far uphill in pursuit of chikor. These little partridge are delicious to eat. We always reached the Rest House at the end of each stage, before 5 o'clock, often earlier. Then Gyalgen would produce another hot meal.

It is curious how quickly one forgets the dismal parts of an experience. In retrospect I see this journey to Leh as a sun-lit path winding among green oases or forbidding mountains; two weeks of exciting new adventure, of beauty and delight. The aching tiredness, the Rest House always round the *next* bend, the small irritations, seem to have faded from my mind. The only trouble which has not faded is my deep-rooted dislike of riding—a deep-rooted fear, really. This was the subject of continual argument between Eric and me.

"If you come to Asia you must ride," Eric said.

I have gradually learnt that he is right. Along mountain paths, narrow and twisting, walking is pleasant; when endless miles of dull desert stretch round you, it is a wretched business. A good, sturdy pony will cover the distance comfortably and fast. But I never learnt to enjoy riding. Each new pony was an ordeal. They seemed to alternate between half-dying animals, moving at a reluctant crawl, and spirited ponies I could not control. No one agreed with me and I began to suspect that it was not always the ponies which were at fault. With rare exceptions, I preferred to walk; to the complete mystification of our servants and all caravan men, I rode as little as possible.

As we approached Leh, the capital of Ladakh, the scene changed once more; only this time it was the people and the architecture which were different. The country was still one of striking contrast between grey desolation and green oasis, but now the atmosphere of Tibet and Buddhism predominated.

While it is delightfully unfanatical, religion plays an important part in the country. It is evident everywhere. Whether he understands it or not, to the Buddhist the holy formula, "Om mani padmi hum", is an essential and important thing in his daily life. At each repetition of the prayer he gains spiritual merit, and a greater chance of a higher rebirth after death. He need not repeat the words himself. They are printed on flags which flutter on high passes and lonely hills; they are carved on stones and built into long "mani walls"; they are written on the drum-like prayer wheels which can be whirled round by the passer-by, or turned, still more easily, by water-power or the wind. The devout spin small prayer wheels, like rattles, as they wander along. Every revolution of the wheel, every flutter of the flag, the mere act of passing the walls, provided that they are passed on the left, means so many more prayers accomplished. Most of the walls have a "chorten" at each end. These shrines, so distinctive a feature of the Ladakh country, contain the ashes of dead lamas. Mixed with clay the ashes are formed into little patterns and put in a niche in the chorten.

It is the lamas who are expected to take care of the religious side of life. The small population supports monasteries all over the country. Perched high and precariously on rocky crags, their commanding position seems symbolic of their power. Inside, the buildings are less impressive, a curious haphazard mixture of squalor and ancient culture. In dim mysterious rooms, evil with the smell of rancid butter burning in little lamps, fantastic gods and calm, inscrutable Buddhas are represented in mural paintings and great idols. Painted banners, brocades, silver cups, little drums made from human brain-pans, massive cymbals, tawdry tinsel and tattered streamers, a cheap enamel tea-pot and a stiffly posed photograph of the Abbot, are all jumbled together under a heavy layer of dirt and dust.

I tried to regard these shrines with reverence. It seemed insensitive merely to patronize and stare. These good intentions were sadly defeated at Lamayuru, on the road to Leh. Perhaps I was tired and the sharp climb up to the monastery completed my exhaustion. Half-way round the dark, inner shrine the smell of rancid butter overcame me. Without any explanation to the startled monks I ran outside and was violently sick on their doorstep. Everyone was concerned and sympathetic which only added to my embarrassment.

Some of the lamas are men of learning and philosophy, students of the holy books in the monastery libraries, but the large majority are as ignorant and primitive as the peasants. Living in comparative idleness, they are a heavy drag on the country. From nearly every family one son enters the easy-going monastic life, so that their numbers never decrease but the birth-rate is effectively checked. Nevertheless the Ladakhi respects the monks and seems to accept the burden of supporting them as cheerfully as he accepts everything. He does not appear to burn with nationalism, with religious ardour, or with military ambition, any more than he burns with a desire to progress, to be educated or to learn new ways of life. Provided the dirt, the slowness and the ignorance does not fill you with despair or reforming zeal, the spontaneous gaiety, the friendliness and tolerance of these people is enchanting. A girl will offer you a tight little bunch of flowers as you pass; another will hand you some fruit; rich and poor welcome you into their homes with charming self-assurance, to drink their buttered and salted Tibetan tea, or "chang", the fermented barley wine. Everywhere the greeting, "Ju, Jule", follows you like gentle music.

The women carry on the daily work of house and field in their elaborate, heavy head-dresses. It is the most striking feature of their dress. Sown with many turquoise, a strip of cloth, shaped like a snake, forms a triangle over the forehead and hangs down the back. The wealthier the lady the wider and heavier the "snake". If possible a band of coral is attached to the side as well. Standing out from the head, like immense ears, are pieces of black lamb's wool, and from these dangle many imitation pigtails. For the rest the women wear long thick dresses (maroon seems to be the fashionable colour) with girdles, and as much heavy jewellery as they can afford. Big white shell bracelets, like false cuffs, are often worn. However hot the day they wear rough goatskin capes, although the rich may have shawls or magnificent scarlet cloaks.

The men are nearly as fond of jewellery as the women, while their long, skirted garments and pigtails add to the feminine effect. A cloth wound untidily round the waist serves as a pocket and into it are tucked wooden bowls for tea, knives, precious needles or a whip. Among the peasants these picturesque costumes are usually in a sad state of dirt and dilapidation; often the clothes are so patched that nothing of the original remains. Even so they lose strangely little of their decorative charm.

When still six miles from Leh we could see the green, welcoming oasis across a stony stretch of desert. Near us the Indus flowed placid and green. In the distance snow mountains gleamed and lower hills were lightly etched in shades of blue. I had given my horse to Amir Ali and felt completely at peace as I trudged along. My contentment was soon shattered. Coming towards us over the desert, in a dusty, noisy cavalcade was an alarming number of horsemen. This proved to be a deputation of Indian traders come out to escort us into Leh. My heart sank at the prospect of a spirited ride in the middle of this cavalry. It was out of the question to walk. A compromise was reached by Eric galloping on ahead with the main party, while a handsome young Sikh, who spoke English, very gallantly offered to accompany me. He never quite understood what all the fuss was about and I hope never realized what remarkable unhappiness that six miles caused me.

Eventually we reached the main gate into Leh and everyone dismounted. Feeling dishevelled and dusty, my legs still shaking from the ride, but trying to look dignified, I accompanied Eric in a "triumphal" walk through the bazaar. Garlands were hung round our necks; arches and banners decorated the street; at intervals we were handed nuts and cakes, while the ordinary population of Leh stared as one might at a couple of dilapidated performing bears. We were led to the Leh Residency, and escaped thankfully into the cool, quiet refuge.

The house was not then occupied but was ready for our arrival. How luxurious it seemed after the fusty, broken-down little Rest Houses. There were chintz-covered chairs in the drawing-room; a dining-room table was laid with silver and glass; we had to go upstairs to bed; an array of antlers decorated the veranda wall and completed the essentially English atmosphere. From the veranda, and beyond the terraced garden, the view stretched wide and unbroken to the Zaskar Range; sometimes dark and angry in a passing storm, sometimes white and shining against a peaceful sky, or touched with pink by the setting sun.

However delightful a mountain trek may be, coming to the end of it is also a delight. The joy of clean clothes, hot baths, comfortable chairs and beds are ordinary things only fully appreciated in sharp contrast to the roughness of travel. Not to have to move *on* is also something to be well savoured. We had ten days of simple luxury in Leh.

We were again busy with preparations, making all the elaborate arrangements necessary for the final four weeks of our journey. We bought more blankets and long padded coats; we repacked everything, abandoning the battered tin trunks; and we reviewed our food situation. The Residency hummed with traders imploring Eric's help, servants asking questions, visitors coming to call, our puppy chewing everyone's feet and always, hovering sadly in the background, was a deputation of Chinese soldiers. They were from a party of about twenty-four who had run away from the Sarikol area after the rebellion. Now they all wanted to return to Sinkiang with us. They had no money, no provisions, no one was responsible for them.

Eric did what he could but was determined to avoid taking them back to Kashgar in our party.

We did not confine ourselves entirely to preparations for the journey. We found time to enjoy Leh. Here the ancient caravan trade routes from Tibet, India and Central Asia meet, and a strange mixture of people jostles in the bazaar. Dominating the whole scene is the impressive but crumbling old Palace. Only once a year it comes to life, when the ex-royal family of Ladakh pays a ceremonial visit to Leh and occupies a few dusty rooms kept as the State apartments. Then they return to their home at Stok, across the Indus. It was there we met the ex-Queen. In a tiny room near the roof, seated rather unexpectedly in deck-chairs, we drank tea with her and conversed haltingly. Our interpreter was an elderly man in a Ladakhi robe and a homburg hat, who spoke a little Urdu.

We learnt later that the ex-Queen completely dominates her husband and household and is a woman of character and determination. Our polite exchange of platitudes could not tell us much, but she certainly looked a severe little lady under her magnificent turquoise head-dress. The Ladakhi women as a whole are hard-working and independent. They tolerate no nonsense about purdah and harems; they can own property; and polyandry is said to be practised, which no doubt makes their position more powerful.

We were entertained by several charming and cultured Ladakhis. Sitting on cushions, low tables before us, we ate large meals and drank yet more Tibetan tea. This was served in cups each with a stand and a cover beautifully worked in silver or metal. I do not enjoy this soup-like drink and only sipped occasionally. Later I discovered that this indicates a desire for more. Otherwise you must empty your cup and replace the lid. In one house which we visited I was taken to see our hostess's kitchen. She had reason to be proud of it. Beautiful copper pots gleamed on the shelves; it was light and large, every detail in clean and shining condition; the fire was encouraged with ingenious sheepskin bellows; I saw the tall wooden churn where the tea was made.

Our comfortable house, the friendly people and the colourful charm of Leh tempted us to stay. But the weather was getting colder, our party was all assembled, our arrangements were complete and we decided to leave on September 20th.

CHAPTER II

"The Headache Mountains"

On September 19th, Eric was handed a telegram from Delhi. It informed us that "bandits" had been reported on the Karakoram route; a caravan had been robbed of goods and ponies; we were strongly recommended to turn back and go via Gilgit. This was dramatic news and could not be casually dismissed. There were so many things to be considered. A heavy responsibility lay on Eric.

Our party consisted of Doctor Allen Mersh, Mr. Refaquatullah Khan, the new head clerk, Mr. Mohammed Shah, the dispenser, with his wife and two babies, ourselves and our two servants. For an exorbitant sum, half of which we had already paid to him, a Turki trader had contracted to transport us all to Kashgar via the Karakoram Pass. If we turned back we forfeited our money. Pleased as we were to hear that the Gilgit road was now considered safe, should we decide to go that way after all, it meant about three extra weeks crossing the mountains westwards to reach Gilgit. This entailed more expense and the difficulty of finding a new caravan. Every day it was getting colder and the passes were becoming more deep in snow. A final consideration was the fate of the out-coming doctor from Kashgar. He and his family were due in Leh shortly, but they might have encountered the "bandits" and be in need of help. This last-minute crisis seemed too dramatic to be true. In the curious way one believes that spectacular disasters only overtake *other* people, I could not think of bandits and robbery as affecting us. Nevertheless with the inhospitable country ahead of us we could take no chances.

A party including women and small children, having to struggle across the lonely mountains without transport, without food, bedding and fuel, had slight hope of survival. The loss of ponies alone might prove fatal; it was ponies which the bandits would probably seize, if they took nothing else.

For three days we held anxious conferences. We knew no details. We supposed that the robbers were connected with the original Sarikol rebellion; perhaps they were roaming bands preying on the trade route while they had the chance. We pored over maps and considered venturing into unknown country to by-pass the danger area; we contemplated going back to Srinagar; we interviewed Mohammed Kurban, the Turki trader, to try to get his views on the subject. Surprisingly, he made light of the whole report. He seemed willing to risk not only us but his own rich caravan of merchandise. He even offered us his head should we eventually meet any trouble and so prove him in the wrong. Spurred on by this optimistic, if rather useless offer, by anxiety for Captain Binns (the Kashgar doctor) and feeling a general reluctance to turn back, we decided to go on as far as Panamik, five days away. If, at this last Ladakhi village, we had not met the doctor and his caravan, Eric was to continue with a selected search party.

With this unhappy cloud over our heads, the journey began, and it began badly. Eric and I had left Leh at mid-day and had stopped to eat a picnic lunch on the way. By 3 o'clock there was still no sign of the main caravan. In a sudden temper Eric rode back into Leh and there found the ponies and men comfortably idle in their serai. An immediate and heavy fine galvanized everyone to life. Perhaps the biggest shock was seeing Eric hand half the money to some startled children standing near.

The result of this late start was that we camped that night in the cold and dark, in dismal confusion, at the foot of the first of the giant passes which we had to cross. As soon as Gyalgen had made a fire the caravan men huddled round it, ignoring the chaos of baggage, babies and ponies. It was an ominous beginning to our acquaintance with them.

The next day we had a long, slow, gasping climb up to the 17,500 ft. Khardung Pass. There was a narrow, well defined path, but as we crawled up I began to feel the unpleasant effects of altitude, and each step was an effort. I was too nervous to ride. The way down was even worse and oddly enough my headache and sickness increased. All pretence of a path failed, and there was a sharp descent over rock and ice. The ponies, slipping and falling, were ruthlessly kicked and lashed; boxes and baggage rolled down the slope. We began to realize that Mohammed Kurban had provided too few men for the number of ponies. The caravan was quite out of control. Through all this pandemonium struggled the dispenser's wife, a young Mohammedan girl in the cumbersome purdah garment which covered her like a tent, and only allowed her a small mesh to see through. The entire journey she sat on her pony, thus heavily draped, clutching her baby, sick and cold, without any interest in the country or any knowledge of how long her agony would last, a gallant and incongruous figure. She rode over places which I found far too alarming. Once she and her baby were thrown to the ground when their pony tripped and fell. I longed to help her but she spoke only Pushtu; and she seemed numbed into a pathetic resignation.

Beyond the Khardung, the journey to Panamik was easier, although I disliked fording the wide, swift Shyok River. It seemed that the current must sweep the little ponies off their feet. Each day we hoped that we should see the doctor and his party on the road. Each day we visualized worse horrors of robbery and disaster having overtaken them. But at Panamik we met them; and there we all camped down in a shady orchard for a long exchange of news. The doctor told us that they had left Kashgar in complete ignorance of any bandits. One morning, as they rode along, they had suddenly found bullets whistling past them. Throwing themselves flat on the ground they had tried to shelter behind some rocks, and then began desperately to wave a white handkerchief. The attackers were not bandits, however, but over-anxious Chinese troops sent to clear the area. Fortunately their aim was weak, no harm was done, and after scant apology, they allowed the doctor to pass.

The whole problem of our journey was discussed again. More solemn conferences were held. Acting as interpreter between Eric, Captain Binns and the circle of bearded, tough caravan men, sat the Binns' twelve-year-old son. He spoke perfect Turki and was a clear, excellent translator, fully appreciating his responsibility. Although news had now reached us that a previous Chinese force had been routed by the robbers, leaving two of their number dead and many of their horses captured, it was reassuring that there were troops in the area. There was also further information that stronger garrisons were being sent there. With this comfort, and with the stern picture of the Khardung still vivid in our minds, we decided to go on. We spent an extra day in Panamik, visiting some hot springs near by. A little house, divided into two separate compartments, had been built over the springs. There we had our last, and the doctor's party their first bath for a month.

After this peaceful interlude the two parties turned in opposite directions and our trek began once more. There was a motley collection of people attached to our caravan, all hoping to gain "protection" from the British Consul-General, although he had little to offer. In spite of Eric's orders one or two of the refugee Chinese soldiers had come along; there was a string of stately camels led by a minute donkey; and a comic little foursome of three donkeys and a white mule, which were abused and prodded the whole way by a sad-faced boy. For six hundred miles he shouted the same curse and made the same encouraging noises without any variation or pause.

As well as the caravans accompanying and behind us, we were soon to meet a busy stream coming from across the border. This was a welcome sight, as it indicated that the way was now clear. It seemed that the bandits had disappeared as suddenly as they had come. None of the caravans reported any trouble. The drivers were wild-looking men in their clumsy sheepskin coats, high leather boots and a weird assortment of fur hats. But they were a friendly lot. Once we were invited to join a party just settling down to a large meal. In a cauldron bubbled soup and meat from a freshly slaughtered sheep that had been driven along with the caravan. Rugs and furs were spread for us, we were liberally fed and I had my first taste of green tea. This was drunk without sugar or milk and was certainly an improvement on Tibetan tea, I thought.

As we climbed towards the second, and hardest, of the big passes, the temperature dropped considerably, we put on every garment we possessed and did not take any off again for the next three weeks. In the evening we only removed our boots, and then crawled into the double eiderdown sleeping-bags which just fitted into Eric's tiny Everest tent. The doctor told me he even slept in his boots, but they were the high, felt variety. Life is made very simple when it is too cold to wash or undress. With our two servants, we soon became efficient in making ready for the night. To keep ourselves warm and to the amazement of the caravan men, we helped with the unloading, pitching of tents and fetching water. Once we had eaten and got into bed, as the warmest place, the evenings were very long; the small confines of the tent exasperating. The only solution was to go to sleep.

The treacherous Saser Pass, 17,480 ft. high, was kind to us; there was no wind. The ponies struggled painfully over the wilderness of boulders which led up to the two glaciers forming the crest of the pass. These they crossed without accident. But already the sad trail of bones and corpses had begun. On this harsh, desolate route, the pack animals are the chief sufferers. All fuel, food and fodder have to be carried and as the traders tend to overload their animals with valuable merchandise at the expense of grain, the death rate, from underfeeding, exhaustion and cold, is high. Never once, until we reached the plains were we out of sight of skeletons. The continuous line of bones and bodies acted as a gruesome guide whenever we were uncertain of the route.

Our ponies were beginning to weaken. The day after we had crossed the Saser many of them were limping and several kept collapsing sadly and hopelessly. The men showed little sympathy and their only treatment was kicks and blows. If the animals collapsed completely, they were abandoned. Our attempt to revive a dying pony was regarded as quite eccentric and in any case proved useless. I know nothing about the care of horses, but the Turki methods did seem to me unnecessarily harsh and senseless. Long after the march was ended the animals were kept standing without food or water. They were either tied together in pairs, head to tail, or, as I noticed later in Sinkiang, to a tree or a post with their heads held tight and high. To any protests the men replied that these methods prevented illness and nothing would change their views.

The caravan crawled slowly on across the lonely, barren country. One day we crossed a wide, empty plain with snow peaks faint and luminous on the horizon; sometimes we had to go up dry river beds, with their tiring, pebbly surfaces; another day we would wind along narrow paths cut into the steep hill-side, or make our way up a deep, rocky gorge, where the sun could not penetrate, and a turbulent stream cascaded down. For six days our route lay down a river which, one day, had to be crossed and recrossed as many as thirty times. Always the country remained empty of vegetation, a wilderness of rock and stone, snow and ice; when there was no stream to break the stillness, the silence was eerie and hostile. The scale of the country was immense; on either side of our trail it stretched away for hundreds of miles in unrelenting desolation and grandeur. We often felt cold and exhausted, the journey seemed hard and endless, but there were moments of supreme beauty to reward us. The moon flooding a valley and catching the river in its light; black crags high against a vivid blue sky; the sun creeping slowly above a hill and bringing to life all the colour in red and yellow rocks; the blue-white of glaciers contrasting with black rock. There was magnificence in that stark country

For six days after crossing the Saser we had not dropped below 15,000 ft. and then once more we had to work our way up to 18,290 ft. at the Karakoram Pass. Beyond lay Sinkiang. The Karakoram Pass was a gentle one. It was an unspectacular, gradual rise up and and almost equally unspectacular descent. But it was a significant moment when we crossed the border into Chinese territory. Only one march away lay the place where the famous bandits had attacked the caravan. In spite of the feeling of danger which hung over the country immediately ahead, I was excited to be in Sinkiang. We were roughly half-way on our journey from Leh to Kashgar.

Two days before this the men had had a cruel disappointment; on reaching a place where, on a previous journey, they had buried grain, they found that the supply had gone. As they had been relying on this, the wretched horses were doomed to even scantier rations than before. They were very weak now and two had died. The first casualty had been my riding pony. As I so seldom rode it, Eric suggested that it had died of boredom. It had always been a lazy creature and for two days before its death had enraged me with its funereal crawl. I felt guilty to think of the abuse I had showered on it, now that I realized it had been, literally, dying on its feet.

Besides the unexpected shortage of grain, the men were running short of fuel. This was nearly the cause of a mutiny—by our party. An alleged fifteen-mile march having stretched to at least twenty miles, we demanded a halt. The men implored us to go on a little farther, promising us wood to burn. But hard experience had taught us how elastic was their idea of distance. As it was getting late, with snow falling from a leaden sky, we refused. An angry argument ensued. Finally the men gained their point and we were forced to go on. To our amazement we soon came to some scrubby bushes growing amongst the stones, the first plants which we had seen for nine days. From now on such occasional twigs, and a little yak dung, provided us with a meagre supply of fuel until we reached the plains.

This quarrel was not the only one we had with the caravan men. But they were a tough, independent lot and they usually had their own way. Our main grievance was their refusal to start early. They were quite unconcerned about time and distance. They liked to get up late; to linger round their fire, drinking tea, before collecting the ponies which wandered loose all night, and then to march until after dark. We disliked pitching camp in the cold and dark and did our best to avoid it. Threats and abuse were of no avail and even an attack on their morning fire with a bucket of water, had no lasting effect. The only time they elected to rise early they completely overdid it and roused us all at 2.45 a.m.

This haphazard progress finally resulted in one of the coldest and most miserable camps of our journey, with our tents pitched on a steep incline, in deep snow, just below the 16,000 ft. Yangi Dawan (New Pass). We had started late, forded a wide river four or five times and then struggled up a long and narrow gorge towards the Pass. The ponies kept falling among the huge boulders and caused endless traffic blocks in the narrow ravine. We crawled upwards and as it was growing dark, with threatening clouds and mist closing in on us, we realized that there was no hope of crossing the Pass that night. Although the men had known what lay ahead of them, they had made no attempt to start early and so get us across the Pass in reasonable time to find a camping place on the other side. We felt extremely bitter and as a punishment confiscated some of the men's precious fuel to warm poor Mrs. Mohammed Shah and her babies.

That wretched camp was the last high one. Crossing the Yangi Dawan the next day in falling snow with the forbidding, grey mountains of the Kun Lun looming out of the swirling clouds, we began to drop steadily. Two days later we reached the first Turkestan village marked on the map. We had been looking forward to this exciting return to habitation. All we found were two little mud huts, hardly distinguishable from the brown earth, and an old, old man sitting in the sun. He was "telling" beads on a rosary. We wondered how anyone could scrape a living from that desolate land. At another collection of huts farther on, the people were more prosperous; they invited us in to drink tea and to eat their flat, round, plate-shaped

3

bread. But they were shy and drab. They lacked the gay charm of the Ladakhis, now so far back across the frontier.

However, their little house was much cleaner and more pleasant than the barrack-room of a Chinese garrison we encountered the next day. Coming round a bend we suddenly found a rifle levelled at us and a suspicious soldier demanded to know who we were. Remembering the experience of the Binns, we were extremely careful and polite. We followed him up to the "fort", a dilapidated building of stones, perched on a wind-swept hill, where we had tea while an exchange of compliments was relayed through four languages—Chinese into Turki, Turki into Urdu and finally Urdu into English. It was an elaborate and cumbersome ceremony. The small garrison had been sent to search for bandits and although they had seen none, the officer was reluctant to let us go on until he had received orders from his headquarters. The prospect of staying in that cold, unattractive place, encamped just outside the walls of the fort, among the horses and garbage, was almost unbearable. With complicated politeness and many more speeches, we thanked him for his "hospitality"; by making exaggerated excuses about our shortage of food and a sick baby, we managed to persuade him to let us through.

We began to feel that our troubles were nearly over; we had crossed all the big passes; we were down to a more reasonable altitude and we had not met any bandits. Tedious days of river crossings, and one more steep, arid little pass lay ahead of us. But the river we now had to ford so often was a clear, deep green; it flowed along between walls of red and grey rock, sometimes splashing over pebbly shallows, sometimes forming into still pools. Gnarled willows bent into the water, and along the banks a variety of shrubs and bushes, now turning red, gold and yellow made a welcome flame of colour. We had grown almost hardened to the impressive but austere scenery of rock and ice. The sudden delight of colour and vegetation was like a cool drink when you are not desperately, but rather unconsciously thirsty.

One afternoon the peace was shattered by some shots which echoed from side to side of the narrow valley. I was walking alone, far behind the caravan, and I knew there were no chikor for Eric to shoot. I hoped it was the Chinese troops practising, but feeling dismally unconvinced I went on. As I usually walked I had continuously to "hitch-hike" across the rivers; either riding pillion behind Eric or mounted high behind Mohammed Kurban on his pile of bedding. This time I found Gyalgen waiting for me with his pony, at a crossing. I asked him about the shots but he laughingly reassured me, and as I scrambled up behind him, told me that my "bandit attack" was no more than Mr. Khan firing at some wild goats with his pistol.

Leaving the green river we made our way through a steep, narrow gorge and over the difficult little pass. The ponies had to be pushed and hauled up the rocks and their loads scraped against the high walls on either side. Once over the top, we began to drop down through dry, sandstone hills. The route now inflicted its final hardship—a severe scarcity of water; an ironical contrast to the many days we had spent struggling across the endless rivers.

Aqmasjid, near the foot of the pass and a place marked on the map, held out some promise of a drink. We visualized springs and green trees. In reality it was another sad little mud house which seemed to grow out of the dry, dusty ground. As we reached it an old man without any feet, came stumping along behind a donkey. This was the owner of the house who had been four miles to fetch his daily supply of water, carried in skins on the donkey's back. He invited us into his pathetic little home and ordered his wife to bring out her store of bread, which was broken before us on the floor with a muttered prayer. I thought the woman looked sadly at her meagre supply of food, spread out so lavishly. I tried to recompense her with sugar and tea, and gave barley sugar to her mystified small boy. It is odd to think how many people in Central Asia have no sugar in their daily diet. To them it is a luxury and not the necessity we have learnt to consider it.

Our caravan men were conspicuously uninterested in the choice of good camp sites. They were sensitive neither to the beauty of the scene nor to such small comforts as were available. We were rarely given much choice in the matter, but when one evening our tent was pitched beside a dead donkey we did complain. After leaving Aqmasjid they chose a more unattractive place than usual. When we questioned it they said we were near the only water supply for miles. The water was a miserable trickle oozing up from the mud and horribly polluted by all the caravan animals which passed. Our evening cup of tea, to which we had looked forward so eagerly, had a disgusting taste, closely connected with horse, and we threw it away hastily. Rather than drink this water, we went thirsty for the next twenty-four hours.

To make matters worse the following morning's march was one of the hottest and most tiring of the journey. For the whole of that morning the path was of loose, deep sand. A hot sun glared overhead, while the low brown hills and sand dunes stretched on and on into the shimmering distance. I shared my pony with Gyalgen, alternately hating the riding and the walking. At last the horizon was broken by tall poplars; although they seemed near, it was a long time before we reached the oasis. It was the first permanent habitation we had seen for eighteen days. The excitement was intense. The small village, collected round a Chinese Customs Post, seemed like a busy centre of civilized activity. Here the trees were still green, the irrigation channels bubbled with water. Delight in this coolness, the promise of shade and drink, relief that the main severity of our journey was over, made our entry into Pussa a most wonderful one. It seemed to me as if bells should ring, guns should fire to celebrate the occasion. But the people of the village only stared at us quite calmly, as we rode in.

Before the officials saw us, Eric and I crept away to an orchard and in its peaceful shade devoured one melon after another. Sinkiang is famous for its melons; it boasts at least twenty-six different varieties, although we did not sample them all at the time. Later we were invited into the Customs House where a young Chinese, in loud tweed plus-fours, was writing out his elaborate forms of rice paper with a paint brush. Mohammed Kurban had brought with him a large supply of goods which had to be "negotiated" through the Customs; a delicate business which took over three hours. While we waited we went on eating and drinking an endless quantity of fresh milk, grapes, melons, eggs, and tea flavoured with cinnamon. I felt no impatience at the delay. I could have eaten indefinitely. I sat hugging the thought that we had reached comparative civilization, had no more passes or rivers to cross, and had something to drink.

Late in the afternoon we left the green oasis and set off across the wide, dry desert. The hills were fading away behind us in the dust haze which hangs like a cloak over the country so much of the time. The sun shone dimly through the haze and gave the scene a weird moonlit appearance.

We had tried to arrange by radio telegram, before leaving India, that the Consulate lorry should meet us at Khokia, the oasis where we camped that night. But we had not received any confirmation of this and owing to the uncertainty and slowness of communications, we could not be sure that the rendezvous would be kept. If it was not, we had ten more marches ahead of us, instead of a two-day motor drive. We waited a day at Khokia; we were glad of the rest, of the chance to wash, above all, to go on eating. But by the second day our hope of meeting the lorry had begun to fade and, with a feeling of anti-climax, we started the slow journey once more. I nursed a melon to console me across the hot, flat sand beyond the oasis. We listened eagerly for the sound of a motor but heard only the interminable jingle of the ponies' bells. My lofty desires to abandon "modern" travel; my longing to try the simple life had evaporated a little. Two days in a despised machine now seemed infinitely preferable to ten more on a horse or my own feet.

Mr. Khan was riding ahead of us and suddenly we saw him, high on a sand dune, waving his arms and shouting, "Lorry! Lorry!" There in the empty desert was the Consulate party which had come to meet us, with the famous old Ford which Sir Eric Teichman had originally driven across the Gobi from China to Kashgar. The acting Consul-General had received our telegram just before starting out on a tour. By further good luck he had heard

of our arrival at Khokia. Everyone talked at once without
listening to anyone else; more melons were produced;
some of our luggage was transferred on to the truck and we
all packed in with difficulty. Our pony men jumped on to
the now spare horses, and with a very cursory farewell,
continued their journey. We had no reason to feel attached
to them, and at times I had disliked them, but we had
shared a hard journey together and it was not without
regret that we saw the familiar caravan disappear so abruptly.

Having never before motored on any but well-made
roads, I had to readjust my ideas of speed. On the soft
sand the ponies had the advantage, and although at first
we roared past them at an exhilarating 10 m.p.h., they soon
overtook us when we sank in up to the axles. It was
humiliating getting out to push our lorry while the caravan
rode past. Even the three brave little donkeys and the
white mule overtook us, their driver still cursing and prodding them along.

We struggled through the worst of the desert, with
periodical collapses in the sand, and eventually came to
the semblance of a road where we could travel at 15 m.p.h.,
or more. At Karghalik, the first large town we reached, we
were given a sadly hostile welcome. In the narrow street a
truculent young Turki soldier suddenly barred our way,
brandishing his rifle. He refused to listen to anything we
had to say, firmly repeating that he had no orders to let us
through. It was an infuriating hold-up, so late in the evening
and so near to the rooms and the meal that had been
prepared for us. The soldier was adamant, and not at all
reluctant to use his bayonet with which he threatened
anyone who came near him. He eventually allowed us to
send a messenger for orders and also to buy some melons.
For nearly two hours we sat, sucking the fruit and trying to
conceal our fury, while a fascinated crowd buzzed around
us, at a healthy distance from the scowling sentry. At last
a man galloped up with permission for us to enter the town.
We never discovered the reason for this pugnacious
exhibition—if any. We drove on to a large building with
a garden, where a civilized four-course dinner was awaiting
us and we slept in beds once more.

The next day we covered the remaining 168 miles to Kashgar in eleven hours. Driving by way of Yarkand we followed a straight road through alternating desert and oasis. In comparison with the roads of Sinkiang which I learnt to know, it was good. But speeding was effectively checked by the many water channels which cut across it at frequent intervals.

At about 9 o'clock that night the massive walls of Kashgar loomed up out of the dark. The city gates were opened for us and we drove in. The little oil lamps of the bazaar twinkled all round us. It seemed unbelievable that we had arrived. To be entering the ancient town, which had been our goal for so long, felt like a dream. It was nearly three months, to the day, since we had sailed from Southampton.

CHAPTER III

A Domestic Chapter

THE DREAM-LIKE ATMOsphere of our arrival did not fade for a long time. In fact, I wanted it never to fade. I did not want to "get used" to Kashgar, or to forget the extraordinary fact that I was in Central Asia. This feeling was not as pretentious as it may sound. There was no peculiar merit in my being in Kashgar. I did not aim to instruct anyone about it, nor to be "the first Englishwoman" to do something or other. I only wanted to keep alive to the significance and interest of the country and the people all round me. In the large, comfortable Consulate it was all too easy to slip into an unimaginative, domestic slumber; to nod gently over one's own small affairs. Yet a chance to see this part of the world would most probably never come again and I did not want mentally to sleep.

In 1946 air travel to Kashgar was still restricted to the use of a few Chinese officials. From whichever direction the ordinary traveller approached it, the journey was rough and the comforts few. Arriving at the British Consulate the sudden transition from the harsh desert to a well-appointed English home, seemed, literally, fantastic— as if by a turn of some magic ring, the whole place would disappear. This sounds over-lyrical, and by some Western standards the house left plenty to be desired. But for me

40

the first impression of luxury and comfort, after the hard
journey, was never quite dulled. The present house was
finished in 1913, and whatever its faults in design, (for
instance many of the rooms were dark and sunless, two
guest-rooms were at the end of a rough, stone corridor,
beyond the kitchen regions), it was a solid, well-built
house; very superior to the modest, native-style mud
house which Lady Macartney describes as her first
home in Kashgar. Such things as glass in the windows,
which I took for granted, were a luxury to her; her furniture
was mostly home-made and comical. I walked in to a
completely furnished, ready-made home. It was strange to
think of the many ideas and tastes which had built up this
whole. Now I was free to add my own individual touch.

In thirty-three years one expects a succession of English
people to make a house habitable and comfortable, and considering the difficulties, they have done it. There was little
to be bought locally; the craftsmen were poor and nearly
everything had to be brought over the mountains from India.
I never solved the mystery of some of the massive bits of
furniture; they must have been transported piecemeal, like
an old English house taken to America. But the best
legacy of the line of Consuls-General, was the library. In
the drawing-room there was a magnificent collection of
Central Asian literature, as well as over 300 books on such
widely divergent subjects as the "Life of Mohammed"
and "Hunting Insects in the South Seas". There was even
an "Arithmetic in the Mongol Language", and twelve portly
volumes of an "Encyclopedia of Religion and Ethics".
Some of the more ponderous books were still uncut and
perhaps had been brought for their furnishing value, as in
many old libraries in England. In the big bare room upstairs, chiefly filled by a ping-pong table, was an astonishing
collection of fiction, including a large "crime" section in
lurid paper covers. Again I pondered on the changing
tastes and interests which had built up this heterogeneous
library.

A much more recent collection was that of the gramophone records. Someone had brought up a beautiful
E.M.G. gramophone and there was a varied assortment of

records, from complete symphonies to out-of-date dance tunes. It added strongly to the unusual character of my life to sit listening to familiar Mozart or Brahms concertos in a place I had hitherto considered so wild and outlandish. Sometimes the raucous, *shouted* songs of the Turkis floated in to drown my music and to remind me of where I was.

Taking no personal credit for the comfort and culture we found in this remote British Consulate, they so far excelled anything else we found in Sinkiang that we began to wonder why. We did not criticize the Turkis when discussing this question, they were a small race, lacking opportunity. But all the Chinese officials we met, civil and military, senior and junior, seemed content to live a sadly bleak existence, in this country they considered as exile. There seemed to be no desire to make their houses attractive, (with *Chinese* taste); their rooms were gaunt and uncomfortable, perhaps decorated with something ugly from the West. It was rare to meet a man with interests, occupations and pursuits outside his job; there was no spirit of vitality. It would not matter that Chinese interests were different from ours, if there had been a real keenness and enthusiasm for something. Our Consulate showed traces of the varied enthusiasms of so many different people. Ordinary people, not necessarily rich or learned—but men who felt a need for pleasant things round them and who brought their individual interests with them. There were excellent photographs enlarged to make pictures in the drawing-room, a store full of horns and heads from many shooting trips, the well-planned garden, a "Game Book", properly printed and bound, full of entries, a book noting the migration of birds, the library, gramophone and games. All these things had taken trouble, time and enthusiasm to collect.

It is not exclusively English to produce such a variety of interests, nor exclusively Chinese to produce so few. Of all the profound and fundamental differences between the East and the West, this difference of attitude to life "in exile", struck me as the most significant. It is only fair to admit that I have not been to Central China. I do not attempt to plunge into a comparison between English and Chinese civilizations. It would be rash and ridiculous. But living among Chinese, Indians and even Russians in Kashgar, I never ceased to wonder at the bareness of their lives; to wonder, also, at the spring from which comes so much keenness, enthusiasm and vitality in the West.

This chapter has got out of control. Such a subject could be enlarged to cover several pages.

Life in Kashgar gave us time for such endless discussion. Eric was not over-worked and "running" the house was not an arduous job for me. I had a staff, which at first seemed embarrassingly large. After the war years I was more accustomed to receive orders than to give them. Eventually the charm wore off and I struggled with the laziness, deceit and inefficiency of native servants. It had little to do with their niceness as people, but it was troublesome.

Gyalgen was my major domo. Through him I ruled an ancient Turki cook, a cheerful but unintelligent boy called Rosa Beg, the gnome-like washerwoman, a water-carrier and a gloomy man who did so little that I got rid of him. The last member of the staff I could never quite look in the face—he was doomed to deal with our primitive sanitary arrangements. Gyalgen's brother, Lhakpa, who had come up to Kashgar with Eric six years before, was still there. He was a masterful character who bullied the entire Consulate. To Eric's sorrow he had lost much of the honest humorous quality he had shown on past mountain expeditions. He had become stout and suspiciously prosperous.

Gyalgen learnt to speak Turki quickly, if roughly. My tentative efforts, with elaborate grammar and flowery constructions soon collapsed and I only learnt a few simple words. So I was dependent on Gyalgen. He gave orders and reprimands, did the shopping, waited at table and generally supervised. But he was as new to running a house as I was. He never developed into the silent, immaculate servant who appears so discreetly in all films about the East. He usually looked more prepared for an expedition to the hills than a dining-room. Although extraordinarily clumsy and heavy-handed he was full of good intentions and was an ingenious inventor of stories to keep me pacified.

During the summer months we wondered how to keep

the lawns cut without a mowing machine. Having our own cow, we decided to put her out to graze on the fresh green grass, and so serve the dual purpose of feeding her and cropping our lawns. A little later the cow went dry. When I questioned the lack of milk Gyalgen replied, with injured logic, that if we insisted on giving the cow fresh grass how could we expect any milk. I was left to work this out for myself. A battle I waged during our first year was over tea. Gyalgen was highly skilled in producing undrinkable tea. I bought new kettles, tried different teas but never solved the mystery. The elaborate process of boiling the water three times in a series of doubtful-looking saucepans may have had something to do with it. This, Gyalgen explained, evaporated the salt. I did not attempt to argue. He never conceded a point and was always determined to have an answer ready for every question. But in spite of his obstinacy I grew fond of him. He was such a friendly, kindly, sympathetic person. I think, at heart, he wanted to serve us well and wanted to prove that everything in the establishment was running smoothly and reasonably.

With our own cow, some hens and a good vegetable garden, the only food we bought in the bazaar was flour, rice and meat. As inflation then raged in Kashgar, prices sometimes jumped hourly and I tried to avoid local purchases as much as possible. The rest of our needs we ordered from India; an elaborate way of shopping as I had to look ahead at least three months and was so often disappointed. Parcels were limited to 4 lb. in the winter, 10 lb. in the summer and frequently arrived battered and broken. But we were fortunate to have the use of our own mail service, a privilege the Chinese, intermittently, tried to stop. After August 15th, 1947, when India gained her independence, the post became very uncertain. Riots, wars, transport difficulties racked the two new Dominions. My attempts to "shop" were useless, and although I had laid in good stocks of essentials, when stores were finished we had to improvise or do without.

In spite of many disappointments, the weekly mail day was eagerly awaited. On Tuesday mornings we woke with that tingle one feels on all special days. Although affected by events outside their control, such as the 1945 Sarikol rebellion, the Punjab riots and the Kashmir war of 1947, the mail runners themselves never failed. If they were a day late it was frowned upon. Considering the hardships and difficulties of the route—over snow-covered passes, risking avalanches, crossing rivers swollen by melting ice in summer along narrow mountain paths—it was remarkable how promptly and regularly our post was delivered.

The mail service was a well-planned system of runners and riders, with shelters and provisions for the men, organized along the route. The first part of this unique service was from Srinagar to Gilgit. Working in pairs, relays of runners went day and night to deliver a daily post. A journey that takes the ordinary traveller a fortnight was completed in six days. The second part of the route was from Gilgit to Misgar, where the Indian telegraph system ends. Again working in relays two runners took six days to cover this distance. But they only worked during the day and there was only a weekly delivery. Taking from five to seven days the third section was covered by relays of runners working in threes, between Misgar and Tashkurghan. Finally the mail was carried on by two riders to Kashgar. Riding hard they reached the Consulate in six days. Each pair had a twenty-three days' rest in Kashgar before making the return trip to Tashkurghan on the twenty-fourth day. It was a hard life, especially in winter, but the job, at our end, was popular. There were long rests and the chance to make a little extra money on allowances and trade.

After the magic words "The mail has come", there was a solemn ceremony of unlocking the bags and distributing the letters and parcels. Once the letters had been read and the parcels unpacked, a sad flatness descended at the thought of a long week to wait for the next mail. Sometimes the mail bags were empty and then the disappointment and flatness was acute. I tried to train myself to expect nothing, to have no hopes and anticipations, but I never quite succeeded—the one post a week meant so much.

The Consul-General's house, the garden laid out in four distinct levels, the handsome terrace overlooking a wide view of fields, river and hills, was divided from the rest of the Consulate by a large gateway and guard-room, where men in rich red uniforms were on duty. Outside these lordly grounds were bungalows for our doctor, the Indian clerks, the dispenser and the Chinese interpreter. A mud tennis court, a squash court, offices, garages, a dispensary, an ice pit and a complicated "village" for all the rest of the Consulate employees completed the grounds. In spite of efforts to check the Consulate population, it was uncontrollable. Remote relations of the staff accumulated in the small houses. Inquiring the identity of some boy, I would be told he was "the son of the sister of a gate-keeper's wife—he was an orphan". There was no more to be said. When we had an outbreak of typhus in the Consulate the danger of this family loyalty was even more obvious. No threats, nor fear of the disease, prevented sympathetic friends and relations visiting the sick. When one of the men died, everyone crowded in to wail round the corpse. It was useless to struggle against the strength of Mussulman beliefs and customs. On this particular occasion serum was dropped by parachute over Gilgit and a special relay of runners rushed it up to Kashgar in record time. We only had the one fatal casualty and the epidemic did not spread seriously.

There was also a tendency to accumulate old retainers who had served the Consulate. There was one ancient man who always greeted us in English. His accent was perfect as he bowed and said slowly, "Good morning, sir. Good morning, madam." He had to complete the whole sentence like an automatic machine, once the penny has been put in. The first time we met him I was delighted, and entered into a friendly conversation. But the old man knew no more English. Like a parrot he had said his piece. I fell into the same trap myself, with the Chinese. Thinking to please I learnt a few words of thanks and politeness. Immediately it was assumed that I spoke Chinese, and I was embarrassed by a flow of conversation, to which I could not reply.

Before we reached Kashgar Eric and I had discussed the problem of how I should use my time in a place where there were no friends, no organized entertainments and very few obligations. With endless, empty days stretching ahead it is fatally easy to fritter away the time. Quite contentedly, and unnoticed, the days fade past with nothing accomplished. So we both set ourselves a mild routine and eventually became so attached to it that we resented any outside interference.

The day began with an hour's walk before breakfast. Later Eric bought a pony and I walked alone. We nearly always went the same way—down to the winding river, through the fields, past the groups of busy water-mills and back in a complete circle. The initial effort of getting up was always unpleasant, but once we were out it seemed worth the struggle. We followed the gradual change of the seasons and crops. On winter mornings we got up in the dark; the frozen earth, the bare trees, the bluffs of crumbling loess and the mud houses, built from this same loess, all presented a uniform dust coloured picture. There were no evergreens in Kashgar and there was nothing to relieve the monotone except the gleam of the river and the frozen streams. Then the sun rose and for a short time flooded the scene with colour. In spite of the bleakness I enjoyed the winter walks. There was the sudden flurry of a wild duck from the river; the clouds of steam rising from the water as if it were boiling; the fantastic shapes of ice hanging from bridges and trees; and ice coating the mills with heavy patterns.

With the coming of spring, in March, there was a beauty more exciting than that of an English spring because of its suddenness and much greater contrast. The fruit trees broke into delicate pinks and whites. The willow trees, lining all the streams became a mist of subtle green. Looking down on the scene from our terrace, we watched this light mist develop into stronger colours, followed later by the tall slender poplars coming into leaf. In the fields we traced the wheat, cotton, rice, melons and tall ungainly maize through the seasons.

The melons were an important crop; they were larger, sweeter and more varied than I had ever dreamed of. The owners often slept out in the fields to guard their property; as I passed early on summer mornings I could see figures still fast asleep on their beds or on high platforms. After the harvest the fruit was stored underground and lasted almost until the small spring melons were ready once more.

Following the melons and the wheat, came the brilliant green of the rice fields standing deep in water. Then gradually, all the crops were harvested, only stubble was left and we were back to the bare brown of winter.

An unpleasant feature of the walk in early summer, was the plague of baby frogs. The path was a carpet of these small, hopping, floundering creatures. I dislike frogs but I dislike treading on them even more. So I had to walk gingerly with my eyes always on the ground. They liked to penetrate into my bathroom, too, and I would find a lost, surprised-looking frog peering at me from the bath. When we returned from a mountain trip in August, all trace of the plague had gone. Only occasionally I would find an elderly frog, stranded and grown old in my bathroom. But Kashgar was delightfully free from serious pests. People said there were scorpions, but I never saw one. The mosquitoes were not severe. We spent a lot of money on a net "house" to cover our beds, but only used it twice to justify its existence.

In the summer when the snows melted in the distant mountains, the rivers grew in volume. The bridge we crossed each morning was swept away and no one seemed inclined to replace it until the water dropped. So for many weeks we had a daily rendezvous with our two donkeys. Their official job was to bring us water from the river. In little wooden buckets, balanced across their saddles, they carried up all our water-supply. But at 7 o'clock on many summer mornings they met us at the ford and having, reluctantly, carried us across the river, returned to their proper duties.

A figure we met regularly each morning was the Consulate communal water-carrier. He was stone deaf, hard working and had a shy, attractive smile. He also had a keen sense of respect and discipline. The difficulties and complications he tied himself into, in order to regiment his three donkeys, were most comical. Seeing the approach of the august Consul-General and his wife, he would begin a

"A WIDE, EMPTY PLAIN WITH SNOW PEAKS ON THE HORIZON"

THE SASER PASS

OUR CARAVAN MEN

THE BRITISH CONSULATE-GENERAL, KASHGAR

THE FRONT DOOR OF THE CONSULATE-GENERAL

harassed shouting and prodding to force the donkeys into a strict line, their faces turned discreetly away from us. I felt like an old Emperor of China, on whom the crowd may not gaze.

Donkeys were a very characteristic feature of the Kashgar scene. They were everywhere. They were used for everything. A lordly, supercilious string of camels was usually led by a tiny donkey; parties of elderly, portly Turkis, almost submerging their mounts, trotted by like miniature cavalry; sitting on the extreme stern of his donkey a boy would pass at a fast trot, his dangling feet flaying ceaselessly to keep up the pace; round, moving bundles of grass would go by, nothing of a donkey visible but four delicate feet. People rarely walked in Kashgar, nearly everyone owned a donkey and used it to go even a few yards. In spite of their "monstrous head and sickening cry", I grew ridiculously fond of them. They looked so patient, so submissive; their eyes were liquid and sad. Yet they possessed an obstinacy and determination which revealed character. They were so much more staunch and gallant than most ponies. Their tortured cry rose in a variety of ludicrous notes, dying suddenly away as if they had become ashamed of the noise.

Perhaps the most important feature of our walks was the mountains. Looking north there was a low line of hills to frame the immediate scene. Looking south-west was a magnificent view of the Pamirs—a line of stately, shining ice mountains dominated by the strong buttress shape of Kungur (25,145 ft.). The delicate twin peaks of Chakragil (22,180 ft.) were, perhaps, even more beautiful. The view of the mountains was important to us because it was so rare. The curse of Kashgar was the persistent dust haze. Throughout the year it descended like a pall for weeks on end; blotting out the near and distant hills, dimming the sun and dulling everything. Even on expeditions into the hills we were dogged by its enveloping gloom. Then sometimes a severe wind storm roared down. You ate, smelt and sneezed dust; it penetrated every inch of the house. But it did, very often, clean the air and for a few days the mountains were sharp and clear.

4

If we were early enough, on one of these fine mornings, we saw the whole line dyed pink by the rising sun. Between such a bright magical view, and the complete black-out of the dust haze, lay a variety of moods. Sometimes mist hung low and the higher peaks appeared to float in space above it; on a stormy morning we could only catch a glimpse of the familiar shapes looming mysteriously through cloud; sometimes the mountains were colourless but distinct, like a shadow thrown on a screen; sometimes Kungur and Chakragil seemed unreal in their majestic height—exaggerated by cloud or mist.

The range was an impressive background to our Kashgar life. To us it was so beautiful it seemed almost inevitable that everyone else should feel the same. But Mr. Khan once said, genuinely puzzled, "I have noticed how you look at those mountains and I have looked at them myself, but I don't understand what it is you admire." So there was nothing inevitable about our enjoyment after all.

To return to our routine, it only consisted in setting ourselves firmly to read or to write for specified times. In Kashgar I had a unique opportunity to read books I had always wanted to read but never attempted in the busy, domestic life in England. Now I had no excuse to postpone reading Tolstoy's *War and Peace*, Boswell's *Life of Samuel Johnson*, and others. It was a new delight to be able to read without interruption or a feeling of guilt nagging in the back of my mind. We did not allow ourselves to flick through a novel or sit listening to dance records to pass the time. This sounds a little smug, but as I have said, with nothing and nobody to control one, the rot of frittering can soon set in.

During the spring and summer there was tennis three times a week. Eric never played but I usually joined the doctor, the clerks and a few Chinese who came regularly. The standard was not high and often very comic. Mr. Chu, our Chinese interpreter, had a style peculiar to himself and effective only on rare and spectacular occasions. I was told that in the past many of the Consulate employees used to play football. To the astonishment of the Turkis Ella Maillart had joined a game during her visit to Kashgar.

There was also a volley-ball ground. But when I was there all enthusiasm for games had died.

Polo is said to have originated in Hunza, and there used to be many Hunza men in the Consulate. Some time before Eric's arrival in Kashgar in 1940, a fatal accident, during a game of polo, had put a stop to the sport. Then Eric was persuaded to organize a game once more, although he had never played before. They had not been playing for more than two minutes when a man was thrown from his horse, dragged and killed. This second tragedy put a final end to polo, and the football-cum-polo field was turned over to melons and fruit trees. A story is told that the victim of the second accident, just before he began to play, was told by a small boy that he would very soon die.

The Russian Consulate-General gave occasional cinema shows; in the town there was a "Club" where more Russian films were shown under the auspices of the so-called Turki Cultural Association. With a view to balancing this one-sided propaganda Eric's predecessors worked hard to order some films from India. We eventually received six "documentaries". This caused a great flutter. First the films had to be passed by the local authorities, but we had permission to give a *private* pre-view of one film for our own amusement. A large screen was erected on the volley-ball court and when everything was ready Eric and I were summoned. We saw to our horror a large expectant audience of Turkis. Entertainments were so rare in Kashgar; the news of a free cinema at the British Consulate had spread rapidly through the bazaar and our gatekeepers had done nothing to keep out the crowd. Scenting trade, sellers of bread, sweets and melons had set up stands with little flickering oil lamps and were crying their wares. There was an air of carnival. It was impossible to turn the people away and yet we had promised the authorities to keep the show private. Feeling very guilty we showed our one film. It proved to be an extremely dull documentary about Radio Delhi. As an attempt at propaganda for the Turkis nothing could have been more unintelligible. As soon as it was over Eric and I crept hurriedly away.

Later, when all the films were officially released, we had another show. It seemed to me that the audience was considerably smaller and one cynic had brought his violin to wile away the time. All the commentaries were in English and the films dealt with life in India—Hindu India— a most unimaginative selection. After a long picture about the coco-nut and all its by-products, a Turki was heard to comment on the extraordinary things they could do with melons in India! This rare excursion of the British Consulate into the field of propaganda was not a success, I thought.

Our prestige received another blow shortly after this episode. In order to celebrate such occasions as the King's Birthday or the Mussulman festivals, it was the custom to have a show of dancing, singing and comedy turns. A handsome awning was erected for us and the office staff; carpets were spread and after dark pressure lamps flared and spluttered. In the gloom, sheltering behind a low wall which divided off the tennis court, were all the women. Some heavily veiled, some peering out now and again, while a few were bold and enjoyed a good view. The first of these shows I attended was made up of local Consulate talent. The Hunza men gave an impressive sword dance; a sweeper proved to be an expert Turki dancer; there were mock battles by grotesquely masked opponents; the head mail carrier, a fine old man of over seventy, did a sprightly dance, as light on his feet as a young ballerina. I enjoyed the family atmosphere and the fun of seeing familiar figures "dressed up". I suspect the turns were hoary with age and by now traditional. But lack of variation is not considered a fault among most Eastern people.

It was Mr. Khan's decision to hire professionals that caused the second fall of prestige. The Turki Cultural Association agreed to let a troupe of dancers and singers come to us for the evening. Again rumour of a free show at the British Consulate had collected a large audience from outside. But there was no sign of the performers! Message after message was sent; our lorry went out to fetch the troupe; but still no one came and still the audience increased. Various answers were sent to our frantic appeals. The performers were having their supper; the performers had been called away to entertain at a wedding. We were "losing face" rapidly. Fortunately the band (a violin, a tambourine and an ancient form of xylophone), had arrived and we managed to get one or two of our own men to dance. Later six disgruntled and apathetic men belonging to the professional troupe appeared. Under pressure they went through their repertoire, in a spiritless, half-hearted way. The absence of the girls chilled the whole atmosphere of the show. I was feeling embarrassed and wretched. Suddenly I suggested to Eric that he and I should give a turn. We must do something to enliven the miserable evening. Turki dancing does not appear complicated. The music is rhythmical and the dancer, with arms outstretched executes a continuous chassé step with few variations. The only difficult feat is a head movement with the head kept vertical and the shoulders remaining still. There was no need to attempt this, so choosing a tune we knew Eric and I proceeded to circle round, chasséing gently. I ended by sinking to the ground with waving arms in the approved style of all the female dancers I had seen. This modest exhibition was greeted with huge applause and we hastily closed the show. Whether the fiasco was due to a genuine muddle over arrangements or deliberate sabotage, I do not know.

So the days passed in the small, Consulate world. The pleasant monotony only occasionally broken by our own little parties, by celebrations, by limited contacts with the Chinese officials and the Russian Consulate. Our soothing routine satisfied me; expeditions to the mountains and week-ends in the country balanced the quiet days and provided another satisfying side to life. We had a wireless to keep us in contact with world news. I felt we were in a backwater, but the main stream was so troubled and unhappy that I had little desire to return to it. So long as Sinkiang's ever bubbling, subterranean discontents and problems did not break into a storm, I was contentedly happy.

CHAPTER IV
Shooting

WE DID NOT SPEND ALL OUR time in Kashgar in domestic routine or entertainment. Our aim was to get out of the Consulate as much as possible. Although soon after our arrival, in October, the scenery became bare and severe, and the cold grew sharp, there was the exhilarating interest of shooting to occupy us. Every Sunday we spent somewhere in the country, or perhaps, went away for the whole week-end. There were usually Consulate men keen to join us. The Hunzas especially enjoyed shooting.

But the important figure was Mir Humza, our driver-mechanic. He was an impressive Pathan, tall, bearded and adorned with large, yellow fang-like teeth. The ferocity of these was mitigated by his gentle eyes and sudden smile. He was an unfathomable character. Aloof and dignified, he had none of the servility and subservience common among Indian servants. He said exactly what he thought; his word was law and we obeyed him unquestioningly. He was calm in every crisis, and there were many on our various expeditions. While he could be extraordinarily considerate and kindly (he once insisted on Eric stopping the lorry while he led to safety a woman on a terrified pony), he was harsh and severe to his assistant mechanic. Yusuf led a most harassed life.

To our surprise we once found Mir Humza tending a diseased dog. On one of our trips into the hills he had come across a wretched dog with an infected sore. This was not unusual, but consideration for animals is so rare in the East and Mussulmans consider dogs unclean. Mir Humza tended this one for several days, with rough but well-meant treatment.

Although illiterate in the accepted sense, he was remarkably well educated in many ways. His knowledge of mechanics, electricity, carpentry and wireless he had acquired for himself. He carried on successful, although possibly quite illegal, trading which made him prosperous. Out shooting he would hand tips to the local beaters with lordly generosity; he always travelled with such efficient equipment as a Primus stove, and a handsome Thermos. But in spite of his powerful position in the Consulate he was never anything but quiet, deferential and extremely hard working. Few people could have kept the battered old Ford going as long as he had. He loved it like a child and nursed it through many illnesses. Over particularly difficult country he would run ahead of the lorry, searching for the best route. It is rare to find such keenness in the East. He seemed to like his work for its own sake.

Shooting was another of his enthusiasms. But he seldom shared it with anyone; he preferred to hunt alone. Silently and persistently he refused to co-operate and this sometimes resulted in spoiling a shoot. He might unwittingly drive the birds away from Eric or upset his tactics.

On most Sunday mornings in winter we would go to one of the rivers and then try to organize the "guns" and the beaters into a plan of attack. But no one seemed to understand what was wanted. Except for Mir Humza, the men had no idea of shooting on the wing; they liked a careful stalk for a sitting bird. The beaters wandered aimlessly about in the wrong directions. But on good days the duck came over in clouds and Eric had no need of any strategy. Crouching near the river or hidden behind a bank, oblivious of the cold, we would spend a whole day while formations of duck flew past us and above us.

A solitary teal flashed by, swift and low; high in the sky

difficult to see, a dozen Mallard in V-formation, faded into the blue; two noisy Brahminy flew clumsily past and some black and white Pochard settled, unsuspecting, on the water near by. Suddenly we would hear the distant honking of geese and excitement reached a high pitch as Eric struggled to change his cartridges, and the untidy flight approached. Usually they altered their direction before they were within range. Special glory was attached to the shooting of a goose. I suppose because they were large and yet difficult to bring down, it was generally considered a supreme achievement to get one. Once Eric hit one and we were exultant; to our disappointment the bird flew unconcernedly on. Eric continued to shoot duck until again we heard geese approaching. To our amazement the flight passed low over our heads and we saw that one of the birds was specked with blood. It was the wounded goose returning. A second shot brought it down. Eric, Gyalgen and I returned triumphant.

But later that season the triumph was completely eclipsed. We had had an unusually poor day and returned almost empty-handed.

Casually we asked Mir Humza about his day's shooting.

"All right," he replied.

"Did you get a goose?"

"I got seven," he answered with almost insulting humility. It was his supreme moment.

Later we discovered that Mir Humza seldom shot a flying goose; he stalked them with elaborate care. Although against his principles, Eric tried this technique. He was often disappointed. After a tedious crawl on his stomach over damp ground, some unpredictable sound would alarm the birds and they would flap heavily away. But occasionally when the ground gave good cover and the birds were busy feeding Eric would creep nearer and nearer, while I waited at a distance, breathless with excitement. To shoot a goose became something vital and urgent, quite out of proportion to the value of the meat and quite unreasonable. Crawling on, inch by inch, Eric would finally leap up to fire and if a bird fell the waiting beaters would dash forward to cut its throat. No Mussulman may eat flesh that has not been "Hallaled" in the orthodox way. Only another Mussulman may perform the rite; murmuring "God is Great" he cuts the bird or animal's throat, if possible before it is dead.

Very rarely we were asked to join other shooting parties. Once a Chinese General suggested that we should visit a small lake where he said the duck were numerous. After a tiresome drive over the primitive country roads, we reached a stretch of water covered with little black coots! The Chinese fired enthusiastically at the sitting birds, while Eric was enormously admired for hitting one of the wretched, slow-flying little creatures on the wing. It is difficult not to make fun of a different way of shooting from our own. To me the English conventions seemed so established and "right". I suppose there is no reason why other people should think so.

When Saif-ud-Din, the Commissioner of Education from Urumchi, invited us to a shooting party, we again visualized our own form of sport. As an experience it proved amusing, as a day's shooting it was nonsense. In the morning we drove to the house where our host was staying and were entertained with the inevitable glasses of tea and ancient cakes. After a long wait and halting conversation, the Russian Consul-General and six of his staff arrived. In a fleet of cars, most rare in Kashgar, we then drove out to a village about four miles away. Once more we were led indoors and an identical display of tea and cakes was spread upon the floor, only this time brandy and wine were added. We began to suspect that "shooting" was an euphemism for "drinking" party. Eventually, however, horses were produced and everyone, except me, rode the exhausting distance of about 600 yards down to the river.

Still Eric and I clung to the idea of serious shooting. We crouched near the river and waited for the duck to come over. But a vast concourse of guests, attendants, pony men and interested villagers flocked up and down the river bank. Nearly every self-respecting duck flew upstream never to be seen again. Eventually a few misguided birds returned and Eric managed to shoot two on the wing. Again this extraordinary feat was regarded with amazement.

Both birds fell in the water and while one of our men plunged in to fetch them, the crowd shouted instructions and advice to him, to us, and to each other. It was an animated scene but the complete end to the day's shooting. For some time the guests wandered aimlessly about. More food was spread on the ground and we all gathered round, but no one ate. The Russian Consul-General made Eric aim at an egg with a ·22; with everyone watching I was relieved when he hit it the first time.

Meanwhile our host had ridden off across the river. Suddenly in the distance we heard a cannon-like explosion and a cloud of smoke rose into the sky. Unfortunately nothing resulted from this impressive display.

The next move was back to the village, where the serious business of the day began. In the same house as before we now found a table and chairs had been produced, and an extensive Turki meal was ready for us. Steaming plates of pillau, platters of meat, bowls of soup and the excellent Kashgar bread "rolls" were all accompanied by more wine and brandy. The day ended with a second half-hearted attempt to shoot. With misplaced enthusiasm Eric rode far up the river in search of duck and everyone had to wait in cold dejection until he returned. Clearly one was not expected to take the shooting seriously, any more than one is expected to be absorbed by cricket at the Eton and Harrow match.

I have never been able to make up my mind about the ethics of shooting. I have no desire to do it myself but I certainly enjoy sharing in the excitement and eating the results. It seems inconsistent to hate to see the eyes of a dead deer and yet to view a dead chicken with unconcern. To a non-vegetarian why is the death of a gazelle more tragic than that of an ordinary sheep? The whole problem of "blood sports" is a well-worn one. Personally I solved it with complete inconsistency. I loved the chase, the thrill of achievement, the suspense as we waited for duck to come within range; the peculiarly exhilarating sound of all game birds on the wing and the whole delight of a day spent in the open. But how often I hoped that Eric would miss as a fine formation of duck, colourful, free, and so strong in their flight, passed over us. How often, in the stony desert I have pretended not to see a group of gazelle feeding peacefully in the sun. To claim that "shooting for the pot" was fair seemed a quibble. It could be no consolation to the bird or animal and at no time were we so short of food that we had to shoot game. Yet the meat *was* appreciated and enjoyed. I remained in a sentimental, illogical muddle of feelings about the whole question.

We varied the duck shooting with days spent in the hills chasing chikor. When disturbed these small, grey, red-legged partridge race uphill and, only when compelled, fly swiftly for a short distance. Eric always tried to take them by surprise while they were feeding low down. But once they were startled he enjoyed the furious chase uphill. It was too exhausting for me and when he and the chikor were out of sight I had to wander rather aimlessly on my own.

At a much higher level lived the ram-chikor, or Himalayan Snow Cock, a fine bird sometimes the size of a small turkey. During a summer trip into the hills north of Kashgar we had met a Kirghiz, called Kurban, who promised Eric good ram-chikor shooting near his home. Late in December of our second winter, we set off, with the doctor, in search of this alleged game. In a lonely valley, with rocky hills all round, we found our friend in his tiny, two-roomed mud house. He gave us a cheerful welcome and offered everything we could want—chikor, ram-chikor, gazelle, ibex. After many disappointments we had learnt to take such gay promises with a large pinch of salt. Already we had searched in vain for chikor, lower down the valley. But only a few hundred yards from the house, we put up a covey and immediately the birds and Eric were running uphill, soon lost to view behind a crag. The hills were thick with them, their loud, raucous cry seemed tantalizingly near, although they were hard to see against the grey of the rock.

Earlier in the day a wind storm had threatened and by evening it was blowing hard. With his usual unfathomable reasoning Gyalgen had pitched our small tent in open space, denying us the protection of walls or trees. There was no room anywhere else he explained firmly. After a good meal in the warmth and security of the house, we were abandoned to the storm while Gyalgen himself slept indoors. All night the ropes strained, the tent flapped and rocked and dust and debris were hurled against it. I tied a handkerchief round my nose and mouth and, dressed in everything but my boots, huddled unhappily into my double sleeping-bag. It was a miserable night.

By the morning it was quiet and clear. A calm dawn broke over the hills and gradually the sun crept into our valley. Following Kurban's instructions we went up the main valley until he led us into a narrow gorge running into the heart of the hills. Eric, the doctor, Gyalgen and I hurried after our guide. Kurban always walked fast and lightly. Among the hills he was as nimble as a goat, swift, secure and silent. We climbed steadily, frequently having to clamber over fallen boulders and round the chaos of rocks in our way.

At last we branched abruptly out of the ravine, up a steep gully on to the open hill-side above. Suddenly in the still air we heard the clear whistle of ram-chikor, ascending in a short, broken scale. Kurban was vindicated. He and Eric climbed off in one direction while we three made our way round the side of the hills in another, planning to meet at the head of the small valley lying below. Unknown to us Eric had seen some ram-chikor on the hill-side near our rendezvous. Unfortunately we did not see his frantic signals as he raced to cut us off. As he was nearly within range, but still hidden, the doctor sighted some chikor and fired. The prized ram-chikor whirred over our heads with their penetrating call of alarm and were lost. It was so rare to find good cover for stalking these very suspicious birds and for once Eric had found perfect ground. It was a sad disappointment.

We saw many more ram-chikor that day. At one point Gyalgen showed me about a dozen moving spots on an opposite hill-side.

"Wild goat," he said.

Creeping nearer, they seemed to me to move in a very odd manner for goats.

"They are ram-chikor," I said excitedly.

It took a long time to convince Gyalgen and, in fact, the "spots" were so large that I could hardly believe they were birds myself.

We spent eight and a half hours climbing up and over and along the hills. Sometimes from a high ridge we saw across to the Pamirs—faint and majestic away to the south-west. In between lay a curious smoky mist, more blue than a dust haze, and only the higher hills rose clear and sharp above it.

The enthusiasm of our guide was infectious. He enticed Eric farther and farther on, while the rest of us laboured at lower levels. On the way back there seemed no reasonable route down into the ravine again. Although extremely tired I had to follow Kurban along the tops of the hills until he led down a rocky, precipitous slope. Held up by Eric and Gyalgen I crawled unhappily after him. The floor of the ravine felt as comforting as land after a stormy sea passage.

All the way down the little Kirghiz was searching for game. No one had shot anything and he seemed to feel responsible. But he had fulfilled all his promises to show us birds and just before we emerged from the ravine a magnificent ibex bounded across a cliff above. Eric fired and missed. Again I suffered a mixture of feelings. I wanted the excitement and triumph of bringing home an ibex; but it looked so handsome leaping along the rocks; I should have hated to see it fall. Just before it disappeared it stood for a moment silhouetted against the sky, black, with its high horns held proudly—then it was gone.

Eric and Kurban went to pick up the ponies which they had brought to the mouth of the gorge, while we three hurried back to the lorry. I was aching with tiredness and had suffered from thirst all day. I knew there were melons waiting in the lorry and the thought gave me sudden energy. We found the melons but the lorry was deserted. Although Mir Humza and Yusuf had not been with us all day, we expected them back by now as it was nearly dark. I felt completely incompetent to drive the truck over that rough country and did not know how long to wait. Soon Yusuf joined us with the startling news that Mir Humza had shot himself in the foot. While racing uphill after game he had slipped, and his gun had gone off. He had had a painful journey back to the camp on Eric's pony. Fortunately the accident did not prove serious and he had not broken any bones. But Mir Humza did no more shooting for many tedious weeks.

We had several more expeditions with Kurban. His enthusiasm and energy never flagged. One week-end Eric got three ibex. We spent Saturday night near Kurban's house and woke next morning to find snow falling. It was grey, forbidding weather all the time we were in the hills. I found I slipped continuously on the snow-covered rocks and slopes and so I did not take much part in the shooting that time. Even Kurban admitted that the route he planned to take, on the Sunday, was a difficult one. At such an admission I turned back. Usually our guides insisted that "the road is easy".

Some weeks later we again visited the now familiar gorges and hills, but we made a camp at the entrance to the main ravine. On our first evening Eric hit an ibex. It was the largest we had got so far and one of eight which bounded along the hill-side in front of us, as we wandered up the ravine.

The next day we were out for eleven and a half hours. Eric was determined to get a ram-chikor. Kurban and a cousin led off up a long shoulder and all day we kept high among the hills. The gradients were not severe and the going was easy. As we climbed higher the low hills spread out below us and snow-covered mountains appeared above them. It was a day of clouds and greyness but occasionally the sun caught the ice and snow far away; the air was cold, the picture boundless. A curious line of old volcanoes showed black and red-streaked among the dun-coloured hills.

The ram-chikor were everywhere. Coveys of thirty or forty flew screaming away from us. Eric tried many times to stalk them, as the rest of us lay motionless, not daring to cough and hardly to breathe. But it was no use. He never hit one. We wandered on and on, hearing the mocking whistle, creeping round each corner full of hope, but always the birds eluded us. The day had been an exhilarating one;

but as dusk fell and we turned back with nothing, I realized how remarkably tired I was. We dropped steeply down to one of the ravines and trudged back to our camp. We saw the dancing flames of a fire in the lonely dark. It was supreme delight to sit round the fire with tea. Suddenly the desert and the hills were shut out and we were isolated in a tiny island of warmth and rest.

There were a few pheasant in the neighbourhood of Kashgar, but we seldom put up more than six or seven in a day's shoot. I found these days the dullest of our shooting expeditions. The small woods and rough grassland which the pheasants inhabited, were drab in winter. Everything was a uniform dust colour. Often we trudged about for several hours finding nothing, so that when a bird finally flew up from under our feet, Eric was almost too startled to fire. It was remarkable how tight the pheasants sat. We could cross and recross the same piece of ground before a bird would get up in heavy, clumsy flight. We were always hearing of places where pheasant abounded and always visiting them with hope and inevitable disappointment.

A wealthy Turki landowner, who had some business in the Consulate, often told Eric about the quantities of pheasant on his land. Their numbers were legion, they were uncountable, in fact, we should visit him for a week-end of glorious shooting, he said. At that time we had not learnt about the pinch of salt. We believed the wealthy landowner.

So one Saturday morning, in February, a large party left the Consulate. The doctor, three Indian clerks, Hafiz, the Jemadar, a collection of servants and ourselves. It was the usual dusty and exhausting progress for about thirty miles.

Except for the main roads leading out to Yarkand, Urumchi and, for a short way, towards Irkestam, there were no made-up roads at all. The cart-roads winding through the oases were a travesty of the word. When we drove along them I felt guilty about the train of disaster we left in our wake. Dogs flew out at the lorry and got entangled under the wheels; ponies, donkeys and camels reared and danced, flinging off their riders; carts were dragged hastily to one side while the drivers hung on to nervous ponies or bullocks. Once we approached a camel sitting by the road-side, a high load of grass on its back. Seeing us coming the owner covered the animal's eyes with his arm and clutched anxiously at its head. His precautions were useless. Terrified by the sound of the motor, the camel reared up on its hind legs and the man was completely buried as the avalanche of grass tipped forward.

A thing I could never understand was the unbelievably slow reaction of many of the peasants. Being so unused to motors I should have thought the roar of an approaching engine would be startling in the extreme. But frequently we could almost bump into a man before he noticed the horror behind him.

We reached the house of the Turki landowner to find a large display of food waiting for us. The familiar Kashgar bread, plates of pomegranates, sun-flower seeds, monkey nuts and melons were all laid out. We made impatient inquiries about the pheasants and soon horses were arranged for Eric and the doctor; to the concern of our host I announced that I would walk. None of the Indians came. All afternoon and evening I trudged about the near-by woods and fields and it was well after dark before we all returned—empty-handed. We had a multitude of beaters with the portly figure of Hafiz in command, but I don't think we even saw more than three pheasants.

Completely unshaken our host promised us excellent shooting for the following day. Twenty miles away, he said, there were vast numbers of pheasant. It was arranged that while everyone else rode, Lhakpa and I should go by "mappa"—a small horse-drawn vehicle with two high wheels, no springs and a wooden platform covered by a coloured, rounded hood.

On Sunday morning I began one of the most painful experiences of my life. It was just punishment for my cowardly fear of riding. All the bumps, ditches, holes and ridges of which I complained on our lorry drives, were intensified. While the driver perched on the shafts—leaping off most skilfully to lead his pony over the more difficult places—I tried every corner of the mappa in a

AN EAGLE PERCHED ON HIS OWNER'S HEAVILY-GLOVED
WRIST

THE "TUSHUK TAGH" RANGE

search for relief. I sat far inside the cab in dark obscurity;
I crouched, I knelt, I lay with my feet outstretched;
finally I decided that the extreme edge of the platform,
with my legs dangling out, was the most comfortable
position. I have read of Europeans travelling hundreds of
miles in a mappa, before the advent of motor cars to
Sinkiang. I feel that I must be spoilt and degenerate,
lacking stamina because of easy mechanical transport. By
the end of a mere forty miles I felt shattered and spent.

At last we reached the place where "pheasants lived in
huge quantities". Everyone dismounted and Hafiz began to
question a local farmer. Yes, there used to be a lot of
pheasant, he said. But that was two years ago. He did not
remember seeing any lately. The mappa ride had not left me
in a good temper. I cursed our host, all Turkis, mappas and
pheasants. Having come so far we decided to explore in the
woods. But the farmer was right and we saw nothing. The
return journey was relieved by lunch and frequent excur-
sions into woods and low scrub. We put up about four
birds but shot nothing. The riders then branched across
country while Lhakpa, I and the mappa made our painful
way back by road.

Our host awaited us with bland inquiries and was again
quite unabashed by the dearth of pheasants. He made no
single apology nor attempted to explain his original bright
promises. We never discovered the object of his invitation.
It was certainly not for the pleasure of our company; it
cost him unnecessary money and he appeared to have no
axe to grind with Eric.

We went sadly, and a little angrily, back to Kashgar.

In one or two particular places we used to find snipe.
Then the serious business of shooting duck or geese was
suspended and Eric concentrated happily on the small,
darting birds. This search for something so insignificant
never failed to astonish the Turkis. As we wandered among
the marsh-land and streams they would follow us with
animated directions about good duck-shooting areas. I
think they thought that Eric had been unable to hit any
duck and so was consoling himself with these ridiculous
little birds.

5

After we had been in Kashgar over a year, often lamenting the scarcity of snipe we put up some on our routine morning walk. So Eric began to take his gun out before breakfast and to explore the marshy fields near our house. An odd coincidence was that on the very first occasion he had his gun with him, a snipe flew up from a ditch only a few yards from our back gate. Never before had we seen any so near and never before had we had a gun with us.

During his wanderings in the near-by fields, Eric encountered a bright-eyed, eager little boy who said he knew of a place thick with snipe. We were sceptical; there was another small, long-billed bird which might easily be mistaken for them. But the boy persisted; he even agreed to come with us into the Consulate to have his flood of words translated, for we had only caught the gist. So one morning we followed him to unknown fields across the river. Immediately his sharp eyes pointed out a snipe, and another and another. The difficulty was that he could not understand Eric's reluctance to shoot them on the ground. He became quite desperate as Eric walked firmly up to them, instead of firing immediately. Before breakfast we had collected half a dozen and were all delighted with each other. Eric because the boy had found him a good place, the boy because Eric shot things, gave him the empty cartridge cases and some unusual fun.

He was a charming boy. His cheeks were rosy and his face round and cheerful. He bubbled with enthusiasm and was so quick to understand what Eric wanted. We heard him explaining to interested passers-by that we did not *want* to shoot duck. In fact duck shooting was altogether too commonplace. The Turkis were mostly so apathetic and lazy, so willing to stand and stare, until there was any hint of work, that this little boy was a delightful exception.

On all our shooting trips we attracted crowds of villagers. As they collected in large, noisy groups they invariably drove away most of the game. They were always full of loud and incoherent advice, but immediately the idea of beating, retrieving or showing the way was suggested, there was a strange melting away of numbers. Perhaps this is not peculiar to the Turkis, most people prefer giving advice to active help. But we were pleased with the energetic little boy with the sparkling eyes.

Two ancient sports still popular in Sinkiang are hawking and eagling. Eric's predecessor had been fascinated by the former and wanted us to buy his hawks. But one abortive afternoon out with the birds confirmed Eric's preference for shooting. Training the hawks may be a fascinating interest. It certainly seems a delicate business.

According to Lhakpa's information the trainer has to carry the captured hawk about with him everywhere for several weeks. He takes it into the bazaar to accustom it to men, to horses and to noise. He allows it little sleep; even at night he must walk it about to wear down its resistance. It is kept hungry and only allowed a small amount of blood-less meat each day. An ordinary, juicy bit of meat makes the hawk too fat. When the bird is in a state of hunger and submission, a long piece of string is attached to it, the trainer holds a piece of meat in his hand and calls. Gradually the bird learns to come to the food, learns to know his master and can then be trained to catch small game. A hawk can catch hares and pigeons quite easily, but is not very successful with duck. It can only fly fast for a very short distance; it cannot catch the duck on the water; two things which reduce its value considerably. Admittedly from little experience, it seemed to us that unless the hawk could see sitting ducks, on land, half asleep and therefore slow to take off, it had slight chance of catching one. The hawk must see the duck before the duck sees the hawk.

One morning three men on horseback arrived at the Consulate, after a week spent eagling near the hills. They gave us two gazelles and a fox, part of the large "bag" caught by the eagles. The birds perched on the men's heavily gloved wrists; little leather hoods covered their eyes and at intervals they gave loud, penetrating cries. They were magnificent in size but evil-looking in their fierceness—with huge curved beaks and wicked claws. When the hoods were taken off glinting, brilliant eyes made them yet more frightening. The men told us that it takes about a year to train an eagle for hunting. According to one owner they can live for twenty or thirty years.

The hunters go out into the desert on horses, and when any game is seen they race to cut it off before it reaches the hills. Then they release their eagles. For a good rider it must be an exhilarating sport—watching the huge bird flying strongly to sweep down on its prey and then galloping up to retrieve the animal. But I never saw it in practice.

CHAPTER V

The Elusive Arch

TWENTY MILES FROM Kashgar, on the road to Russia, a spectacular line of hills rises above the low sandstone cliffs. They break the sky-line in a series of sharp pinnacles, jagged spires and huge buttresses. The most striking feature of this curious little range is an archway high up in one of the spires, an immense hole bored by Nature.

Eric had first seen this intriguing arch as he drove away from Kashgar, on his way back to England via Russia, in 1942. On his return in 1946 he determined to explore the place, little guessing what an elusive goal it was to prove. During our first winter in Sinkiang the arch loomed in the background of all our plans. After each failure we determined on another effort to reach it.

In gay ignorance our first attempt was to drive out to the range one Sunday morning in January, in the belief that a few hours' climbing would bring us to the arch. We drove the first twenty miles along the semblance of a road, the greater part of it across empty desert.

Until I went to Central Asia my idea of a desert had been the conventional one of rolling, yellow sand dunes—cruel, perhaps, but essentially "romantic". Mirages, sheikhs and swift camels embellished the scene. As in films, the last two were continuously to be found in fine silhouette, the setting sun behind them. The deserts I saw in Sinkiang were very different, a much more austere, drab scene. Wastes of grey stone, sometimes relieved by struggling scrub, stretched flat and endless to the horizon. There was often an effect of shining water in the distance, but not the complete scene of trees and delight that taunts men in novels about the Sahara. There was an attraction about these deserts, nevertheless. The limitless space and lonely monotony, the silence and size were impressive and awe-inspiring. The camels were there, too, but they were in slow-moving lines, padding gently along as pack animals. In the same way as a human figure seen in a picture of mountains gives the mountains greater significance and height, so it was the little parties of donkeys that made the deserts appear emptier. Sometimes we would meet a solitary man driving his one donkey across the huge country. He made the scene seem infinitely more lonely and vast.

At a massive, decaying old "potai" (a Chinese "milestone") we turned north and went up a frozen river. It was an uncertain surface, but delightfully smooth and restful after the desert. Before we reached the foot of the range, and with the arch still in sight, we decided to walk. As we approached one of the wide gorges leading into the hills, the arch disappeared. We spent the day clambering about the sandstone hills and exploring up the first gorge we had reached. Until we left the hills we did not see the arch again. We began to realize that a bigger task faced us than we had thought, and that we needed more than one day for our search.

For nearly a month we waited for clear weather, free from the dust haze. But it was obviously useless to go on waiting and finally we made preparations to spend a weekend away. We decided to leave after lunch, one Saturday in February.

At 11 o'clock that morning our decision was shaken by a high wind which began to blow with dramatic force. All the loose dust from roads and fields was whipped up into a thick fog, obliterating the country more firmly than ever. Our servants prepared to unpack and to abandon the trip. But having learnt how often these storms subside, as quickly as they arise, we made them wait until the afternoon. At 3 o'clock there was no change, the wind still tore along in fierce gusts and dust penetrated every corner of the house, laying a fine film on everything. But we felt obstinate and refused to cancel our plans. After some delay the lorry was loaded; a crowd gathered to see us off; at about 4 o'clock we drove out of the Consulate.

Even in the closed cab of the lorry the dust poured in. For the four servants in the open seats behind, it was far worse. When they got out they looked like white ghosts. We made slow progress against the wind and along the rough track. All we could see was the immediate desert, with an occasional lonely caravan of camels, looming up out of the gloom.

We turned north by the familiar potai and continued farther than before up the frozen river. Then the ice failed us; suddenly we drove into soft shingle where the wheels churned frantically and uselessly. Mir Humza and Yusuf were always ready for these emergencies; with much shouting and pushing, working with poles and spades, they soon got us on to firmer ground. Only in the struggle the unhappy Yusuf had a finger-nail torn completely off.

Avoiding the soft ground, we bumped our way along and soon afterwards turned into the same wide gorge as before. In the failing light we selected a camp site, hoping to get some protection between the high walls of the ravine. But the wind had lost none of its energy. When we climbed up out of the gorge, it lashed us with such force that we could hardly stand. We made a hurried survey of the arch to try to memorize its position. We knew from previous experience that once we plunged into the maze of country leading into the hills, it disappeared from sight. Eric studied it through a telescope, getting rather an obscure view until I pointed out that the cover was still on the end of the glass!

By the time the tents were pitched and the fire lighted, it was quite dark. Tea and supper became one continuous meal; we all sat round the fire, under the dim stars, forgetting the wind and content in the sense of freedom, space and well-being. This evaporated when we went to bed. The ground was hard and stones lurked in unexpected places. The wind kept up a ceaseless roar and rattle and threatened to carry the whole tent away. It was a long time before we fell asleep.

The anticipation and excitement of the day before seemed ridiculous at 7 a.m. the next morning. It was cold and still dark. Having slept in our clothes we only had to struggle into our boots, but to leave our sleeping-bags at all was an effort. Breakfast only partially restored our enthusiasm. Then a sudden, unexpected view of the distant Pamirs roused us. The line of snow peaks hung above a blue mist, their lovely shapes touched with pink from the rising sun. The wind had dropped and left this rare and wonderful clearness. With high expectancy we set off up the ravine with Lhakpa and Gyalgen.

Of course, the archway had disappeared. But we knew its position and our previous exploration had shown us a good way of approach through the wild maze of pinnacles turrets and gorges. The ravine we were in grew narrower and narrower, deeper and deeper, until the sun was blotted out and we could touch the walls on either side of us. The foothills of this weird little range were of sandstone and shale—the formations looking firm and massive from a distance, but often crumbling away when we began to climb. For some time the going was easy. We followed along the bottom of the ravine and were only occasionally checked by a hard wall of sandstone, where I and our dog had to be pushed and pulled to the top.

The golden retriever puppy we had brought in Kashmir appeared to have survived the hard Karakoram journey quite well. She looked healthy and ate a great deal. But either she was naturally a stupid dog, or the six weeks of that unusual existence had affected her. All her reactions were slow; we had great difficulty in house-training her; attempts to make her retrieve met with no success; she hardly responded to our affection and did not appear to distinguish us from all the other human beings around her. Apart from food, only two things roused her enthusiasm. She went frantic with excitement over stones thrown into water and she never failed to be fascinated by shadows. Big stones thrown into a river or pebbles dropped in a puddle made her delirious with joy. She would often plunge into a river after the splash of a stone and would always dig furiously in a puddle. But she took small interest in the fall of a duck in the water. She chased her own, or anyone else's shadow with tireless energy, but showed no desire to run after a stick or a ball. She developed into rather a buffoon of a dog. We were fond of her in a mild way, but we missed the affection and the keen alertness of most puppies. She came with us on all our expeditions and invariably caused a lot of trouble.

When in Kashgar for the first time Eric had had a beloved, half-breed retriever, which he called Khombu, after the home of the Sherpas, a secluded valley of Tibet called Sola Khombu. We decided to call the new puppy Sola.

To return to the arch. The cairns we had built last time showed us which of the many turns and twists of the gorge to follow, and so saved precious time. At last we reached the big "overhang" which had checked us before. It was a high wall lying across the gorge and shelving outwards like a mantelpiece. Its hardness was deceptive and the foot and hand holds too treacherous to be trusted. A steep climb round by-passed this obstacle, and to slide down the soft, crumbling hill-side, back into the ravine, did not take long. But gradually the ravine began to fade and we branched up the dry bed of a tiny stream. The sharp ascent was hindered by thorny bushes growing in our way.

We emerged on to a flat tableland, a sudden and dramatic change from the narrow gorges. As we had been making height steadily we were now well above the dust haze—a clear, tremendous view spread round us. Above soared the most majestic of the spires and buttresses. We knew that somewhere amongst them was our elusive, and still invisible, arch. Below lay the fantastic complication of hills and gorges through which we had made our way—

dwarfed now and looking like a child's game in the sand. Beyond this labyrinth stretched the flat desert, mile after mile leading to more low sandstone ranges on the horizon. Above these the snow range was still visible. The peaks were no longer sharply clear but were etched in faint, gleaming lines—only sparkling in places where the sun caught the ice. They seemed disconnected with the earth and unsubstantial.

The high tableland cut off our advance and we realized that to get any nearer to our goal we must drop down into a new ravine, leading into the hills. The precipitous walls of this gorge looked uninviting. Their surface was hard, but not hard enough for safety. So we set off "across country" to search for an easier way down. Once the winding gorges were left the going was tedious and slow. We were forced to scramble up and down the steep, insecure hills while thorny bushes, and a continuous cloud of dust from the loose earth, added to the difficulties. After about an hour of this I was exhausted; I decided to wait in a sunny coomb and so avoid a particularly nasty climb we had reached. It seemed a long wait in that lonely silence, and when the wind began to blow once more, it became a very cold one. To keep myself warm and occupied, I finally struggled up and over the difficult pitch, crawling cautiously along a narrow, crumbling ledge. I shouted into the emptiness and to my surprise was answered from far below. Round a bend in the deep ravine came two tiny figures which waved up to me. Their steps echoed for a long time after they had disappeared. Apparently Eric and Gyalgen had found a way down, while Lhakpa had turned back (to bring me some lunch).

It was now too cold to linger so he and I decided to return. Having built a cairn, to mark the half share of melon which we had left for the other two, we turned for home. In that wilderness of hills it was not easy to remember the way back to our tableland. Twice we were cut off by a precipice and had to retreat. To avoid a particularly high cliff we took an alarming route across a steep, loose slope. The angle was unpleasant and the hand-holds liable to break away. I clung on precariously, kicking small steps, edging my way along and not daring to look down at the sheer drop below. We seemed to have been there for hours, and only Lhakpa's staunch support got me across. We reached the stony, grey plateau at 3 o'clock.

"I wonder where the others are?" I remarked as we peered down into the ravine once more.

They were there below us, on their way back!

Suddenly they turned and began to climb up towards us making slow progress. Presumably they wanted a short cut. We watched them from above while Lhakpa implored them, in English, Urdu and Tibetan, to go back by the long way. Even promise of the melon did not tempt them at first. Inch by inch they climbed up while we waited, always expecting the treacherous "holds" to crumble away and send them hurtling down to the bottom. Sola added to our anxiety by whining and making ridiculous attempts to join them. The wind was strong now and whipped the dust into our eyes; it must have troubled the climbers still more. It seemed an eternity before they gave up the struggle and turned back; not until we had watched them reach the ravine, did Lhakpa and I leave for our camp.

We made one false start by leaving the plateau down the wrong stream-bed. This brought us to a sheer drop of about twenty feet and we realized that we had never come up anything so difficult. We had wearily to retrace our steps to the tableland and look for the original route. Going downhill made the journey home much easier but there were still the steep walls to negotiate, which seemed more severe with only one man to help me down instead of three to help me up. We always threw Sola down first and then I would lower myself nervously on to Lhakpa's shoulders and so slide to the ground, nearly knocking the litttle man over in my clumsy descent. An arrow drawn in the dust showed us where to climb up, to avoid the big "overhang". Once more we clawed our way, clutching at roots which came out of the loose soil and at hand-holds which fell away at a touch.

The last hour was quite easy, we followed the familiar ravine as it wound down and out into the plain. But by now we were tired and stiff; it seemed an interminable way to our camp, and round each bend there was always another. At 5.15 p.m. we saw the lorry and there was tea ready for us. Unfortunately it was rationed, because our water supply had run out. Three-quarters of an hour later Eric arrived, and Gyalgen limped in ten minutes after him, exhausted but still cheerful. After I had seen them in the ravine the first time, they had followed it up until they were cut off by two frozen water-falls—sheer walls of ice. Having cut steps up the first one with long labour, the second had defeated them owing to lack of time. Even so it was quite dark when we started for home.

The afternoon wind had not abated and now it was behind us or following us at the same speed. Our own dust was blown up in front of the headlights, shimmering and shining and reducing visibility to nothing. Over the rough desert surface we tried to race the dust in a wild progress. Towards the end conditions improved and we could see quite clearly. At 8.30 p.m. we reached home where a welcoming fire, a bath and a good dinner were ready for us. It had been a strenuous week-end and the mysterious arch still eluded us—guarded by its tortuous approach. But the clear, magical views and the weird charm of the country had made it an eventful trip.

A third expedition to the range (which we had christened in Turki, "Tushuk Tagh", or Cave Mountains) was thwarted by the lorry. It was not noticeably a colder day than usual nor was the wind especially strong, but every few hundred yards the radiator boiled and we found the water was freezing as we drove. Continuous and lengthy halts while Mir Humza lit a fire under the lorry, made us so late that we decided to turn back. As soon as the wind was behind us all was well—a ridiculous anti-climax to our plans.

About five miles beyond the potai there was a village called Ming Yol. Eric's new plan was to go to this place, talk to the villagers there and try to find out if any of them had ever visited the arch. One week-end in March we drove once more along the familiar desert road. In Ming Yol we were immediately surrounded by the inevitable, interested crowd. But they were cautious and we discovered, through Gyalgen, that they thought we were Russians. Having been assured that we were not, and that our intentions were innocent in the extreme, all the men of the village entered into our plans with vigour.

Public opinion insisted that the right man to guide us was one Usman Akhun. He was a keen hunter, he knew the hills and both he, and his father before him, had long tried to find a way to the mysterious arch. He was a remarkably nice-looking man, with a strong, keen face. We discovered later that he had been to Russia and Afghanistan and was a much travelled, self-possessed, intelligent man, very superior to the ordinary Turki villager. We nicknamed him Toughy. He seemed quite willing to come with us into the Tushuk Tagh but said emphatically that it was impossible to find the arch.

Leaving Ming Yol, with Toughy and a friend to guide us, we drove across the desert towards the range. A species of broom was then in flower and big clumps of brilliant yellow relieved the grey, bare country. Following one of the many gorges which split the hills, we managed to get the Ford much farther into the range than we had done before. We seemed to be in one of the main valleys and we had vain hopes that it would lead us by a direct and easy path to the foot of the arch. I think Toughy was more interested in shooting than in our strange search; he was determined to lead us to good ibex country.

At 8 o'clock the following morning a large party, consisting of Lhakpa, Gyalgen, Mir Humza, Toughy and friend, with Rosa Beg, Sola and ourselves, started off up the ravine. We had hopes of seeing some game but as everyone talked in a penetrating shout we had to abandon the idea. Although alleged to be an expert hunter, Toughy never seemed to consider silence at all important; he addressed everyone as if they were deaf.

This gorge was not as narrow as the previous one we had explored, nor did it wind along in such exciting twists and turns. But we were again captured by the dry, silent country, the strange shapes and contortions of the sandstone hills, the feeling of mystery attached to our search.

We had even begun to wonder if the arch existed at all or was an optical illusion, only visible from a distance.

This expedition really belongs to Eric. He has described it vividly elsewhere. As soon as Toughy led us out of the ravine, up a steep boulder-strewn hill-side, the country became too difficult for me. We finally reached a climb I could not tackle, and left alone with Sola I watched everyone disappear into the hills above. The hill-side was still in shadow; it was a very cold wait. Sola was not content with my company, she spent her time whining and barking and trying to follow the rest of the party. Later a cascade of stones heralded the return of Lhakpa who, grown portly and short of wind during six idle years in Kashgar, had found the going too difficult. Toughy's friend, a mediocre character, also joined us and we three spent five weary hours waiting for Eric to return. Having left me with the promise that he would not be long I expected him every moment. The echo of distant shots convinced me that he was near. But the shots were fired by Mir Humza. Later I discovered that Eric and Toughy had been tempted higher and farther by a tenuous route up into the centre of the main mountain group. They finally reached a gorge so narrow that they had to move along it sideways, in complete darkness. The return journey was hazardous and even Toughy's bold spirit had nearly failed.

Ignorant of all this adventure I became restive and irritable. By 2 p.m. I was also exceedingly hungry. Three rules I learnt on this trip I never broke again. Always to carry a piece of bread and a book, and to keep all my jerseys tied round my waist. I had foolishly given my extra clothes to Gyalgen to carry—and Gyalgen was lost among the hills with Mir Humza and Rosa Beg.

Lhakpa, Sola and I returned to camp and to a large meal of bread and delicious mulberries from our garden. Later I wandered alone up yet another gorge. I have always disliked being alone in a house. I people it with a hundred ghosts of my own imagining. I have seldom minded walking by myself in lonely country. But that evening my imagination seemed to be out of control. I had a constant idea that I heard footsteps behind me. So strong was this belief that I sat and waited on a rock for "Eric" to catch me up. There is nothing original about this feeling. I suppose most people have experienced it at some time. But the actual *sound* of steps was quite definite that evening.

As we drove out into the desert in the evening light, the Pamirs struck us almost physically with their beauty. They were exceptionally clear, with the dying sun slanting across them. After the confinement of the gorges the sudden space and glowing colour was spectacular.

We had failed once more in our search. The difficulty of the country he had explored alone with Toughy, convinced Eric that the arch was unattainable from the south. So we decided to attack from the north. In early April we made a tentative reconnaissance up a valley beyond Artush. Leaving the main Urumchi road after ten miles, we branched off into the desert and had the most uncomfortable drive I had yet experienced. It was a dull, uneventful week-end, but it confirmed us in our plan to explore the Tushuk Tagh from the north and we had been able to select a possible route.

A fortnight later we again set out on the Urumchi road. After leaving it we laboured for about two and a half hours up a stony river bed. We continuously crossed the stream and occasionally got stuck in treacherous patches of soft ground. At rare intervals there were indications of a road; through a village there was even a stretch of firm, fine earth; but most of the way was over unrelenting rocks and stones. We were thrown about from side to side of the lorry and over the severe bumps hit our heads against the roof. At 5.30 p.m. we were tempted to stop by an inviting patch of green grass lying at the foot of high, conglomerate cliffs. There we camped for the night.

We made an early start the following morning and turned south up a dry river bed, towards the jagged lines of the Tushuk Tagh, just visible through the dust haze. We stopped at a Kirghiz encampment to ask the way. After some delay a crippled and ancient man greeted us nervously. We found that all the younger men had disappeared when they heard the lorry. Again we were thought to be Russians. Remembering a previous era of Russian-directed rule the

Kirghiz thought we had come to take them away for enforced military service. Having assured the old man that we were only there for our own amusement, he relaxed a little. But he knew nothing of the arch. It was nowhere visible from this side of the range.

We crawled on up the valley, later branching off it to the left in the direction of our hills, and climbing steadily in second gear. A line of low hills appeared to cut us off from our goal. But we found a valley leading into them and again we branched to the left. The valley grew more and more narrow. We had to break down some of the soft walls in our way and nurse the lorry through the passage. Finally the valley merged into the low brown hills. We camped where we had stopped, at about 9 a.m.

From there we walked. Over the small hills we went until our range lay clear ahead of us; a wide, stony valley led easily on towards it. The many gorges on the north side were gentle, but we had to decide which one of them to choose. There was no sign of the arch. But by now we were familiar with the line of spires and buttresses and we knew that it lay to the right of the main block. Selecting the widest of the valleys leading into the hills, we followed along its flat but pebbly floor. On this side the hills were of firm conglomerate, towering above us in fine, solid shapes but in places patterned like gigantic honeycombs. When the valley divided sharply to right and left we were faced with another decision. Eric chose the left-hand turn because it looked the bigger of the two.

Soon after this divide the valley narrowed suddenly to a dark passsage and our way was blocked by a damp wall of rock. We climbed up without difficulty and Sola was pushed up after us. Although extraordinarily lethargic on our daily walks, when, in spite of beatings she spent most of her time eating dung, she appeared to enjoy our expeditions. At any rate she protested violently if left behind at some difficult climb, and preferred to be dragged up and thrown down, rather than be abandoned.

There were no alternative routes now, we could only follow up the valley. At every corner we expected to find our way barred by an impassable rock wall. Three more walls had to be negotiated but they were not severe. One was a smooth drop of some eleven feet up which I had to be dragged but no one else had any difficulty. We had Gyalgen, Mir Humza and Rosa Beg with us. This climb led us into an attractive little dell full of shrubs and a few small pine trees. The discovery was unexpected among those arid, bare hills and we even began to have hopes of finding the legendary fruit garden which is said to exist in this odd little range.

At the head of the green coomb was another small climb where I was helped up ahead of the others. Beyond, the valley narrowed once more and developed into a steep, rock-filled nullah, curving away to the left. The hills soared on either side and ahead of me. High up on the mountain in front there appeared to be a small patch of snow. I was surprised to see it at that low altitude. Then Eric joined me and his reactions were quicker than mine. He gave a gasp and pointed to the patch of "snow". With a sudden shock I realized that it was the *sky* I had seen. I ran excitedly round the bend. There, high in the mountain at the head of the valley was an arch.

As we panted up the dry nullah, Eric damped my excitement by saying it could not be "our" arch, it was too small. The rocks led on to a very steep but grassy slope—this seemed to lead to the foot of the arch. When we reached the top of the rise we found ourselves looking straight across at the immense curve of the arch. Its upper half soared above us but the walls continued down into an unfathomable gorge below. It was as if we stood on a platform some few feet away from a gigantic window. It framed a view of mountains beyond. It was impossible to gauge the height of the arch accurately. But now that its full size was revealed Eric did admit that it must be the right one. The one we had seen from a distance, the one we had searched for so long.

The walls of the arch were smooth and clean; they swept round like a beautiful structure carefully made by man. We could not see the base, the supports disappeared into gloomy depths. But it was easy to see why we could never have reached our goal from the south. The end of the

6

gorge below us was blocked by a solid mountain; only deep, extremely narrow defiles led the way out—defiles too narrow and difficult for anyone to penetrate. Owing to the tilt of the strata the approach from the north had been a comparatively easy one. The wonder was that we had unerringly chosen the right route, among the many possible ones, to lead us so directly to our long-sought goal.

We spent the day trying to photograph the arch, climbing a near-by hill, eating lunch and unashamedly exulting in our triumph. In itself the arch was an impressive phenomenon but our search had added spice to it. We wondered if any-one else had ever visited it before. A hunter might have done. But the rock walls we had climbed were high for a shepherd to drive his flock that way and we never met any locals who knew of the place. We liked to nurse the illusion that we were the first to reach the secret valley. In any case we had found it for ourselves, without a guide.

Later we revisited the arch in order to show our dis-covery to the doctor. It was a stormy week-end and we had several sharp showers of rain. I had almost forgotten the feel of it. The cool refreshing wetness was something I had never appreciated until I came to a country where it rains about twice in the year.

Having spent all Saturday near the arch, on Sunday we decided to explore one of the other valleys leading into the range. The day was fine and clear after the storms, and the air seemed washed by the rain. We had an easy walk up to the watershed; no rock walls barred our way. Near the top of the final grass slope, Mir Humza sighted an ibex. The party climbed up in silence, all hoping to see it, but it had disappeared among the high crags. To my disappoint-ment there was no view from the watershed; only a deep gloomy gorge leading away to the south. Through the dark, narrow V of this gorge was the promise of a view of the Pamirs. To see them in their full glory it was obvious that we must climb up to the ridge above us. There were two alternatives. To follow a narrow shelf which ran along the cliff-side or to climb straight up the face of the rock wall. Eric advised the latter as I could then benefit from a direct pull on the rope, which we had brought with us. Feeling very unhappy I tied on between Gyalgen and Eric.

Although Eric has climbed mountains since the age of fifteen, I have never done more than walk among them. The feel of mountain country and the beauty of hills I have always known. But steep places frighten me and I had never before attempted anything that I could, strictly speaking, dignify by the name of a "climb". Difficulty, of course, is relative to the climber's skill. I do not want to give the impression that I now tackled something difficult, as the term is accepted among climbers. It was certainly a sheer rock face and a fall would have hurled one into a deep gorge, of which the bottom was invisible. But the rock was firm, the foot and hand-holds were good and in climbing terms it was "easy". This was scant consolation to me; my fears had little to do with reason. It was Gyalgen's gentle, soothing encourage-ment and not Eric's logical assurances, that got me to the top. We were often to have arguments about "difficult" climbs during our expeditions. Fear of heights in some degree, must be familiar to everyone who has been among mountains. Presumably the real climber gains confidence as he learns the technique—learns to control his feet, his hands and the rope. He must learn mental control, too. Although Eric never asked me to tackle anything that he considered severe, he did, quite rightly, ask me to try small climbs which he knew were easy and absolutely safe. He was convinced that with practice I should learn how to move and also to control my unreasonable fears. It was like our argu-ments about riding and I found it hard to follow his advice or to believe his assurances. But in this case the rewards seemed to me so much greater that I tried harder to conquer my fears. I only introduce the sorry story of my personal cowardice to explain that "difficult" climbs relate to my own low standard.

The reward of my first "climb" was very great. To the north and south snow peaks stood high and sparkling against a bright sky. The soft misty-blue folds of the lower mountains merged imperceptibly into the deep red-browns of the smaller hills. On either side flat deserts and wide river valleys rolled up towards our range. The hills immediately around us were a complicated pattern of shapes. They rose in sharp and delicate spires, in heavy blocks, in pyramids like those of Egypt; all were divided by the huge canyons. From our narrow ledge we peered down into one of these terrifying ravines. It took nine seconds for a stone we dropped to hit the bottom.

My enjoyment of the huge scene was a little spoilt by the prospect of having to go down again, always the disadvantage of climbing up. This time I chose the slanting shelf. With the rope to prevent me from slipping and two men to guide me from in front, I crept carefully down on my seat. It was an easy descent and I regretted my silly apprehension.

Now that we had found our arch we felt a little aimless. We almost regretted that the zest of the search was gone. But Toughy and his friends had whetted our appetite for adventure in the Tushuk Tagh by stories of a beautiful garden, hidden somewhere among those remarkable hills. Only the pure in heart could reach this paradise, it was said. Huge gates barred the way to all who were evil-minded. Taking our purity of heart for granted we decided to go once more to Ming Yol, to ask Toughy to guide us to the garden. We were also anxious to tell him of our discovery of the arch.

If he was impressed he did not show it. I suspect that he did not really believe us, when we told him of the route from the north, straight to the arch. However, he agreed to join us again and we drove to the same main gorge as before. We branched off it into the smaller ravine where I had wandered alone. When we had pitched camp, we started a lengthy search for water. There was none within an hour's walk of the tents. We had to be content with our "tinned" water, which always tasted faintly of petrol.

The next morning a party of eight left the camp. Lhakpa had found the two previous trips, on the south side of the range, more strenuous than he liked. When he first came to Kashgar, he explained to us, he had been an "animal", now he was a "man". This development, we understood, was a mental one, for physically Lhakpa had deteriorated. In his place we had Yusuf, and for some extraordinary reason the Consulate tailor had joined the expedition.

Gyalgen always insisted on bringing Rosa Beg on these trips, to help him with the cooking and general work. The Consulate was developing grand ideas in Gyalgen also; he now considered it undignified to be seen washing-up or peeling potatoes. But, although town-bred, Rosa Beg was active among the hills; he was always eager to come with us and entered fully into the spirit of our expeditions. While not conspicuously intelligent, he worked hard and was firmly imposed upon by all the other servants. He would often attack some quite difficult climb with wild impetuosity and then be unable to extricate himself. Grumbling at his stupidity Gyalgen would have to help him down. With Mir Humza and Toughy to complete the party we started at about 7.30 a.m.

Whatever he really thought about the legendary garden, Toughy was quite definite about the place he was leading us to that day. It was a lake in the hills and round it grew trees, grass and flowers. This was sufficiently intriguing for the moment and we followed him up the gorge. It very soon became harder work than any of the previous ones I had explored. At intervals massive falls of rock and debris blocked our path and it was not always easy to find a way over them. Again I had to be pushed from behind and pulled from in front, with Gyalgen, as usual, nursing me over the worst places. The tailor had some difficulty, too. The permanent smile that normally adorned his face was fading rapidly and I suspected that he was beginning to regret having come at all. Through no fault of her own the way was much too difficult for Sola. But as we had brought her we did not like to leave her, miserably barking and alone at the foot of some rock wall. Once she was forgotten and the long-suffering Rosa Beg was sent back to retrieve her. But she was surprisingly gallant, she seemed quite determined to share in the expedition.

After alternately climbing over the great boulders and following the smooth, easy floor of the gorge, we came to a place I thought impassable—at any rate for me. But instead of having to climb over the rocks in our path, I found I could crawl *under* them; a tiny tunnel led through to the country beyond. On such small chances my hopes of seeing the lake depended; I was always expecting to reach some barrier I could not tackle. Creeping under the rocks on my stomach I edged my way out into a wide valley. This was a complete and startling contrast to the narrow, severe gorge. There were shrubs growing and fair-sized trees; we began to feel that a magic garden might well lie somewhere near.

The easy walk along this valley soon ended when Toughy led us up the hill-side to avoid a really severe rock-fall, which blocked the end of the valley. The hill-side was steep and crumbling; both the tailor and I were put on the rope with Gyalgen, to give us moral support. I was glad to have someone with me, if possible, more nervous than I. Once we had by-passed the rock-fall the going was easy. The way had contracted into a deep gorge once more, like a high, narrow corridor. We came to several rock walls in our path, similar to the ones we had encountered on the way to the arch. The final one was the most difficult and to add to my troubles a stream trickled down from above—wetting me as I struggled up.

Having got so far I was determined to reach the lake. But I was still expecting to be prevented at every corner. However, the last lap, although exhausting, was straight-forward. The passage-like gorge led out into a rough steep hill-side. Having laboured to the top of it we looked down into a small, secluded, green valley. It seemed like a miniature Promised Land. Full of excitement we ran down into it.

The famous lake was something of an anti-climax. It had dried to a small pond and was a muddy patch of water. But the valley was no disappointment. Sheltered among the massive walls of the mountains—some of which rose in sheer, smooth sweeps—it was covered with shrubs, green grass and tiny flowers. In a country where little grows without irrigation, this discovery of natural grass and vege-tation was especially entrancing. For long we lay, by the water, eating and dozing and contented.

Later we explored farther up the valley and were amazed to see a flock of sheep. I cannot imagine how the shep-herds persuade them up the route by which we had come, yet there was no path leading into the valley from the north. Perhaps they know an easier approach from below? We were reluctant to leave the enchanted valley, but on the way up Eric had noticed a climb he thought intriguing and he wanted time to explore it. He and Toughy left us and we went back to camp. Down the dripping rock wall, through the dark passages, along the unwholesome by-pass to the series of big scrambles, we went. The tailor, Sola and I again had to be helped. I felt sorry for the tailor because whereas I was expected to need help, he was heavily chaffed and mocked by the others. Sola had an irritating habit of halting at some steep drop but backing away when anyone went to help her. Unless she was secured and pushed down first, she remained protesting but reluctant at the top. By now her paws were cut and bleeding; she was very tired. Slowly, with a rather drunken roll, she covered the final easy stretch to the camp. We both ate a large meal and went to sleep.

Eric and Toughy had another of their alarming climbs and did not get back to camp until nearly 7 o'clock. I was beginning to feel nervous. I had no idea how or where to organize a search party. We had just decided that the climbers might have returned down a different gully and would meet us at the big fork, when they appeared. Toughy was enormously impressed by Eric's climbing, but I gathered he had no wish to tackle that particular area again.

We drove home in the dark and found Lhakpa about to organize a search. It was then 10 p.m. and he was getting anxious.

CHAPTER VI

Entertainments and Visitors

MOCKERY AND JOKES against the Englishman abroad have been as monotonously popular in England as in any other country. Our "outposts" are diminishing and perhaps with them our alleged arrogance. The prosperous Empire builder of the nineteenth century is now an historical figure. Meeting Chinese, Indians and Russians in Sinkiang I learnt, with surprise, that there are nations more parochial, more narrow and prejudiced in their own favour, than my own. I am unashamedly proud to be English. I would not change to any other nationality. But this does not effect my keen interest in the customs, ideas, manners, clothes and food of other nations; nor with a genuine admiration for many of these things. I did not find this interest reciprocated. There seemed to be a reluctance to admire foreign things, a reluctance to sample foreign foods and an unrelenting conviction, among each peoples, that their own ways were unquestionably the best.

The Turkis were looked down upon by the Chinese, the Russians and our Indian clerks alike. They were dismissed by all three as backward, barbaric. For all their obvious failings, Eric and I found ourselves alone in our liking for them, in our interest in their way of life. I suppose this difference is another aspect of my "hobby horse", the lack of a spirit of inquiry in the East. (The Russians we met were nearly all Asiatics.) So the further I ride the more I reveal an unattractive superiority complex in the English! But it does seem to me that it is better concealed, and at least it allows for wide interest in, and admiration for others as well.

An ill-concealed war raged in our Consulate between the Indian clerks and the Chinese interpreter. Admittedly Mr. Chu was a temperamental character. He would rush into Eric's office, bare his chest and announce that he had been "hit". But although the blow usually proved an imaginary one, he did have reason to feel injured. He suffered continuous small snubs, injustices and irritations. When he and his family finally left, after nine years in the Consulate, open war was declared. No one appeared to help them with their luggage and the loading of the lorry, and we suspected quiet sabotage. It was a childish exhibition of spite and we were sorry that Mr. Chu should have left with such bitter feelings about the Consulate. Both sides were to blame and both sides were uncompromising in their feelings of superiority towards the other.

Through this complicated maze of personal and national dislike we tried to steer a peaceful passage. A dinner party was a delicate affair, with conversation running a sluggish course, and eddies and currents to be avoided. We all gave small parties to each other, but frequently no Indians appeared at Mr. Chu's table and the Chus were not present at an Indian dinner. I do not know what they all thought of our meals, but rudeness about each other's food was very thinly veiled. There was no desire to sample new cooking, to experiment and learn.

Mr. Chu's successor, a dapper little man called Mr. Yang, was somewhat more diplomatic with our Indian staff. But he unreservedly condemned everything Turki. He found Kashgar rude and primitive and regarded his life there as a bitter exile. To him everything unfamiliar, from an English dinner to a Turkestan town, was suspect. He was a good interpreter and served Eric well, but I pitied him his unhappy, constricted days.

Outwardly, at any rate, life in the Consulate was reasonably smooth. It was a small community and that invariably results in a certain amount of friction.

The only occasion on which Eric and I entertained *all* the Consulate employees was at Christmas. It never seemed a real Christmas to us. It is when such festivals or family anniversaries come round that you feel the remote isolation of foreign places. Then all the interest of travel, the fascination of "new worlds", fades away and you long only for home, for a familiar country-side, for people that speak the same language and follow the same customs.

So at Christmas the charms, interests and attractions of Kashgar faded. It seemed a distant, alien place and attempts to stage an English Christmas were doomed to failure. It was not only because the bazaar could offer nothing in the way of presents and decorations, nor because holly and "Christmas trees" did not grow, but because the festival meant nothing to the people there and our traditions were unknown to them.

It was known, of course, that Christmas was a Big Day for the English, and to celebrate it various customs had grown up in the Consulate. The day's programme followed certain rules and we could but conform. First of all, the office staff and Indian traders were received in the drawing-room. Tea and cakes were handed round, and vodka to the "infidels" who drank it. Most of the guests accepted everything handed to them and ate nothing, piling their plates high with unwanted food. Hardly anyone spoke. Except for a little forced conversation ("How long have you been in Kashgar?") among the English-speaking men, the party sat in serried rows. The signal for departure came and the guests went silently out.

Immediately after this gaiety came entertainments for all the lesser Consulate staff. A long stream of gate-keepers, watchmen, orderlies, water-carriers, mail carriers and servants filed into the big dining-room. A vast table was spread with cakes and fruit, and this time there was no question of wastage. As each man sat down he seized a cake and within ten minutes the table was clear! When the guests had swallowed one or two bowl-fulls of tea, which we helped to pour out, they filed away again. Each man salaamed respectfully as he passed us, but not a word was exchanged. An oddly rapid, silent party, more like a plague of locusts attacking a harvest, than a celebration.

The children's party in the afternoon, was a more cheerful affair. In the big library upstairs, a shouting, jostling mob of both sexes, all ages, shapes and sizes, was controlled by Hafiz with a huge stick. We began the party with "musical chairs", the children obeying our shouts and instructions with confused obedience and gradually grasping the idea. Buns, dipped in treacle and tied high on a string were much more popular, the aim being to gnaw off a bun without using the hands. A triumphant, treacle-covered little boy soon won the struggle. An egg and spoon race was a more elegant competition for the girls; my feeble attempts to pick up an egg were watched with polite patience.

Eric then demonstrated cock-fighting, rolling in undignified abandon on the floor. A speciality of ours, where the opponents lie, blindfolded, on the floor and hit each other with rolls of paper, was a success. A queue of boys waited for a turn, and although no rules were observed there was some fine, fierce slashing. All round the crowd pushed, struggled, laughed and cried, while Hafiz threatened in vain. The dust whirled thickly and the atmosphere was choking. An attempt to make the little girls dance petered out owing to the acute shyness of the performers.

Then at last the children were told to sit in a large circle, while biscuits, cakes and popcorn were handed round. Each child held out a hat for a share, and even the uncooked potatoes (for a potato race) were gratefully accepted. We left them all munching their little stores. An exhausting party, but by far the most cheerful, genuine one of the day.

Christmas Day ended with a staff dinner in the evening. My first Christmas in Kashgar the lamp was dimmed for the dramatic entry of the lighted plum pudding, only to find that cheap Russian brandy refuses to ignite. I had to remember to order two puddings, one without alcohol for the Mussulmans. How I missed the holly on the pudding.

In all the celebrations of Christmas Day the women could take no part, shut away by their Mussulman rule of purdah. So I decided to give them a "purdah party" on Boxing Day. I had no idea of the number of women hidden away in the rabbit warren of the Consulate. I simply laid out as many cakes as remained from Christmas Day and opened a tin of cigarettes "in case anyone smoked". The servants were forbidden to come near the drawing-room, and one or two more unorthodox of the women offered to bring in the tea.

Before the first purdah party I gave, Mrs. Chu and I waited until, very late, the guests began to trickle in, shedding their long white coats and little veils, in the hall. Everybody had made an effort to put on their best clothes; they wore round velvet caps, gold embroidered, or fur hats over a chiffon scarf, brocade, silk and velvet coats of every colour, elaborate but cheap jewellery, hair plaited into a hundred tiny pigtails with sometimes a black curl plastered down the forehead; the hideous fashion of joining the eyebrows with heavy black paint across the bridge of the nose was a popular one. In spite of all this finery, no one left off her heavy Russian boots.

Soon all the seats were taken, the tea and cakes were rapidly disappearing, and I found that everyone smoked! Cakes and cigarettes were often secreted inside the coat, for future use. The trickle had grown to a flood; more and more women poured in; I and my helpers worked frantic-ally; searching the house for chairs; impatiently ordering more tea from the men in the kitchen; opening new tins of cigarettes; and finally snatching a secret store of cakes, which had been kept by the servants, and hurling them into the fray.

There was no stiff silence and restraint. The room bulged with women; those who had no chair sat on the floor; everyone talked at once and screamed across to friends opposite; helpers picked their way about with trays of cakes and tea, falling over crawling babies or bumping into each other, so that tea poured on the carpet and cakes were trampled underfoot. The babies were being fed by their mothers, or were howling, others chewed any available cake, ash tray and cigarette, or made a quiet pool to add to the general fun.

Gradually the storm died down, the food was finished, the cigarette tins were empty, and the exhausted helpers sipped their tea.

Then someone suggested dancing. A woman fetched her long two-stringed "guitar", and one or two reluctant guests were persuaded to perform. The two elaborately-dressed and elderly wives of the Jemadar opened the show with a slow shuffling dance; a plain but self-possessed girl sang one of the harsh Turki songs; and finally two pregnant women took the floor and they shuffled, too. But the interest was half-hearted and the performers embarrassed. Mrs. Chu spoke Turki and I asked her to announce that the party was over, how delighted I had been to see them all and so goodbye. Everyone thanked me profusely and streamed into the hall where veils were carefully put on again before going out.

Lhakpa and Gyalgen were disgusted with the chaos left in the drawing-room and railed against the greed, dirtiness and even dishonesty of all Turki women. In spite of Lhakpa's Turki wife, the two Tibetan brothers never ceased to complain about the local women. They disapproved of their idle, hidden lives. They explained to me how hard the Tibetan women work, how virtuous they are in every way. Certainly I was not impressed by the Turki women. Their main interests were entertainment and new clothes. Divorce was a simple matter and changing husbands seemed to be another of their pastimes.

Although I counted ash trays to see if any were missing, I enjoyed the unaffected hearty atmosphere of my purdah parties far more than the stiff, embarrassed parties of men.

Another annual entertainment was the King's Birthday—a date officially fixed in June. England seems curiously lacking in National Days; this event, which is inconspicuous at home was unfamiliar to me. It was an occasion for all the officials and the members of the Russian Consulate-General to pay Eric a call, which he had solemnly to return. In the evening we gave a dinner party.

My first year in Kashgar the prospect of this party filled me with terror. I did not feel that Gyalgen, the aged cook, or I, could contend with the situation. However, everyone helped and I found so much of the ceremony was laid down by tradition that my help was superfluous. Under the command of Hafiz, flags draped the Consulate like a ship. A charming decoration planned for the evening was a myriad little lights all round the roof of the house and patterning the garden. Small earthenware saucers, filled with wicks and oil, were to shine like many glow-worms.

It was decided that we should give an entirely Indian meal, and I was gravely informed that Mir Humza (being the best cook in the Consulate) would arrange it all. We watched the weather anxiously. Not for rain as one does at any English out-door function, but for a dreaded wind storm. It looked threatening and by 6 o'clock we were still arguing whether to dine inside or out. The majority voted "out" and a table for thirty was laid on the terrace. All the drawing-room furniture and carpets had been arranged on the lawn.

By 7 o'clock our guests began to arrive; gaily I tried to hide my anxiety about the gathering clouds. Dinner began and the wind rose. It became increasingly colder and I fetched extra wraps for some of the women. We managed to reach the pudding stage with everyone politely ignoring the obvious discomfort. Then the fury of the storm broke. The wind hurled itself down on us with venom and whirled up the dust. We hurried our guests into the dark, empty drawing-room. Open windows splintered, servants bumped into each other fetching lamps and chairs; I came across a pail of water sitting incongruously in the middle of the floor.

In one's own language it is possible to turn a calamity into a joke. Through interpreters it is not so easy. The unsmiling faces of our guests seemed to quell all my efforts to "laugh it off". Gradually everyone was seated; we tried to hand round the remainder of the dinner and to ignore the wind whirling in at the broken windows. The wretched storm passed more rapidly than it had come, leaving me completely exhausted.

The night was still when everyone had left except the Chinese Commander and his wife, General and Mrs. Chao. With a kindly tact which no one else had attempted to show, General Chao asked if we would light the little lamps he knew we had arranged. Men were hurriedly summoned and we did achieve a small display. Seeing how attractive was this fairy-land of twinkling lights, I was more bitterly disappointed than ever at the collapse of our plans.

We were not the only people to be embarrassed by sudden wind storms. In 1947 General Chang Chih Chung, then Governor of Sinkiang, came on a visit to the South. People said that it was not a wise political move, but whatever the local feeling, the event could not be ignored. Elaborate preparations were made; the town was clumsily decorated with banners and triumphal arches; the Governor's drive from the aerodrome was cheered by organized processions of school children, youth brigades and police; official calls were exchanged at the two foreign Consulates, and finally a dinner party for two hundred guests was arranged.

It seemed an ambitious number to entertain and, to add to the difficulties of the organizers, on the night of the party a violent wind got up. Dinner had been laid out on an attractive roof-garden; electric light had been installed and a show of press photographs arrayed round the main table. There was no possibility of altering these arrangements—there was no available room large enough to seat two hundred people.

After a short prelude indoors, where some of the guests were seated stiffly round a table laden with fruit, nuts and cakes, we all moved out into the gale, to take our places at the enormously long dinner table. It was a chaotic scene. Napkins, name tickets, leaves from the vine overhead whirled and raced down the table; the roar of the wind made it difficult to hear anyone speak; guests were more occupied with fetching coats and wraps than with finding their seats; the photographs flapped and strained and finally had to be taken down. In the midst of the uproar it was incongruous, and calming, to see a large congregation of white-turbaned, devout Mussulman guests saying their evening prayers. Eventually dinner began.

The usual excellence of Chinese and Turki food (the dinner consisted of both varieties) was ruined by the numbers and by the uncontrollable weather. When the dishes reached us they were congealed and unappetizing. No one made much attempt to eat them. Conversation was equally heavy. Unless we could speak the language of our immediate neighbours, our attempts to talk through an interpreter, far down the table, were drowned by the wind. The complication of language was extraordinary. Chinese talking to Turkis in Russian; an American guest we had with us translating into Chinese for me; Russians speaking fluent Turki and contrariwise; an elderly Turki talking in French; I felt so confused that I thought I should soon join in animatedly in Polish or Tibetan. As it was, my efforts to talk to the Governor met with little success. He was painfully distracted and made no attempt to listen to bellowed translations from Mr. Chu.

Endless "toasts" between individual guests and the startling flash of the press cameras (so unexpected in that curious setting), were the main distractions of the tedious meal. Speeches were impossible. The Governor reduced his to a few sentences of apology and it was doubtful if even these were heard. Eric's carefully prepared speech had to be abandoned.

After dinner, the same group of guests moved back into the inner room. The atmosphere was somewhat easier and more relaxed than before. A Turki band, which had played strenuously throughout the evening, now accompanied a lusty, male chorus singing songs in praise of the Governor. I wondered what he was thinking. The wind had done its best to ruin his unwieldy party.

Not all Kashgar parties were so tempestuous but most of them were long and tedious. Chinese etiquette demands that an impressive relay of dishes be produced, regardless of whether they are eaten. I soon learnt only to peck at each dish. On one occasion unusual interest was added to an invitation to dine with General Chao—the promise of a Chinese opera after dinner.

When we arrived a large party of Russians, Chinese and Turkis were already sitting under an arbour of vines in the garden. Eric and I were firmly separated, and while he went to join the men, I was ushered towards a group of

"THE DRY, SILENT COUNTRY" OF THE TUSHUK TAGH

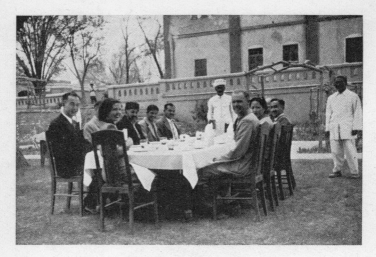

A STAFF LUNCH PARTY

ERIC AND MR. CHU GOING OUT ON AN OFFICIAL CALL

ladies. Our hostess was a colourful figure, flashing with jewels and lipstick, wearing the straight, high-necked Chinese dress that is so seldom becoming. She spoke uncertain English, nearly as difficult to understand as Chinese. But as no one else spoke at all it relieved the strain of complete silence and the exchange of helpless smiles. I wondered if we were to be segregated all evening. But after a long wait dinner was announced and we all moved indoors together.

The party was divided at three tables. It is the custom in China for husband and wife to sit together, so we found ourselves, with the Russian Consul-General and his wife, sitting in the places of honour opposite our host and hostess. A Russian who spoke very halting English and a Chinese who spoke Russian, were there to interpret. Not without difficulty, conversation limped along. Suddenly a brass band outside began a rousing tune which successfully drowned nearly everything we tried to say. The music seemed to be an uncertain waltz but volume was its main characteristic, and it thundered joyously throughout dinner.

Chinese food is usually excellent. They make subtle-tasting soups; know what to do with vegetables and have an impressive repertoire of intriguing dishes. One dish at a time was put in the middle of the table and we all dipped in as we felt inclined. I began by using chopsticks, but found I was achieving so little that I had to revert to the more clumsy knife and fork. There were sea-slugs and squid, elegant varieties of sea-weed, chicken in a dozen unrecognizable forms, sweet potato and lotus seeds, soya beans twisted into strange shapes, ducks feet, dried mushrooms and preserved eggs, ancient and highly coloured. The famous bird's nest soup, I never tasted. Mr. Chu solemnly told us that it is considered a great luxury and is very expensive.

"But no one really *likes* it," he added.

The sweet course came in the middle of the meal and small bowls of hot water were provided, in which to rinse the chop-sticks. The General's favourite story was of the ignorant man who proceeded to drink this water. But I had

7

guests who drank from the finger bowls provided with the
desert. After the pudding the procession of courses began
again. Not until bowls of plain rice appear is the end of a
Chinese banquet in sight.

To the accompaniment of bangs and brassy trumpetings
from the band, the party dipped and nibbled at the bewilder-
ing amount of food, and offered endless "toasts" to one
another's health in the ugly smelling rice wine.

The long meal ended at last and we were taken over to
the garrison theatre. It was a large hall with a proper
stage, lighted by electric and oil lights. As the General's
party came in the audience of soldiers began a rhythmical
clapping, and yet another brass band burst into life. The
programme was divided into two plays; a synopsis of
each had been translated into English and Russian.

The performance opened with a play entitled "Killing
Wife at Monastery". This was a moving incident from
Chinese history of over a thousand years ago. To avenge
his murdered father and satisfy his mother, the hero has
to kill his wife, the daughter of the murderer. Although
her father had been the original villain, the lady is a devoted
wife and daughter-in-law. She often prays in the monastery
for those she loves. It is there that her husband finds her
and has to reveal to her her dreadful fate. After a harrowing
scene between the two, the lady seizes the sword and com-
mits suicide, to help her hesitating husband. When the
implacable mother sees the severed head of her daughter-
in-law she is overcome with grief and hangs herself.

True to classical tradition this cheerful story was half
spoken, half sung, to the deafening accompaniment of a
proper Chinese band. Although hidden from view this
seemed to consist only of drum, cymbals and gong. The
music seldom stopped throughout the performance. It
was more completely tuneless, to our ears, than any
Eastern music I have ever heard. The female parts were
acted by men. Although the "heroine's" face was painted
chalk white and the surrounds to her eyes deep red, the
effect was not as clownish as it sounds, but oddly frail and
appealing. I was envious of "her" rich brocade robes and
complicated hair style. She sang in a convincing falsetto

and used her hands in all the beautiful and traditional gestures of the Chinese theatre. Seeing this theatre for the first time the meanings of the gestures were unkown to me. I believe in all classical opera there are definite rules to be strictly followed.

As in the days of Shakespeare there was no scenery and the properties were mostly symbolic. A far higher standard of imagination was demanded of the audience than is asked in the West nowadays. For example, the monastery was indicated by a table with two candles, brought on without any lowering of the curtain. It was a little disconcerting, in the middle of the tragic scene between husband and wife, to see an unconcerned small man in a white coat, strongly resembling a dentist's assistant, wandering on to the stage with a necessary chair or table. He would wait patiently, ready to hand the husband his wife's severed "head", long before she had committed suicide. At intervals he would bring in a pot of tea to refresh the actors. Other intruders on to the stage were soldiers tending the oil lamps. Walking briskly about they were quite unmoved by the suicides and passions around them.

But however quaint the stage management, however incomprehensible the words, however exhausting the music, the two principal actors had the ability to convey emotion, and to act convincing parts. I felt really concerned about their tragic situation. It came as a shock when a new and very grotesque figure suddenly leapt on to the stage. I tried for some time to fix his antics into the story of the monastery. But he belonged to the second play. There was no breath of a pause between the two and we were now swept into what appeared, to the uninitiated, to be a knock-about comedy. It was in fact written by a philosopher of olden times. The story was of "King Monkey" and "King Ox" and the struggle of the former for supreme power over "King Dragon", under the sea.

"This is not a true story," my hostess whispered in kindly explanation.

King Monkey was a delightful and irrepressible character, his face an ingenious make-up of red, white and blue. But for me, ignorant of the philosophical meaning, the story seemed to be only a light background for very clever acrobatics, juggling and fencing. Figures whirled in and out; two youths somersaulted and leapt wildly and brilliantly; a procession of small boys marched across the stage or executed a short dance with swords; elaborately dressed "Kings" with increasingly grotesque make-up, appeared and disappeared; it was a confusing, amusing, colourful, kaleidoscope of people with King Monkey as the recurring and most brilliant figure. He reminded me of a good Bertram Mill's clown, his humour understandable in any language.

All this was accompanied by the relentless, ear-splitting clash of drums and cymbals, and the quiet attendance of the dentist's assistant. He and his tea-pot were nearly always there, and at intervals the exhausted acrobats would have a quick drink from the spout. How the soldiers, trimming the lamps, and the whirling dancers, avoided collision, I do not know. At last, after complicated adventures, King Monkey was subdued by an ancient Buddha. As his final duty the dentist's assistant came carefully forward to draw the curtain and the show was over.

It had lasted exactly two hours; a fascinating entertainment, and not too long. I am told that the normal length of a Chinese show is nearer four to six hours. Few Europeans would have strong enough nerves to endure the band for so long.

Another entertainment by Chinese soldiers which I thoroughly enjoyed, was a display of dancing by lantern light. In the open we found bobbing, flickering clusters of paper lanterns, made into intricate patterns and shapes, representing anything from a dragon to an aeroplane. In the darkness the lights were like something seen in a dream —beautiful, grotesque, unreal. Then began a definite play. Mr. Chu confessed that he could not explain it. It was a simple legend in a dialect he did not know. It did not matter, the scene was such a fascinating one. A long, illuminated, paper dragon curled and twisted itself in a dance reminiscent of the Conga; a decorated, lighted boat dipped and swayed—an exquisite young "lady" was seen in it from the waist upwards, "her" oddly military legs running round below. The dream intensified as a circle of men on stilts suddenly appeared. Stern warriors, attractive "girls", frank clowns circled high above us to the incessant clashing and drumming of the band. They walked, skipped, hovered, strange, elongated figures with vividly painted faces. This, I thought, is something of real China—a show ancient, weird and beautiful.

Sometimes we were asked to professional Turki entertainments by the Turki Cultural Association. I genuinely enjoyed the first two hours of dancing and singing. Although the words were unintelligible to me the music was attractive, the costumes colourful and the whole production far more polished than I had expected to find. It did not take long to realize where the training and organization came from. There were dances with a strong Russian flavour, several definitely Cossack numbers and at each performance we saw, a girl sang a prayer-like chant to Stalin. The Russian ability to use traditional Turki music and dances and to form them into attractive, well-balanced numbers, was undeniable.

We always attended with the Russian Consul-General and his wife. Tacitly assuming that she knew all about the programme, I once asked her how much longer the performance would last. We had already sat on the hard, narrow chairs for two and a half hours. Her knowledge of English was sketchy but she replied confidently, "Six years".

Later on, after the suppression of an anti-Government plot in 1947, this "Turki Club" was taken over by the Chinese. But they did extraordinarily little in the way of propaganda themselves. Occasionally they showed an old Russian film, gave a Turki or a Chinese show, but we were no longer invited to the elaborate performances we had first seen. Entertainment at the "Club" was advertised by the loud, ceaseless beating of a drum from the roof-top. From mid-day until evening the rhythmical drumming went on. On hot summer days the sound penetrated to our garden— a perpetual noise which made me restless and uncomfortable as drums always do.

Like marathon dancing competitions in America, endurance seemed to be the main requisite for entertainment in

Kashgar. When the Russians gave a party it was larger and longer than the Chinese ones. Whether this is typical of Soviet hospitality I do not know. It may have been peculiar to the Russian Consul-General in Kashgar at the time. Although we persisted in giving small, intimate dinners, (except for the King's Birthday) the Russians only invited us on state occasions. They had a big hall, with a stage, where guests could be seated at long, low tables facing whatever performance had been arranged. Sometimes it was a film show, sometimes Turki and Russian dancing. We ate and drank in between the numbers and everything was well arranged. Four hours of such entertainment was pleasant. But when the professional show was over, the guests were expected to dance among themselves. On uneven carpets, to barrel-organ music from a gramophone, watched by mystified Turkis and our Indian staff, the ordeal was severe. I always felt our extraordinary gyrations, in undignified embrace, must convince the East of its extreme superiority.

Our efforts to leave were vigorously resisted. This was not polite protesting, a matter of form, but aggressive refusal. Every hour we would make another attempt to leave until by 2 or even 3 a.m. we would abandon politeness and go. I never understood the meaning behind this half-humorous, half-angry fight to keep us until the early hours. It was obvious that everyone had exhausted their powers of conversation. Interpreters were drooping, many guests were frankly asleep but still our host whipped on the flagging spirit of the party.

At a New Year's Day celebration we attended, the inevitable battle had raged intermittently since midnight. I had, as usual, enjoyed the first few hours. The room was beautifully decorated with a "Christmas tree" and imitation snow hung from the ceiling. The cabaret had been attractive. But in the early morning, as guests began to wilt, paper streamers and confetti were produced. It reminded me of a "gala night" on a ship, in a rough sea. A few hearty spirits working hard, a few definite "casualties" lying asleep and the majority struggling to survive the strain. I caught sight of our three Indians, sitting in a dignified row, occasionally dozing. Being forbidden alcohol they were sternly sober; they made no attempt to speak, to smile or to conceal their inexpressible boredom. Suddenly a stout young girl descended on them with extreme coyness and paper streamers. She left them garlanded but unmoved; calmly they brushed themselves and went back to sleep.

In Kashgar I was more conscious of, and more mystified then ever by, the kudos and significance attached to drinking. Personally I like wine and I am in favour of everyone drinking as much, and whatever, they like. But why the tedious insistence on it? If a person dislikes oysters, or can only eat a few, he is not regarded as odd and somewhat weak. But it takes courage to announce a dislike for alcohol. Of course it is far worse for men than for women. There must be innumerable young men who have never dared to reveal a distaste for whisky or a reluctance to drink too much.

Prussian officers, I have read, used to be *trained* to drink. With typical efficiency, they made what should be a pleasure into a solemn duty. Judging from my small experience amongst Russians in Sinkiang, they seem to have a similar idea, but omit the efficient training. Drinking became a duty. There was no escape from the ceremony of endless "toasts". At my first few dinner parties in our Consulate I made the uneducated mistake of sipping my wine as I felt inclined, and imagining that my guests would do the same. The only toasts I was accustomed to were standard ones at the end of the meal. I discovered that neither the Russians nor the Chinese drank except when invited. They must have considered me very inhospitable. An invitation meant draining the glass to the bottom and any reluctance was regarded as an insult. Men who preferred wines to vodka or brandy were labelled "women" by the Russians. Our non-drinking Mussulman staff never escaped this epithet and monotonous mockery. The whole question of alcohol began increasingly to exasperate me. Eventually I abandoned all efforts to please, I drank exactly as much as I chose to drink and no more.

Both Eric and I found that this firmness did not usually affect the Chinese. We suspected that the majority of them did not care for excessive drinking and only felt that hospitality required it. General Chao always drank his "toasts" with a hideous grimace. This was understandable if he drank Chinese rice wine. Its smell is as unpleasant as its taste. But a great deal of conventional conversation about wine was always indulged in. The curious, but familiar, admiration for a "good drinker" was always forthcoming.

On one occasion the General invited us to a dinner in honour of a departing Russian Vice-Consul. The accent was strongly on drink. No time was lost in offering "toasts" all round. With great pride General Chao pointed to a stout, rouged, Chinese lady who, he assured us, could drink four bottles of brandy without flinching. The champion seemed determined to prove her ability as quickly as possible. Concentrating on the Russians, she toasted them each in turn, insisting that they drain their glasses as she did hers. The rest of the party drank timid little "toasts" to one another and pecked at the variety of dishes which loaded the table. But interest centred on the champion who was now standing up to make a long speech about the Friendship of Nations. Our host continued to applaud every glass which she drank, while imperiously she waved away empty bottles and summoned new ones.

I got a little tired of the performance and tried to divert the General with a Chinese wine game. But he was fascinated by the lady's powers and continued to tell us that she was a wonderful drinker. I turned my attention to the food, thankful that I was not being forced to drink.

The star performer had now reached a very flushed stage. Her speeches had become longer and more fierce. Even her ardent admirer, General Chao, indicated that she should sit down and have a rest. She refused vigorously, clutching an empty bottle and thumping her portly bosom, like a grotesque Tarzan. The general began to look displeased. The champion's husband (a quiet, negative little man who did not drink at all) tried to calm her. At the suggestion of restraint she became aggressive; her reddened eyes flashed; she waved a bottle high and shook off her husband's hand; she shouted louder than before. We learnt later that on being laughingly accused of drinking cold tea, instead of brandy, she had become enraged and abusive. Three generals bore down on her and, not without difficulty, forced her, struggling and screaming, from the room, to be seen no more.

It was an embarrassing episode, but our host ignored it with commendable calm and the party continued.

The majority of Chinese we met appeared to have a small capacity for drink and were rapidly defeated. Whether they have adopted the Western reverence for alcohol and "good drinkers" or have always felt it I do not know.

When we first talked of Kashgar Eric told me that there would be no society but that of the Chinese, the Turkis, the Russians and our own Consulate staff. But since 1942 the Government of Sinkiang had changed considerably and with it the policy towards foreigners. The Chinese Central Government began to grant visas and, particularly, to encourage journalists. We found ourselves entertaining quite a stream of visitors. On two occasions we had all our guest-rooms occupied.

First came two Swedish missionaries who lived in the rooms at the end of the stone passage. They had all their meals with the doctor. For four and a half months they were a delightful and valued addition to Consulate society.

One day in April 1947, as I was deep in the making of a cake, Gyalgen announced the arrival of a Russian lady. As the ladies of the Russian Consulate never called without the Consul-General, I was startled. It transpired that the gate-keepers had sent the news, and to them any white-faced, unknown woman was a Russian. However, our visitor was a young American journalist, just arrived from Urumchi. With remarkable initiative and courage Miss Stephens had made her way to Kashgar from Central China. After a three weeks' stay with us she continued her journey down to Khotan, on horseback. It must have been a hot and unpleasant ride along the straight, relentless road to the south. We did not see her on her return as we were then away in the hills. In August we heard with dismay of her death in an aeroplane accident, returning to China. After the hardships and endurance of Central Asian travel, undertaken alone; after long separation from her home, to which she was then planning to return, this last-minute tragedy was very cruel.

The news of the accident was brought to us by another journalist. Mr. Robertson, an Australian, arrived at the Consulate one day in late August, with his American fiancée. They were with us for nearly two months and eventually returned with us when we visited Urumchi. During their stay a charming American couple passed through Kashgar on their way to India. Our house suddenly hummed with gaiety. We tried to persuade Mr. and Mrs. Ransom to stay with us for the winter; even talking until 2 o'clock in the morning we had not exhausted subjects for conversation. Perhaps they were worn out by our animated arguments? All our favourite theories and problems were released and made fresh by new opinions. They only stayed for ten days and then continued their world wanderings.

In January of the following year, a French journalist visited Kashgar. He refused our invitation to stay at the Consulate. I think he felt, quite rightly, that he would be in better contact with the country living with the Chinese and the Turkis. But as he spoke good English we had another chance for long conversations. It was inevitable that living alone so much, Eric and I should have grown familiar with each other's arguments and opinions. We delighted in the stimulus of new ideas.

I was surprised to have visitors in the remote isolation of Kashgar. Except for an English friend of ours they all came by lorry from Urumchi. The road has greatly improved in recent years and with all the help and kindness given by the Chinese authorities to foreigners, the journey is no longer hazardous, although it can be tiring. Unless policies or local conditions change, it seems that Kashgar may lose some of its peculiar isolation.

CHAPTER VII

We Visit Two Mountain Valleys

OUR FIRST VISITORS ARRIVED
at the end of December, 1946. The two Swedish missionaries Mr. Moen and Mr. Robintz, reached Kashgar after a
weary journey via China and Urumchi. Having been
expelled from Sinkiang in 1938, when the whole flourishing
Mission had been closed, these two had now returned to
review the local situation. At least they hoped to claim
compensation for their confiscated Mission property. They
both spoke excellent English and immediately we fell into
animated conversation. They were full of interests: they
liked natural history; they were fond of the Turkis and
could speak their language even better than English; they
enjoyed tennis, shooting and seeing the country; having
known Kashgar for so many years there was much we
could learn from them. This meeting confirmed my feelings
about Eastern and Western cultures. These two Europeans
only differed from us in language and a few customs; their
enthusiasm for life, their humour and variety of interests
were something familiar and very valuable. We felt free
to discuss any subject without restraint.

One of the properties of the Swedish Mission was a
bungalow built in the Bostanterek Valley, among the foothills of the Pamirs. Members of the Mission used to go
there for a rest during the summer. As Eric was helping
the Swedes with their affairs, and the property had to be

inspected, we all decided to visit the house together. It would combine business with a pleasant holiday. Eric informed the Chinese authorities that we wanted to go. After long delay, Eric had a reply saying that a secretary from the office concerned, would accompany us; he wanted to go there and back in a day; we must be ready to leave the following day at 9 a.m. I should not have thought it was possible to live anywhere in Asia for five minutes without being aware of the huge extent of the country. In Sinkiang distance was complicated by the lack of roads. Yet without making any attempt to find out where Bostanterek was, the Chinese secretary was proposing to travel about a hundred and twenty hard miles in one day, and complete his business as well!

Ignoring this wild "order", we prepared for our first serious expedition to the hills. We arranged to be away for eight days. In mid-March the four of us left the Consulate with the usual retinue of servants and two Chinese officials. Although the Swedes had always done the journey on horseback or in carts, we decided to motor the first thirty miles to Opal. At any time that country road was a particularly bad one, a rough sea of ridges and ditches. But in March the spring thaw was at its worst and we soon regretted our decision. Every few miles we bogged down in the glue-like mud of the road. While Mir Humza and Yusuf worked frenziedly and impressed various passers-by as well, the lorry strained and roared in vain. Progress was painful and when at last, with relief, we left the melting mud of the oasis for the open desert, we found ourselves thwarted by soft sand. We had to lay strips of matting under the wheels, drive the length of these and then begin the process all over again.

The journey took eight and a half hours. I could not help wondering if the distance and the difficulties were making any impression on the optimistic Chinese gentleman.

In Opal we were received by the Beg, or Head Man of the village—a wealthy Turki who had probably levied a quick tax on the neighbourhood in order to entertain us. This system, which I knew lined the Beg's pocket quite satisfactorily, always embarrassed me. But we could not avoid staying with the most senior man of the place and could do nothing to alter the local custom.

The next day the lorry was left behind and a cavalcade of horses and camels started out across the desert, towards the mountains. The range was clear and the ice peaks sparkled in front of us. Lower hills to the north were coloured in browns and deep rusts. The immediate country was monotonous and I was very glad indeed not to be trudging across it without a pony. But the space, the variety of colour in all the hills and the excitement of new country compensated for the dullness of the miles. A tantalizing feature of that ride was being able to see Bostanterek for many hours before we reached it. It was a peculiarity of Central Asia I was often to dislike. It was as if one persevered on a moving strip of floor but never advanced. I again wondered if the journey was impressing our Chinese companion. He had made no comment about the thirty-mile drive and only announced that he would ride to Bostanterek and back in the day. As we did not reach the place until after 5 o'clock in the evening, he did not have the opportunity.

To the horror of the Swedes, they found their charming little house had been transformed into a fort. A large wall with watch-towers had been built round it and it was reduced to the gloomy dilapidation of all these small outposts. In the 1945 "rebellion" it had been attacked by invading Kirghiz from across the border, and the small garrison had fled. As the house was built on the side of a hill it did not lend itself to defence. A few snipers on the slope above could aim directly into the fort below.

We were told that the attackers did, in fact, continue to fire happily into the fort long after the garrison had escaped. A tragic result of the whole incident was the suffering of the local Kirghiz in the valley. Whatever the truth about the rebellion the invaders had plundered the local flocks and ponies, leaving their owners destitute. Many of the Swedes' old friends came to them for help. With pathetic, yet significant, naïvety they asked if it was advisable for them to go to the present Russian Consul-General for compensation. So convinced were they of the origin of the rebellion.

Now the fort was occupied by a small police force under the command of a stern Tartar officer. He was very agitated about entertaining us and did everything he could to make us comfortable. But we did not care for the gloomy confines of the fort. Once all the business was concluded, and the two Chinese officials had left, we announced that we should like to take a camp higher up the valley. There were the inevitable objections about how cold and uncomfortable we would be, about the lack of habitations and amenities higher up. But we persisted politely and finally the Tartar agreed to let us go. His only condition was that two policemen must accompany us.

Our desire for small, simple camps, free of an escort, was one the authorities never understood. How much their attentions were in order to keep a check on us, how much they were a genuine feeling that certain honours were due to a Consul-General, I don't know. Probably the junior officials were afraid of doing the wrong thing and took no chances. In any case, our liking for simplicity and living in the open, was completely incomprehensible to them. I think we probably "lost face" with our comparatively humble caravan.

The Swedes having decided to stay in Bostanterek, for gazelle shooting in the desert, we went off with Gyalgen, Rosa Beg and the two policemen. The higher we went the nearer we got to the pines. After the brown monotony of the Kashgar winter, it was a delight to see evergreens. They were not very handsome trees and many of them had been ruthlessly cut with, of course, no attempt at replanting. But we found a charming camp site, near a miniature pine and a clear stream.

After lounging through the afternoon, pleased with our camp and idly content, we decided to go for a "walk". The gently failing light of evening is Eric's favourite time of the day. Striking uphill at once we climbed steeply to the top of a ridge on the south side of the valley. Though not spectacularly tall the pines were thick on that slope. I soon took to my hands and knees as we made our way through them, on a sharp incline. The last few feet I clawed clumsily up loose scree and then fell on to the narrow ridge.

The sun was setting. The stern rock and ice mountains at the head of our valley stood up black and bold. To the east the dim expanse of the plains was lighted by the dying sun. Faint lines marked ghostly hills far away. Light, colour, and shape—all formed into a wide glowing picture. We followed up the narrow ridge, through pines and snow. Suddenly, from almost under our feet, a covey of ram-chikor flew out, noisy in their alarm. We climbed on beyond the trees; in deep snow we flogged our way to the top of the highest point of the ridge. There was just time to see the sun's light fade from the scene, leaving it austere and cold. We had a breathless descent. Eric was teaching me to glissade; to use my stick as a brake, then to relax my nerves and slide. I was stiff and slow to learn, often falling or creeping nervously. But I did improve. Going down by a more gentle slope than we had come up, we slid nearly all the way. It was almost dark when we reached the camp, hungry, breathless, full of an intense happiness.

I was concerned about the two policemen, who had no tent and not very much bedding. At over 7,000 ft. in March it was still cold. Later in the evening I persuaded Eric to send them down with a note to the Swedes, who could explain the situation to the Tartar. Satisfied with this arrangement we went to bed. In the morning I was startled to see two figures, huddled in sheepskins by the dead fire. Gyalgen explained that the men had been sent back by their infuriated officer, who, ignoring our message had ordered them to stay at their posts even if they froze! He seemed to confirm the traditional character of his race.

We spent two nights at our little camp and during the day time climbed round the near-by hills in pursuit of ram-chikor. Our last day was particularly strenuous as Eric and Gyalgen were led ever higher and higher in their excitement, while I panted in the rear. Eric stalked several coveys of ram-chikor, leaving Gyalgen and me waiting at a distance, watching anxiously as he crept slowly nearer to the birds. But he was always defeated.

Along the tops of the hills we climbed until we reached the head of the valley and the forbidding mountains faced us. In places snow lay deep and when I floundered up to my waist Gyalgen came a long way down again to rescue me. Whatever his faults in the house, on these mountain trips I loved him dearly. He never seemed to tire; he treated all my outbursts of despair and cowardice with calm encouragement; he stoutly maintained that I was almost capable of tackling Everest; he would usually wait to see if I could manage some narrow ledge or airy corner. Only occasionally he would jib himself and Eric would have to go on alone. He did not mind snow and ice, he once told me, but rock climbing frightened him.

Having returned to our camp that day, we still had a two-hour walk back to the fort. We were all three stiff and weary. The policemen, after their reprimand, had tried to accompany us among the hills. But they were so unused to it they had to abandon the struggle. We were thankful to be on our own and were willing to lie gaily to the officer about their help and support.

We found that Mr. Moen had shot several gazelle but Mir Humza was completely abashed by having fired twenty rounds and hit nothing.

The following day the whole party rode back to Opal. The monotony of the ride was quite unrelieved as a dust haze, resembling a London fog, obscured everything. It lifted a little as we approached the oasis. Looking down on the irrigated country, from a stony bluff above, we were enchanted to see the first signs of spring. A very gentle feathering of pink and white blossom touched the fruit trees. It was lovely returning to Kashgar with blossom all along the road and then to find our own trees bursting into flower. The quagmire of the thaw was over and although the road was rough, we no longer stuck in seas of mud. A different route through the desert avoided all but one small patch of sand.

We did not have another opportunity for a short expedition until early in May. Eric was keen to explore a valley leading to the northern foot of Chakragil. The sharp, graceful lines of this mountain had become so familiar to us, it was exciting to plan a closer view.

On the same day as the Swedish missionaries left Kashgar for India, we left the Consulate on a two-hour drive to

THE CHAKRAGIL MASSIF

the Yamen Ya. This river has a soft, uncertain bottom, unsafe for a motor. So we had arranged for ponies to meet us at the ford to transport our baggage the rest of the way, and we intended to walk. But there was no sign of the animals when we reached the rendezvous. It was a clear, fine day. We could see the snow peaks which now looked so close to us; the wide river sparkled invitingly; we heard the English sound of a cuckoo; and we occupied ourselves stalking teal. After waiting for two hours we began to think that our arrangements had broken down. Then at 2 o'clock our caravan appeared. It had been waiting patiently at the wrong place.

To my chagrin I found that there were five riding ponies, while camels had been brought for the luggage. I had hoped to escape a ride. However, Eric and I decided to walk a little way first and we set off bravely in the heat of the day. As we crossed the river we saw one of the camels, half loaded, rear up at the sound of the departing lorry, and begin an hysterical dance, chased by men on foot and on horseback. It had lost all the usual aloof dignity of a camel and seemed determined to smash our luggage as it capered round. Eventually it was caught and calmed and nothing was broken. I noticed later that this uncertain camel always wore a rope muzzle.

Eric and I trudged along the dusty road and at frequent intervals inquired how far it was to Tashmalik.

"Two potai," (five miles) said one man.

"Five potai," (twelve and a half miles) said our next informant, about a mile farther on. When I suggested it might be one potai he agreed quite cheerfully. The Turki travels until he reaches his destination, a more peaceful attitude than ours. But, whatever the distance, we realized that Eric's original estimate of ten miles had been an optimistic one. I soon changed my opinion about the horses and was thankful to ride for a time; the soft earth roads, through the oases, made pleasant going and gradually I gained confidence in my unknown pony. At "Sunday Bazaar" we tried to buy some dhai, a curdled milk. But as it was a Saturday the village was a dead place.

Soon Eric grew impatient of our leisurely pace and

8

galloped ahead, followed by Gyalgen, Rosa Beg and a guide. Rosa Beg proved to be as impetuous and enthusiastic a rider as he was a climber. Like most Turkis he was familiar with horses and although he knew none of the refinements of a riding-school, he was quite fearless and liked speed. He could induce the dullest pony to gallop. It amused him to come up behind the unsuspecting Gyalgen and whip his pony into a race. I lived in terror of these hearty games in case my horse became infected. On this occasion my pony refused to be left behind and ignoring my protests cantered after the others.

Breathless, but still in the saddle, I eventually rode into Kumerak to find our party eating dhai. People collected round us in interested silence, but they refused all our attempts to pay them for the dhai; they seemed shocked at the idea of "guests" offering money. It was a village of handsome, shady trees, unusual in a country of small willows and poplars which are seldom allowed to grow tall. Fortified by the sour, sharp curds we rode on and out into the desert.

Alternately walking and riding we covered about eighteen miles to Tashmalik. A cool, high room had been prepared for us and we sank down gratefully among the rugs and pillows on the floor. Our hands were washed with warm water poured over them from a copper jug into a copper bowl with a perforated top. Immediately afterwards, flat bread and milkless tea were brought. This was followed by bowls of steaming hot "sukash"—a dish of macaroni with soup, tiny meat balls, vegetables and mint. With the usual dignified charm of Turki hospitality we were left to eat and rest in peace; not until later did our host, with his brothers, appear to greet us. Slipping off their shoes at the door, they bowed, stroked their beards (either real or imaginary, symbolizing Mohammed's holy beard) and inquired politely about our journey and our needs. I admired the handsome room they had given us. Though bare of furniture it was filled with carpets and there was an unusual amount of carving on the beams. The windows were intricate and beautiful screens of carved wood.

The next day, after an early breakfast of eggs and milk,

Eric and I started to walk through the green charm of the Tashmalik oasis. Blue iris grew in our path; little streams had to be crossed and recrossed; the people greeted us with friendly amusement, as usual mystified by our decision to walk. When the oasis ended and the heat of the bare desert beat up at us, we began to think their amazement was justified. So we rode slowly across the rocky, pathless waste. Again the day was clear and ahead of us the Pamirs rose high and magnificent. Now they seemed to hang immediately over us; the bulk of Kungur, dominant and powerful. Far away to the north was the jagged line of the Tushuk Tagh in which we could just determine the famous arch. The blue and mauve of distant hills curving round the horizon, the shimmering haze over the wide, flat desert and a long line of camels rocking slowly across the lonely scene, gave an impression of distance and endless time so typical of Central Asia.

We had to cross a racing river where we watched Sola bravely fighting the current, but being swept farther and farther down stream. Eventually she managed to reach the other side. We passed the camel caravan; the drivers were beginning their long journey through the mountains to India and we wished them luck. Only a few traders come this way, following the Gilgit route. The small, sheltered valley of Hunza, through which they must pass, cannot provide for a large traffic, so that most of the trade must use the harder Karakoram route.

The rough desert seemed interminable. The sun baked into us and the foot-hills which were our goal never seemed to get any nearer. After an hour's walking we curved round to the river again, where we drank endless cups of water and ate some of the battered remains of yesterday's lunch. Soon after this halt our way lay up a valley to the right. It was no less hot or stony, but narrower, than the main valley and more steep. At the first bush we came to we stopped again and had tea made. For nearly two hours we lay under the scanty shade of the only shrub in sight, and that a very prickly one, waiting for the cool of evening.

The cliffs of this valley were in high, complicated shapes, resembling mighty cathedral walls, giant organ pipes, or slender towers. In some places they were a deep red colour, glowing even more deeply in the sun. Rounding a bend, the quite unexpected green of a flourishing oasis, lay spread before us; like a Shangri La hidden in the rugged hills. This was Oitagh. Unknown to us, a traveller who had joined our party for tea, lower down, had invited us all to his house for the night. We should have preferred a peaceful camp of our own choosing, but could not refuse this kind hospitality. Passing by a deep gorge, with a muddy river racing far below us, we waded through a brilliant carpet of irises, the air heavy with their scent. Then towards the end of the village we stopped, and under an ancient willow rugs were spread for us, while our host disappeared into his house to make hurried preparations.

In his small noisy courtyard, surrounded by stables for ponies, camels and sheep, we found a raised platform. Two wooden beds and a table furnished it and there we had to sit, in high state, like royalty or perhaps a side-show in a circus. The servants, our host, the local school-master and various interested neighbours sat below and watched our every movement. Mysterious women flitted past shyly and they also enjoyed the free entertainment. We got used to the publicity in time and buried ourselves in delicious creamy dhai and maize bread. Sukash followed and, of course, tea. Below us the audience and our servants also enjoyed this meal, with loud sucking noises and appreciative belches. As usual the host did not eat with his guests. I never got used to this custom. In fact the host's main object seemed to be to obliterate himself entirely. Uncles, friends, distant cousins usually undertook the honours, and on inquiring who was the owner of a house, a silent figure would come forward from the shadows.

After a short walk in the fading light we went to bed. I had supposed we would sleep on the public platform, but we were shown into a small, dark, mud room, lighted by two tiny open squares in the roof. To the sound of animated conversation in the courtyard, we fell asleep.

It was very disappointing to find on the following day, that a heavy dust haze was creeping up from the plains and firmly blotting out the view. In the curious suffocated light

Eric and I began walking up the valley. The cultivated fields soon ended in thorny bushes; out of the gloom a camel suddenly appeared, contentedly munching this harsh diet. We had again intended to walk all the way and had only kept the two camels for our baggage. But after we had been going for two and a half hours, Gyalgen and Rosa Beg overtook us, comfortably mounted on two mournful ponies. Concern for our dignity, or their own dislike of walking, had galvanized them into finding these animals. So we all took it in turns to ride and progressed slowly up the valley. It was a dull, restricted journey, with little to be seen through the haze, and only relieved by bowls of dhai and a large lunch.

We came to a small, rocky hill covered with stunted pines. These tended to increase our unenthusiastic state of mind, as we had been expecting tall, handsome trees. But as we went on the pines developed and high above we could just see fringes of trees on the hill-sides. I was persuaded to pass a delightful glen of trees, green grass and a sparkling stream, with promises of even better camp sites farther on. Feeling very unconvinced I followed the crowd. Our party had now swollen to a motley collection of cattle, sheep, donkeys and camels, all being driven up to the summer pastures. This procession was enlivened by harassing attacks from Sola.

At last we could go no farther, our way was effectively blocked by a forbidding, black glacier. But we found ourselves in such a beautiful place that we had no desire to go on. Although visibility was still poor, immediately around us were tall pines and slopes of soft, brilliant grass; in such startling contrast to the wide, hot, severity of the desert and the barren hills we had passed, that we felt we had entered another world. There was the usual difference of opinion over a camp site and we spent some time wandering up and down in search of one. Our servants, with various helpful hangers-on, recommended a bare, open plateau; we chose a green slope protected by trees.

After tea we began to explore a little and walked on to the glacier. The dust haze persisted but we could just define faint shapes far above and around us. One pointed peak, a little clearer than the rest, hung so high and isolated in the air that I thought I must have imagined it. There was something exciting about this dimness, exasperating though it was; there was a promise of unknown beauty when the curtain was lifted, like a woman hiding behind a heavy veil.

Early the next morning the veil was lifted. Running out in my pyjamas I saw Chakragil shining in clear, cold majesty. From the floor of the valley a semi-circular wall of ice swept 10,000 ft, up to the line of peaks and buttresses, with the two main peaks of the mountain dominating them all. To our disappointment the miserable dust haze was once more creeping up from the plains. But for a long time yet Chakragil remained unclouded and graceful.

At half-past seven we left our camp in search of ram-chikor. Passing an encampment of shepherds we were watched by a shy but fascinated crowd. One of the men, alleged to be a great hunter, agreed to come with us. He led off up a steep, but well-graded path. First we were tantalized by the quick, harassed call of chikor, and then by the whistle of ram-chikor. As we climbed higher the trees dropped below us but the soft grass continued, lightly starred with tiny flowers. Rocky crags rose above; the birds called in every direction, always tempting us higher; and at intervals we were startled by the piercing scream of a marmot. I was enchanted by these little animals, like miniature red-brown bears. They would sit still and upright near their holes, apparently watching us, and then suddenly dart screaming underground.

On a rocky hill-side we watched two ram-chikor feeding peacefully. After a careful stalk Eric made a dash into the open hoping to get above them. I watched an exciting race as the birds ran up-hill and on to a difficult rock promontory. Eric fired. One of the pair appeared to drop far below among low bushes. But a long search never revealed it.

Later we climbed higher; our enthusiasm for shooting fading a little but still hoping to get a view above the dust. It was thicker now and even Chakragil had become a mysterious shape once more. We lay on a tilted slab of rock, peering over into space. I had felt very unhappy getting there and did not enjoy the prospect of climbing down; our guide's idea of a "good road" seldom agreed with mine. However, we slid down the steep slopes gradually and easily, looking half-heartedly for ram-chikor on the way but seeing none. By 5 o'clock we reached our camp and found tea elegantly laid out on a packing-case, with a royal-looking couch of pine branches and rugs prepared for us by Rosa Beg. That evening we built a large fire of pine wood—a handsome, crackling, dancing fire, with the delicious smell peculiar to pine.

At 6.30 the next day Chakragil was half obscured by moving white clouds. The ice peaks and buttresses appeared and disappeared in the gently flowing mist. We crossed the main glacier, slipping and sliding on the dirty, gravel-covered ice, and reached a small, green valley—a sheltered "alp" which ran up to the foot of the forbidding ice walls of Chakragil. Yaks grazed quietly and untended. Once again we climbed high in search of the elusive ram-chikor, their call enticing us on from pleasant grass slopes to the snow-covered rocks above. When the climbing became too difficult I stopped on a ledge of rock and watched the others stalk two unsuspecting birds. These flew away before Eric was within range, and the climbers had an arduous return journey. Rosa Beg plunged rashly down a difficult snow-filled gully and eventually returned wet and exhausted. For once he acknowledged defeat. He had "nearly died", he said, and willingly agreed to go back to camp.

Eric and I went on alone. We climbed along the damp hill-side, which melting snow had made into a vast bog, and crossed immediately under the walls of Chakragil. The complicated architecture of ice-falls, cornices, hanging glaciers and sweeps of unbroken ice, towered above us, painfully dazzling in the sun. We did not linger there, warned off by the sound of avalanches high above. Then we recrossed the glacier, which was now much wider and cleaner. Deep little lakes lay here and there; fierce streams, cutting their way through smooth passages of ice, raced along and at intervals disappeared below the surface; a threatening roar flowed under our feet. Soon this was drowned by the noise of mighty waterfalls. High up on the opposite side of the valley several streams plunged 500 ft. down a rock face and disappeared below the glacier.

On reaching dry land once more we found another enchanted valley. A carpet of yellow flowers covered the green slopes as well as an almost invisible pattern of smaller flowers. We slept there in the sun. Farther down we saw cattle and sheep grazing; a collection of rough shelters had been built but there were no people anywhere. The contrast of the forbidding but beautiful mountain, commanding the head of the valley, the austere ice and racing rivers of the glacier, with this calm, green scene, made it all the more magical. It did not seem fanciful to imagine some fairy-tale character suddenly appearing to offer us three wishes, or perhaps to demand why we had invaded the sanctuary. Soon we were forced laboriously up to avoid a deep ravine, and then had to work our way down again through thick pine forest. Decayed and broken wood entangled us and the descent was slow. In some places the rotted mould of years was up to our knees. Then we crossed the black ice once more and hurried back to tea.

Completing a circle we had discovered the two gentle green valleys on either side of the glacier; we had enjoyed the contrast of severe ice and grandeur. But it was good to rest. There is a degree of tiredness, nowhere approaching exhaustion, which is enjoyment. I felt deliciously relaxed; I changed into soft slippers, drank limitless tea; lay on Rosa Beg's seat of pines with a book; and I felt completely at peace.

On our last day we planned to explore the glacier which joined the main one from the north. We had already made several friends among the people living in the valley; they supplied us with meat and milk and I responded with simple first aid, from my medicine box. On our way up that morning some men invited us into their tent.

It was one of the round, collapsible felt tents called by the Kirghiz "akois". These tents, or something very similar, have been used by the nomads of Central Asia since ancient times. I have found them described as the homes of the Scythians in the seventh century B.C., and at a much later date Marco Polo describes them clearly.   Other customs of these ancient Scythians, such as the drinking of "kumis", a fermented mare's milk, are still followed by the nomads of to-day. Inside, the tents are colourful and comfortable. Varying with the wealth of the owner, a gay wall of cushions, rugs, quilts and painted boxes is stacked on one side; a wicker screen divides off the kitchen utensils or sometimes hides a family of newly born lambs; there is a hole in the roof to let out the smoke from the small central fire; and all the necessities of life are arranged neatly in the compact space.   On this visit we watched a woman cooking some delicious flat wheat bread for us, on an iron plate over the hot ashes. To be given wheat was a luxury; maize bread is the usual diet and, with dhai, it makes an excellent meal.   Our hosts were two young brothers, as hospitable and friendly as nearly all the people we met in the mountains. Through the chinks in the tent we sensed a peering, whispering crowd of children, collected to see the unusual guests.

Eventually we went on up the side valley, and leaving the dark green pine woods, climbed on to the ugly moraine of the glacier. The dust haze had never quite lifted towards the plains; but again we had a brilliant view of the ice peaks, this time from a new angle. The going was not attractive on the crumbling, steep slope and I was glad to get back to the trees. All the way up the side of the valley, on the edge of the moraine there were sudden little alps of emerald grass and flowers; some of them lying high above our heads, tucked among the rocky crags. Then an ice-fall cut across our path; it was a complicated wall of black ice from which large chunks were continuously breaking off. There was an alarming cannonade from these and from the avalanches higher up; the roar echoed back from the rock on our right, doubling the noise. It was curious to see pigeons flitting unconcernedly about among the ice blocks and crevasses. It seemed a cold and inhospitable home to choose.

Cut off by the ice-fall we turned back and wandered down, keeping to the woods. Then we climbed up a gently rounded shoulder of green grass and returned by another valley. We made frequent halts, lay long on the grass and gazed at the shining beauty of the peaks opposite. There was a feeling of infinite peace, of quiet loveliness and awe-inspiring loneliness. We passed a large herd of grazing sheep, their shepherd fast asleep; startled marmots screamed at us; the evening sun glowed on the vivid grass and on the ice far above.

We made another call on the way home and were again generously entertained. This did not prevent us from enjoying our own large tea. To add to it the wife of our Oitagh host appeared with a lavish rice pudding. She had come up to the summer pastures ahead of her husband. Without him she was much more forthcoming and talkative. She brought her friends to us and asked my help for a sick baby. A nervous but impressed group of women collected round me as I attempted some simple doctoring.

The next day we left our enchanting valley and returned to Oitagh for the night. But before going we wandered once more over the main glacier and into the hidden valley where the yaks grazed. The weather was uncertain that morning and Chakragil changed its moods abruptly. One moment it was clear and serene, then dark clouds covered it and only an occasional peak showed through the gloom. It even rained a little. We had an uneventful journey back to Oitagh; stopping, as before, for a meal or a bowl of dhai; walking and riding in turns and, regretfully, dropping down below the level of the pines.

We had hoped to make our own camp, near a clear brook, before reaching Oitagh. But the friendly wife had assured us that everything had been prepared for our coming and insisted that we could not disappoint her husband. Not wanting to offend her, we returned reluctantly to the house of the public platform. But our host was himself leaving for the summer pastures the next day and everything had been sent up with his wife. Instead of elaborate preparations, we found a house so bare that we had to provide food for our host as well as for ourselves. He seemed embarrassed and silent, and probably cursed his wife's lavish and ill considered invitation.

The return journey to Tashmalik was hot but rapid. After idling back to the solitary bush where we had had tea, and where this time we had breakfast, the pony men suddenly announced that they were anxious about the river. Its volume increased during the day as the ice and snow melted in the mountains. So to save time I rode pillion behind Gyalgen, and he managed to persuade our little pony into a fast walk or an uncomfortable trot. We found the river was already quite deep; twice one of the ponies fell, wetting the rider, although he managed to stay in the saddle.

When we reached the outskirts of Tashmalik, we made a long halt under the shade of willows and paddled in a stream; a glorious contrast to the unrelenting heat beyond the oasis. The final hour's walk, in the comparative cool of the evening, was delightful and unhurried.

We found new quarters had been arranged for us. A ceaseless stream of tea was supplied and varieties of steaming Turki dishes. Every time we bowed our thanks and sank back, exhausted with eating, another dish appeared. At last we finished and lay distended among the rugs and cushions. Shortly afterwards our host appeared and asked, gravely and deferentially, what we would like for dinner!

Wandering out for a final stroll before going to bed, we found a caravan, newly arrived from India, camped near the gate of our house. One of the men was a friend we had made on our journey from Leh. I found it odd to think of him carrying on his severe life of trading across the ranges all this time. The men looked hard and strong; a feeling of adventure clung round them and suddenly recalled, with nostalgia, our long days on the Karakoram route.

We were woken at 4.30 the following morning by an orchestra of rural noises. A cock crowed lustily on the window-sill; there was the tortured bray of a donkey; pigeons sang to one another; a sinister rustling noise inside our room convinced me that there was a rat about. I forced the reluctant Eric to investigate.

"It's not a rat," he said getting sleepily back into bed, "only a goat." So we left it at that.

We had some difficulty in getting breakfast. It was always "just coming". Finally, having had bowls of hot milk and local bread, we left at 7.30.

For two hours we walked, along the flat, dusty road, while

the sun climbed high. Once we stopped to watch the ingenious, but Heath Robinson, machine for pounding rice. Three long poles, worked by water, rose and fell unevenly in a drunken rhythm. When the ponies overtook us we made another halt, at a wayside restaurant. In the cool, mud room, we ate the inevitable, satisfying dhai. I was annoyed to find that my new pony was lame. Having tripped and hobbled for some way, I could endure it no more and decided to walk. But this upset the pony man and he insisted that I exchange ponies with our host (who was accompanying us to Kashgar, to get a visa for India). He seemed quite unaffected by the uncomfortable progress and even induced the poor animal to canter.

As it was Sunday we found ourselves part of a cavalcade making for "Sunday Bazaar". There were superior men riding by on horses; men with a live sheep thrown across the saddle in front of them; women walking with babies in their arms; a woman on a donkey holding three children on as well; panniers full of live chickens or a rattling load of wooden cradles tied on to a donkey; people walking, people riding, everyone had something for sale in the market or was intent on going there to buy. A suffocating cloud of dust was kicked up by the hurrying traffic and I urged on my fat, lazy pony to overtake it. It was as complicated as negotiating London traffic without a policeman in control.

When we reached the village of the tall trees, we stopped again, being believers in leisurely travel. This time we were invited into a house and having provided our own food, tea was made for us and the whole party settled down to breakfast. Our unseen hostess then asked if we would call on her brother. It seemed unnecessary, but we did not want to offend anyone and so in due course were shown across to another house. Here was a room richly furnished with carpets, an array of nuts and fruit on the floor and yet more tea to drink. Noticing a flutter of veils and skirts, and suppressed giggles, from behind a door, I asked if I might visit the ladies. I was introduced to our host's three wives and politely bounced small babies on my knee. The head wife immediately poured out a tale of woe through an embarrassed interpreter. She had, I gathered, no children, but felt convinced that I could provide some medicine to remedy this, and to ensure her producing a large family. I assured her, regretfully, that I had no such magical medicine.

Once more we joined the cavalcade going to market and soon we reached "Sunday Bazaar". The village which had been so dead when we passed through it before was now a scene of hot and noisy activity. People streamed towards it from all directions; round the stalls crowds buzzed and jostled; men shouted their wares and bargained over prices; outside the vortex, little clusters of women and children slept under the shade of willows; a long line of patient donkeys was tied in a field, like a well-organized car park at a race meeting. A newly purchased calf, being led home by an old woman, suddenly broke loose and fled. People made half-hearted attempts to catch it for her. We joined the chase on foot and also tried to head the calf off on horseback. I think we only confused the situation. The last we saw was the calf in the far distance with the old woman still in faint pursuit, hopelessly offering it bread.

In about an hour and a half we reached the Yamen Ya and there on the opposite bank was our lorry. In a wayside arbour, where light refreshment was sold, we found Lhakpa had arranged a delicious array of fruit, brought from the Consulate garden. We were parched and hot from the midday sun, and the cherries, apricots, white mulberries and our first strawberries, were a delightful, cool surprise. We gave our host the first strawberries he had ever eaten. We were home again in two hours.

CHAPTER VIII

Politics and a Picture

I<small>T IS DIFFICULT TO LIVE IN A</small> country and feel no interest in its history and so, inevitably, its present politics. I am nervously aware of all the traps ahead when approaching the subject of Sinkiang's history and politics. Over the first is a film thousands of years old, over the second lies the heavy pall of controversy and prejudice attached to the subject, in any country. It is impossible to draw a black and white picture, it must be blurred, shaded and smudged in places.

I once asked General Chao how long the Chinese had been connected with Sinkiang. As I already knew, he told me that China's power over the province has varied according to the situation in Central China. The date he gave me for China's first connection with this province was 10 B.C. Other opinions allow the Chinese a nominal control since 101 B.C., a more definite one since 60 B.C. It seems fair to say that China has had intermittent power over the province for about 2,000 years. When her Emperors were strong and interested in expansion, they sent armies to conquer the areas to the north and west of China proper. In particular they waged weary war through the centuries, against the Huns; struggling with them for supremacy in Central Asia. But when the Emperors were weak, or uninterested in colonization and Empire building, Chinese influence over neighbouring territories was withdrawn. Sometimes there were great men like Ban Chai, appointed Protector General of the Western Regions (in A.D. 91), holding Chinese prestige high; sometimes Chinese power retreated and only a shadowy claim to control existed. China has always liked to keep up a bluff, not to "lose face", in her claims to suzerainty. She still claims allegiance from Tibet and even the remote little state of Hunza.

From 1911, when China became a republic, until 1942, the control of the Chinese Central Government over Sinkiang has been very nominal. Individual Chinese have had power in the province but they have not owed it to the central authority. Governor Yang Tseng-hsin ruled Sinkiang strictly but wisely, as a complete autocrat, without interference from the Central Government, from 1911 until his murder in 1928. Many people think, perhaps rightly, that the dictatorship of such a man, stern but controlled, cunning but disciplined, is the best form of government for a simple, peasant people. Certainly under Yang, Sinkiang seems to have been more prosperous and peaceful than it has ever been since.

The history of the province after Yang's death is a complicated one of rebellions, civil wars and divided authority; in which the Central Government played a weak part and the Soviet Government an increasingly strong one. Groups such as the White Russians and the Tungans (Chinese Mussulmans), added to the confusion. Gradually, with Russian backing, the Chinese general, Sheng Shih-ts'ai, began to dominate the whole province. There was some unity once more. Under a new type of dictator the country was restored to a certain measure of peace and prosperity. Sheng controlled inflation; he built schools and roads. But there was a price to pay for these benefits. Whether he liked it or not (and nobody knows the exact extent of Sheng's liking for his supporters), he was under strong Soviet influence. It had helped him to power. With its aid he built the roads and schools; under its direction he worked to rid the country of all other foreign influence, and to eliminate the prosperous Turki landowners, and the religious leaders.

Depending on one's attitude to Sovietism, so was the rule of Sheng a good or a tragic period in Sinkiang. It is difficult to deny the Russian element. There is, of course, a difference between the political scene in North and South Sinkiang. What is true of one is not always true of the other. Governor Sheng may not have had a very firm control over the south; he may not have wanted such sweeping "Sovietization" as took place there. But it did take place. During this period the British Consulate in Kashgar was boycotted; the staff had difficulty in buying supplies in the bazaar, no one cared to be seen talking to them; spies were stationed everywhere. British subjects—traders and landowners—were expelled from the country, very often at a few hours' notice. They were turned out of their homes to face cold and suffering on the hard road to India. Some of them died. The Swedish Mission was closed and all its members driven out. Foreigners were not the only victims of this policy. Purges, liquidations and strange disappearances decimated the rich Turkis, the owners of property, money and influence. Acting with, at least, Soviet approval, Sheng was ruthless. How much any ruler affects the simple man in the country-side, is open to doubt. Probably the peasant was grateful for peace in which to till his land or tend his flocks, for a controlled price for his food. But in the towns, among the richer classes, Sheng brought a reign of terror.

His rule lasted roughly from 1934 until 1944. During those ten years he had one rebellion, at least, to contend with. A Tungan named Ma Hu Shan rose against him, but was defeated and fled to India. In 1942 Sheng Shih-ts'ai made a sudden volte-face. For some reason unknown, although conjectures are many, he decided to throw off the Soviet yoke. The whole political scene began to change. Sheng turned to the Chinese Central Government and for two years continued to rule, under their direction—a startling change which I make no attempt to explain. Pressure on the British Consulate in Kashgar was lifted. When Eric went to Urumchi, in 1942, he suddenly found himself treated with polite friendliness and hospitality. The days of boycotting and prison were over. For on his arrival in

Sinkiang in 1940, the new Consul-General had even suffered the indignity of being kept in gaol for four days.

Sheng Shih-ts'ai was removed from office in 1944, and the Central Government of China began to appoint the provincial officials. Its power was on the increase. But another rebellion, in 1945, which broke out in different parts of Sinkiang, added to the already considerable difficulties of a Government recovering from a hard war against Japan and struggling with civil war. Many Chinese officials, in such lonely outposts as Tashkurghan, were murdered in this uprising. A large group of insurgents, centred on Kuldja, threatened to defeat the Government forces altogether. But the main threat, to the capital, was suddenly eased and the Kuldja Group seemed content with certain demands, a greater share in the provincial government and the "organization of racial troops" being two of them. This agreement has caused trouble ever since. The Kuldja Group claim that it has not been honourably carried out. More and more this party has withdrawn to the north of Urumchi, cutting itself off from the province as a whole and increasing the troubles of the Sinkiang Government.

When we visited the capital, in 1947, we wanted to go up to Kuldja; it lies in fine country. But it was not possible. No official would take the responsibility of allowing us to go into this "alien" territory. It was as if Scotland had cut herself off from England and beyond the Tweed nobody would guarantee one's safety. Kuldja lies close to the Russian border. One is tempted to think that the Soviets had again taken a part in Sinkiang politics and had backed the rebels of 1945. Perhaps they continue to back the victorious group collected round Kuldja. But this is only a conjecture.

I have tried not to entangle myself in the complications of Sinkiang history and politics. While living in a country its problems tend to seem more vital and important than they appear to a general public. What seem to me the everlasting and incomprehensible rebellions and revolutions of Latin America are undoubtedly of keen interest to someone living there. I have tried to keep a sense of proportion in regard to the subject. But some idea of the history and

9

government of Sinkiang is necessary as a background, even to my slight picture. There is always much talk of Sinkiang as a future international battle-ground. It is a buffer between two large nations and may, people say, be the cause of a general conflagration. This certainly throws more limelight on the province; it makes its pains and troubles seem more important. But there are so many danger areas in the world to-day, so many tender spots ready to fester and produce a general blood-poisoning, that I do not claim a greater significance for Sinkiang's problems than for any of the others.

Sinkiang, whether it develops big issues or not, has its own difficulties to solve. It has little choice between domination by one or other of its powerful neighbours. A certain percentage of the people favour the Soviets; many of the young men, the intellectuals without much money, the element which is tired of what it considers the inefficiency of Chinese rule. Another group, the richer men, the religious men, who stand to lose by Soviet ideas, supports the Chinese. A minority, idealistic and sadly unpractical, hopes for complete independence.

As I have said, the ordinary peasant probably feels little interest in who governs him. Provided wars do not ravage the land, provided he has enough water to irrigate his fields (and the distribution of water is his knottiest problem, causing his small battles), his life is simple and satisfactory. In South Sinkiang, at any rate, the land is prosperous; famine on any large scale, is unknown. The farmers have an easy task, without hideous pests, tempests, floods and droughts to endanger their crops. With primitive agriculture—with wooden ploughs, reaping by hand, threshing with the tread of animals driven in an endless circle, winnowing with the wind—the Turki still produces sufficient food for himself with the minimum of trouble. The standard of living, at least compared with India, as I knew it before 1947, is high. The average man, woman and child looks healthy and well dressed. There is a remarkable absence of beggars. Because food is plentiful I never saw the gaunt, pitiful ponies which make parts of India so hateful. There are lame animals and others with cruel saddle sores, but the majority of horses and donkeys are well fed.

This easy-going state of affairs is the result of Chinese rule. It is as possible to point to abuses, corruption, inefficiency, and failings as it is in the government of any country in the world. There are practically no hospitals for the people, the schools of Sheng Shih-ts'ai have fallen into disrepair, by modern standards the whole province is sadly backward in transport and industry. But there are good excuses for this. In the first place the Chinese Central Government has not been in control of the province, in modern times, for more than the last four years. Secondly it has had ceaseless wars to contend with, and thirdly the difficulties of building a primitive Central Asian country into a "modern" one, are enormous and profound. It may not even be wise to try. I cannot believe the ordinary Turki would be essentially happier with trains and factories. But that is another question. Certainly I think much *could* be done for his benefit. One cannot withhold modern advantages simply because one likes to see the quaintness of ancient ways. But the would-be reformers who see in hydro-electric schemes and mass production the end of all evils are surely taking a shallow view.

Under the Chinese the Turki has a freedom that he may not even consciously value. Of course, it can be maintained that this benefit is fortuitous because the rulers are casual. They are content to let things drift along, provided they can levy taxes and make profits. But freedom is to be valued. The Turki can live his own life very much as he pleases; he can pray, he can trade, travel and own property. I do not think the average Turki expects the same political freedom as is now demanded in the democratic countries of the West. The whole conception of authority is still different in Asiatic countries. In religious tolerance and in equality among classes the Chinese are far more advanced than many other Eastern countries. If one accepts the fact that the Turkis cannot achieve complete independence then I, personally, think they enjoy many advantages and are wise to remàin under Chinese rule. If only the complicated affairs of Central China can be sorted out, I think the Chinese will gradually allow more autonomy to the people of Sinkiang and do more for them. Even during my short stay the Turkis were being granted more power. Many of the officials were local men and a Turki Governor was appointed. Wholesale, rapid, ruthless methods would bring much suffering to a primitive, simple and religious people. But such a policy is easier to advertise; its reforms glitter deceptively bright. Many foreigners, seeing the slow advances of the Chinese, plunge headlong into the assumption that the only alternative is Soviet domination.

Because one likes simple things oneself; because one finds native ways interesting; because it is "picturesque" to see slow ploughing with an ox and a donkey yoked together, the dignified camels, the women sitting on their doorsteps spinning, two men making a false breeze over a satisfying pile of wheat, while a third tosses it high to free the chaff; because one sees a people apparently unhurried, unharassed by "modern" progress, one tends to laud a primitive way of life. It is like looking back and thinking how delightful it would have been to have lived in the eighteenth century. But like the hero in the play, *Berkeley Square*, one would inevitably find all sorts of unattractive manners and habits, many discomforts to which one is no longer accustomed, if one attempted to live that primitive life oneself. The simple people of Sinkiang may have advantages over us, but forced to live their life one would, no doubt, lose a good deal of one's rosy romanticism about the subject. Eric once asked me if I would rather lead the life of a Kirghiz woman or that of a restricted English housewife. Personally, I regard the latter with considerable horror; I tend to idealize the former. But to be honest, I do not know if I could discard all the ordinary comforts, advantages and entertainments of an English life, for the narrow, though free and open-air existence of a nomad.

I am trying to correct an idea, which seems to have developed from my support of the lax Chinese rule, that Sinkiang is a small paradise of fat, smiling peasants, wanting for nothing. It is not. There is poverty, disease, cruelty, as there is anywhere else. But it is ridiculous to judge a

Central Asian country by Western standards. Ridiculous to think that people are starving because they do not have four meals a day, and are unhappy because they cannot read and do not see Gary Cooper once a week. Some foreign journalists tend to sweep into Sinkiang for a month or two, compare the country with their own, come to the conclusion that all is misery and promptly blame the Government. They want to paint a picture in black and white, mostly black; ignoring local standards and Asiatic standards as a whole.

It is no more possible for me to say whether the people of Sinkiang are happy or unhappy, than for the firebrand foreign reformers. But I do think slow, careful improvements, *suited to the country*, are more likely to help the people than swift, sweeping innovations which would disrupt the whole rhythm. I should begin by organizing doctors and hospitals. I should try, tactfully, to improve the agriculture, to encourage better run "cottage industries". The benefits of standard education, the profits from industrialization, could come later. I only hope they will. But I hope they come gradually.

Abandoning conjectures, my amateur efforts at social reform and quite personal views on the future of Sinkiang I would like to try to paint a small, light picture of Kashgar and its people. I cannot pretend to know anything about North Sinkiang, where there are many more Chinese, nomad Mongol groups and others to form a different scene. I have not travelled much in the oases to the south of Kashgar, but I think there are few major differences between them and the Kashgar one. The people in the hills are certainly different. I have tried to describe them in other chapters. I am not attempting a complicated picture in oils, an art taking years of study to perfect; I am not attempting exhaustive detail. Word pictures of foreign countries, rich with detail and instruction always seem to me difficult to visualize. In any case Sinkiang has already been so competently "painted". If I can, I want only to give an impressionist view.

The colour of soft brown loess dust predominates. The earth, the roads, the houses, the rough "bricks" drying in

the sun, the massive, fortified walls of Kashgar city, the
graves, so carefully built, so soon crumbling back into the
ground, all are the same uniform colour. But in the early
morning and at sunset, if the sun is bright in its rising and
setting, it gives a rich colour to the dull mud walls. They
seem to absorb the light and to glow with a deep, subtle
pink.

It rains so seldom that there is no need to build solid,
efficient houses. Here and there a Chinese barracks, a
Yamen (or government office), is firm and well-finished,
probably distinguished by a wash of blue-grey. But the
native houses rise up from the earth from which they are
built, loose and casual. Or they grow directly out of the
low cliffs, leaning and crumbling, their crazy little balconies
of wood jutting dangerously out into space. Only mosques
are given more care and attention. They are clean and
upright, with carved pillars of wood and lattice work
windows.

The mosques are the meeting-place of the men. Outside
one sit three venerable old men, bearded and turbaned,
studying the Koran; by another a large group gathers to
gossip and discuss their affairs. Islam is an important
part of the picture. High on a bluff, where graves cluster
thickly, stands a circle of swaying, chanting men attending
a funeral. The rhythm develops strongly, reminiscent of
some African tribal music and seeming alien to these placid
people. Then it dies away and the somewhat hysterical
feeling is gone. More often is heard the wailing of a
woman kneeling alone by a grave. She repeats her sobbing
prayer in a continuous, unchanging chant—mechanical,
pathetic. In a field, in the middle of his work, a man stops
to pray. He kneels, bows to the ground, stands up, kneels
again, in the long, complicated ritual of Mussulman prayer.

But these people are not fanatics. By some Mussulman
standards they take their religion too easily. For instance
purdah is not so very strictly observed. Some women hurry
by draped like little moving tents. Their faces are hidden
behind dark "handkerchiefs", a long white cotton coat,
with narrow, unused sleeves, is worn over the head and
clutched round them. But to many women the garments

seem to have become merely traditional, like the "flash" worn by the Royal Welch Fusiliers since the days of the greasy pigtail. So they put on the white coat and the small veil, but throw the latter back over their hats in gay abandon. Sometimes a woman goes by with a silk shawl all over her face and head—as if it had just fallen on her by mistake.

The great walls of Kashgar, raised at intervals to a massive watch-tower, overlook the ant-like activity of the bazaar on the one side, and the leisurely life of the roads and the irrigated fields on the other. Only the bridges, with their arches overhead, and the one Chinese Temple, standing high in the city, with its typical up-tilting roof, mark conspicuously the foreign rule. On special occasions, when the Chinese flag drapes every building, when red bunting is twisted round archways, when slogans, in beautiful Chinese "characters", are written on banners, the rule is more noticeable.

Six miles away from the Old City of Kashgar, the Chinese have built their own, small, New City. It, too, is guarded by a vast wall of mud. There is nothing very superior about this isolated retreat of the Chinese; but the atmosphere there is quite different. There are a few Chinese style buildings; there are Chinese shops with their Chinese owners standing behind proper counters; paper lanterns and Chinese signs dangle outside some of the shops; in the streets are more Chinese than ever appear in the Old City. The women in their straight, standard blue cotton dresses; fat babies with narrow eyes and elderly men unexpectedly wearing homburg hats, add to the foreign feel of the place. It always seemed to me a sad attempt to forget exile.

Normally the Kashgar scene is essentially a Turki one. The hidden women, the bearded, weak-faced men, so surprisingly fair skinned, the fleets of donkeys, the creaking wooden carts with extraordinarily insecure-looking wheels, the gayly caparisoned mappa ponies with their bells and tassels bobbing, the little girls with their innumerable tiny pigtails and round, embroidered caps, a boy wandering along playing on a flute, the melon sellers by the road-side— all these are typical and essentially Turki.

Perhaps sounds recall a place more vividly than the sights one has seen. The sounds of Kashgar are not all beautiful but they are characteristic and so much a part of it. Chinese soldiers on the parade ground, barking out slogans in ugly staccato unison; a miller standing on a high bluff, blowing his horn to summon customers to his mill; the cry of a bread-seller, and the call of a priest at the time of prayer; the gentle whistling of pigeons' wings as they wheel and tumble in the sky. The "tumblers" are a speciality; they play a game of falling like a dead bird only to recover, flutter and play again; a whistle attached to the tail of some of them makes the charming, soft music. There is nearly always a donkey lifting its tragic voice in despair or joy— who can say which? Somewhere a man sings as he goes along. Delightfully unself-conscious he breaks into a song of deafening force. Far away someone takes up the tune. At harvest time a monotonous unvarying song rings continuously in one's ears. I once passed an old man on my morning walk, singing as he drove his two donkeys in their weary circle to thresh his rice. He sang so loudly that he kept his fingers in his own ears to deaden the sound.

The Kashgar people are lazy and placid. They have been ruled for so long, their life is so easy, that they have not developed the toughness of the Esquimaux, the Pathans' love of war, the energy of the Tibetans or the arts of the Kashmiri. But the peasants are as friendly and hospitable, as ready to share a joke as are simple people anywhere. They are exasperating in their indolence and the work they do is not impressive. But if one demands little from them they are charming and kindly. Not high praise perhaps, but these are happy characteristics in a world of fanaticism and frenzy.

CHAPTER IX

Towards the Frontier

IT WAS ON A SHORT EXPEDITION
into the hills north of Kashgar that I began first to know and
appreciate the Kirghiz. This ancient race of nomads has
more character, is a tougher breed than the people of the
oases. Without any deep study of the differences between
the people of the hills and the people of the plains I found
it was usually easy to distinguish the two quite separate
races. The Kirghiz tend to have the Mongolian characteristics of high cheek-bones and slanting eyes, while the
plainsman is a fairer Indo-European type. Gradually I
learnt the many differences between the life and customs
of the two peoples. I had a genuine affection and respect
for the nomads that I did not feel so strongly for the Turkis.

Throughout this book I have called the people of the
oases by the general name of Turkis, to distinguish them
from their Chinese rulers and from the nomad tribes,
such as the Kirghiz and the Kazaks. I make no attempt to
plunge into the complications of Central Asian races and
the fine distinctions of their nomenclature.

In our search for chikor we had often visited a place in
the hills called Ishtik Karaul, about thirty miles from Kashgar. When first we explored in this direction, driving out on
the Urumchi road and then branching off into the desert, we
had been surprised to find the trace of a road across the
stony plain. In many places water had washed it completely

away and everywhere the slight track was disappearing. But we picked up the line at intervals and followed it steadily north, into the hills. The intriguing fact was that *any* attempt had been made to build a road, leading through desert, north to the Russian border. The only consistent explanation we got from the locals was that it had been originally built in the days of the last Tsar. Then about fourteen years ago the rebel Tungan leader, Ma Chung-ying, probably with Russian aid, began to rebuild the road. In 1934 his resistance collapsed and he fled to Russia along this route. Our Kirghiz friend, Kurban, told exciting stories of tanks and motor convoys driving down the road from Russia, in the days when Russian influence was strong in Sinkiang. But I can offer no proof of these stories and only repeat what the locals told us.

Whatever the truth about the road, we had followed it as far as Ishtik Karaul on several occasions. It was not until the end of June 1947 that we planned to go beyond this village and to explore the lower foothills of the Tien Shan.

On this expedition we decided to economize on transport and to make use of our own two donkeys to carry our baggage. We hired two ponies for riding and having driven to Ishtik Karaul met all the animals there. Sali Akhun, the water-carrier, was in charge of his donkeys and a gate-keeper, alleged to be familiar with horses, came to supervise them. The latter was a large man with an innocent child-like expression. He could be so unintelligent it made one gasp, but he was so obviously wanting to help and was so permanently good-tempered that we grew fond of him and he later became Eric's groom. He was familiarly known as Kapak, which Gyalgen informed me with loud laughter means Vegetable Marrow. With Gyalgen and Rosa Beg our party of six was complete.

In late June Kashgar was unattractively hot and fly-ridden. We were looking forward to the cool hills and set off happily from Ishtik Karaul after lunch. We had not walked more than a few hundred yards before it was obvious that the two little donkeys could not carry all our baggage. I did my best to follow Eric's stern views on "travelling light", but strange, bulky sacks and boxes always appeared

—and always with a convincing excuse from Gyalgen. Nothing would part him from a dilapidated lunch basket (half empty), huge baskets of rotting vegetables, extraordinary collections of cooking-pots and an elaborate "kitchen box". He lived and worked in a chaotic muddle which he brought with him on trek. I would make a raid into this chaos; throw away empty tins, amalgamate two half-empty ones, cast out the rotted vegetables and pieces of stale bread so carefully preserved, and argue over some damaged treasure. But in a day or two confusion reigned once more. On this occasion I had again tried to reduce Gyalgen's paraphernalia. But even strict necessities made too big a burden for the donkeys, and we were forced to reload everything on to the riding ponies. The donkeys were now dignified with saddles and stirrups and we all began the journey once more.

At Ishtik we had collected a rather unwilling guide. He appeared to resent the whole expedition and kept changing his advice about water, habitations and camp sites. After four and a half miles he insisted that we halt for the night and was quite uninterested in our protests. We consulted a passer-by, who seemed knowledgeable and friendly, and he assured us that farther on there was water, but no village. Dismissing our surly guide we decided to go on. There may have been water if one knew where to find it, but we did not know, and we did not find any for the next twenty-four hours. Until after 8 o'clock that evening we continued our search, while Eric and Kapak made reconnaissance rides up nearby valleys. Finally we gave it up and made a doleful camp where we had stopped. This was on an exposed plateau of bare stony ground, where a steadily rising wind added to our discomfort. A bottle of milk, mixed with a tin of soup, was shared by everyone and we went hastily to bed to forget our thirst.

It is a great mistake to develop fixed habits. Getting up at 5 a.m. the following morning, without my habitual cup of tea was a severe hardship. It seemed impossible to eat anything and so with an empty stomach I set off into the wind. This had increased during the night and blew into our faces all morning. With an eye jaundiced by the

bad start, the valley we followed seemed to me the most
gaunt and uninteresting I had ever seen. The surrounding
hills were low and lacked grandeur, there was nothing to
relieve the monotony and only one thing occupied my
mind—a cup of tea. It was one of those patches, which
one is inclined to forget when thinking or talking, so
glibly, of the joys of mountain treks. There were inevitably
moments when one was too tired, cold or hot, hungry or
merely irritable, to enjoy the general experience. Living a
simple life the simple things loomed large and important.
On many occasions the scenery had to be very impressive
indeed, to take precedence, in my mind, over a passionate
longing for a drink of water or an end to the day's march.
Again it was a question of mental control, and I certainly
did not have a sufficient share of it. I often wondered
whether men like Gyalgen, Kapak, or any of the Kirghiz
who accompanied us, had more self-control than I had, or
whether they were just more tough? I liked to think they
were more tough, or perhaps, more insensitive. They
appeared to react much less quickly to changing tempera-
tures and while I would put jerseys on and take them off a
dozen times in the day, they would wear the same padded
suit in the cold dawn and the heat of the sun. Such details
as a limping horse, swarming flies or a smoke-filled tent,
appeared to leave them unmoved. Perhaps this insen-
sitivity results in mental dullness in other directions; but
I often envied it, and I suspect could copy it without much
damage to my fancied intelligence.

The whole idea of trekking began to appear a ridiculous
one. The stony valley wound on and on and the few
people we met were infuriatingly vague in their directions.
In fact we hardly ever met a local who could give concise,
accurate information. As it is equally rare when asking
the way in England, I suppose this is not so surprising.
Apart from the lack of interest in time and distance, we came
to the conclusion that limited thoughts resulted in limited
language. The people had not got the words for an elaborate explanation of the route. Instead of saying, "You go
two miles down this valley until a side valley joins it obliquely
from the west. Then 600 yards beyond this junction a

noticeably large, dry water-course on the right hand side . . . etc.", they could only tell you that "not far away you will come to" water, a house, or whatever it might be. And I learnt to hate the word "yaqin", (near) which raised my hopes, falsely, so many times. A place any distance up to twenty miles would be described as "yaqin".

What seemed so long, so dreary and so severe at the time, seems extraordinarily mild in retrospect. At 2.30 in the afternoon we finally reached a Kirghiz encampment and after a cup of water my irritation fell from me. We were invited into an akoi and the merriment and interest all round us was infectious. I began to enjoy myself. The biggest joke of all was the amount of tea we put into the boiling water which the women supplied. It would have lasted them for months they said. They were not a rich group and we asked nothing from them but milk for our tea. We produced our own food and were watched by a fascinated audience as we ate. I was equally fascinated watching the audience.

The tent was full of women and children. The women were unveiled and seemed much more self-possessed than those of Kashgar. I learnt later that they hold a firm and responsible place in society, work hard and are respected. One or two of the girls were extraordinarily pretty and, what I envied most, had attractive heavy silver ornaments tied to the end of their long plaits.

We first met the Kirghiz prepared to patronize them with flashy trinkets from the Kashgar bazaar. But these women with their elaborate jewellery and innate good taste, made us ashamed of our cheap presents. In time we learnt what was appreciated. While they seldom agreed to take money from their "guests", tea, rice, flour, lengths of material and mirrors were welcomed. Presents for the children were also a success and in any case a reel of thread, a cigarette, or anything handed to a woman, was immediately given to her baby. The tents were always alive with children. How any of them had survived was a complete mystery to me. Fresh from all the "modern" views on bringing up a baby I was horrified to see inert bundles strapped into narrow cradles and the whole covered with a heavy blanket. Often a mother would feed her baby as it lay in its prison. I imagine the infant death rate is high.

When our meal was over we were escorted to an encampment farther up the valley, which was considered, I suppose, more able to entertain us properly. We were led to the richest of the akois and introduced to an elderly, dignified lady. She appeared to be a person of some importance and was certainly a delightful hostess. With the usual good manners of the Kirghiz the heavy, felt door of the akoi was held up for us and we were ushered inside. Rugs and cushions were hastily spread, wooden bowls of dhai and cream were brought out from behind the screen. Our hostess immediately busied herself with sifting flour, kneading, rolling and preparing pastry for a rich and delicious "cake". This flaky pastry, made with layers of thick cream and eaten hot, is one of the best, and most indigestible things I know. Whenever we lived among the Kirghiz, in the summer months, we fattened on a diet of milk, cream and dhai. But it is curious that no Asiatics have developed the art of making cheese. Considering the uncountable varieties of European cheese it is strange that these nomads, who rely so much on milk products, have only produced one, very tasteless, dry variety.

Although by Kirghiz standards our hostess was well-to-do, we did not want to inflict six unexpected guests upon her. We supplied the flour but she insisted on being our cook, and was soon busy once more making noodles for all of us and for her own large household. The inevitable sheep was led up for our inspection. The compliment of slaughtering a sheep in our honour, was one I never enjoyed. I felt I was signing a death warrant. In any case I did not appreciate the very long wait and the very tough meat which followed. A rapid meal cooked by Gyalgen was what Eric and I preferred, but like all guests we were at the mercy of our hosts. When the meal was ready, on this occasion, it was enjoyed by a large party who chewed and gnawed at bones and meat with loud noises, while Eric and I nibbled as small an amount as politeness allowed.

Our position, life's history, family and immediate plans having been explained to, and discussed by, everyone gathered round in the central akoi, it was agreed that we could go on the next day. Our hostess's nephew would be our guide. Eric's maps were always a great source of interest. That he knew the local names and main routes, although a stranger, was an unexplainable mystery. I find maps a complete mystery myself.

Early the next day we distributed our presents and said an affectionate farewell. The friendly matriarch came to see us off and told me she always wished to be my friend. The way led up towards a stern little pass called the Kara Teke (12,000 ft.). It was a stormy day and soon rain began to spit down on us. Neither Kapak nor Sali seemed able to load an animal properly. This part of the route was certainly a severe test; the gradient was steep and the path rough. All the way up the pass and down the other side, the small caravan kept halting while a complete reloading was carried out. While the rain increased and the sky darkened, we crawled slowly up, with long and frequent halts. Several times one of the donkeys collapsed and had to be prized off the ground like a limpet from a stone.

The Kirghiz guide was rapidly losing his spirits. At the top of the pass, a sharp, rocky ridge, he announced that he was going back. Entreaties, bribes, threats and abuse finally persuaded him to come on and he did eventually accompany us all the way back to Ishtik Karaul. He was rather an unreliable man; very sociable and voluble when all was well and he could introduce us to other Kirghiz, but untrustworthy about the route and easily depressed.

The descent of the Kara Teke was steeper and rougher than the ascent. Picking our way down among rocks and slates, one man had to hold the head of each horse while another hung on to the tail. The baggage slipped continuously and had to be rearranged. Eric and I got so exasperated with this clumsy progress that we left the caravan and ran all the way down to the foot of the pass. The rain, now a steady torrent, was exhilarating. The black slates of the pass led down to a valley of soft, green grass and small flowers which added to our suddenly vivid enjoyment. We had the feeling of wild delight one sometimes gets in a high wind or in a storm on a lake. We ran on and on and having no coats were soon completely wet, with water trickling down our necks. Not since we left Kashmir had we been in such a severe downpour. A curious contrast to the day before, when we had plodded so wearily and thirstily up the harsh, dry valley.

Where our small, green valley met the wider one of the Chakmak River, we had expected to find a Kirghiz encampment. We had decided to cut short the march and shelter there. On reaching the junction we found no akois, no sign of people anywhere and a desolate scene of rocks, rain and the racing river. Our exhilaration ebbed away and as it faded we realized how exceedingly cold and wet we were. The rain was heavier than ever. While waiting for the caravan we crouched under the meagre shelter of a rock. The one sign of habitation was a small, mud house, on the opposite bank of the river. It was obviously deserted and as its flat roof was invisible to us, I was unhappily certain that it was a ruin.

As soon as the doleful little party of ponies and donkeys appeared, we consulted our guide about shelter and he said there were no villages or encampments for a long way. The poor house opposite was our only hope. We crossed the river which was fast and very cold. In front of the others I ran to the house, murmuring to myself, "Let there be a roof, please let there be a roof."

There was, but the only door was heavily bolted. Extreme cold, the ceaseless, heavy rain and a general feeling of depression, dulled our consciences. Having tried in vain to pick the lock, with a united heave we broke in the door! We found a three-roomed house, with firewood, and everyone, including the donkeys, poured in.

I valued the cold and wet for the glorious contrast of getting warm and dry. This sounds like the madman who beat his head against a wall, because it was so wonderful when he stopped. Sometimes I have felt that there was an element of this madness in my travels. Certainly the roughness made me appreciate simple pleasures, and the return home was always a delight. But mountains give more than this negative pleasure—a depth of happiness and a sense of awe which is a permanent value.

The largest of the three rooms was given up to Eric and me, the men occupied the "kitchen" and the donkeys the "hall". The latter spent most of the time wandering into our room and eating the straw matting on the floor. Gyalgen soon produced tea and food. Finding that our room was cold, and the roof leaked, we joined the men round their fire. Long familiarity with Europeans on expeditions, a natural friendliness and self-confidence has made the Sherpas more at ease with their employers than most natives. Gyalgen was quite willing to share our food, and to sit chatting with us round the fire. It took us some time to persuade our Turki servants to the same easy attitude. They were shy rather than subservient. They always hung nervously and deferentially on the outskirts of the circle.

Towards evening the rain stopped and the sun came out. The storm had left a sharp clarity and cleanness in the air.

The march had been a short one and we were not at all tired. Once again the barometer of our spirits rose. We saw some gazelle on the hill-side above us, leaping delicately higher and higher; we crossed the river and chased chikor; we climbed a small hill and had a wide view over the mountains all round us. The setting sun lit the folded hills; in shadow the deep blues and purples were exaggerated, the Kara Teke was powdered with snow that had fallen during the storm. Life seemed an excellent thing.

We were away by 7.30 the next morning, having tucked some money among the pile of wood in payment for our illegal night's lodging. A few hours later we met a man who our guide alleged was the owner of the house. The whole story was related to him, and also where to find the money. He looked completely startled and confused. In spite of placating smiles from us and voluble explanations from everyone else, I do not think he ever understood what had happened to him.

Progress up the valley was complicated by the many river crossings. Rosa Beg was as usual imposed upon and the others made him ferry us all across in turn, on the donkeys. When very tired on this trip, I tried riding a donkey. It is a special technique to induce one to move, and to move in the right direction. I never achieved it. After half an hour I became so exasperated with the constant prodding and kicking required that I always began walking again. In spite of the loads I often saw Kapak and Sali riding the ponies—perched high like sultans on elephants.

Our guide was right about the lack of habitation in the valley. But his idea of distance was, of course, different from ours. Leaving the river at about 1 p.m. we inquired if there was any water in the country immediately ahead of us. He was firm in his promises of a Kirghiz camp "just over the pass". He suggested that we delay lunch and then enjoy tea and refreshment with his friends. We followed his advice and began an easy but steady climb up to the Testa Pass. At the time it seemed a weary march to me, I think I was feeling very empty, having had nothing to eat since a small breakfast at 6.30. I felt listless, with heavy legs weighted down. But it was delightful country, reminding me in places of the Wiltshire Downs. In startling contrast, and very different from Wiltshire, was the colour of some of the hills. Bright ochre, yellow, every shade of rust and pink leading up to a distinct red, were splashed across the scene.

At the rather indefinite top of the pass, we met one of our guide's relations, the son, I believe, of our elderly hostess. He was returning home with his wife and hearing of our visit to his mother, he was as friendly and kind as she had been. He gave me my first taste of "kumis". Because I was very thirsty it seemed delicious. I have never really enjoyed it since. His wife was a most colourful person. She was young with a round face and a body that also seemed quite round, because of her numerous clothes. Her final garment was a magenta plush coat, handsomely contrasting with a yellow silk scarf over her head. The silver ornaments at the end of her plaits, were the richest and heaviest I had yet seen. Mounted high on her horse she made me feel a very drab, dusty figure as I trudged away down the pass.

Eric left us at this point, to explore a near-by hill. The guide led me on to his alleged friends. I was losing all faith in their existence and finally, in mutiny, sat down on the path and ate some lunch. An hour later, well off our route we sighted a group of akois. As we approached, our reception was chilly. The inevitable dogs flew out and Sola had to be rescued from an early death; men and women stared without smiling and I began to feel embarrassed. However, our guide did some rapid talking and eventually I was shown into an akoi and promptly surrounded by interested women. It was not until Eric joined us that we were all led to the main tent and the atmosphere became at all cordial. Then tea was made, the ceremonial "tablecloth" (a somewhat grubby handkerchief) was spread and small squares of pastry were produced. We retaliated with mirrors, tea and cigarettes. This place was close to the Russian border and, I think, this delicate position may have had something to do with my cool reception. We certainly left on a very friendly note.

Our goal was Toyin-Toba and we wanted to finish the remaining six miles that day. The tea and rest had been pleasant but had taken us out of our way. Now it was getting late and the six miles began to seem very long. It started to rain again. Having come to the hills to escape the heat of Kashgar, we had never expected to feel so remarkably cold. Rain was something I had not provided against in my wardrobe. I had no mackintosh, and on this occasion no coat nor sufficient warm clothes. Seeing a couple of akois before we reached the "official" group at Toyin, we ran to one of them for shelter. The owner was startled but soon recovered and made us welcome. His was a humble tent but he built up a magnificent fire of yak dung and roots and had a plentiful supply of milk. We arrived at milking time when all the sheep were tied in rows and the lambs put in a separate pen. The noise was deafening.

We decided to spend a day at Toyin. Our plan was to ride up towards the Russian frontier. Keeping quiet about this we simply asked for a guide to show us the country. Eric and I mounted our own two ponies and we set off. Among my many reasons for disliking horses, their amours had not been one. But the whole of that day we were burdened with the desperate jealousies of our red and black horses. Finding mine was difficult to control I changed on to our guide's neat, stocky little mare. She, apparently, was the cause of all the trouble. If one of the horses was close to her; the other became frantic. We all three had to ride widely apart in ridiculous isolation. Except for this undercurrent of the eternal triangle I was happier on a pony than I have ever been before or since. My mare appeared to be equally uninterested in both of her suitors. She was placid and firm-footed, but very willing to move when I wanted her to. Working my way up cautiously from a trot to a canter, I soon gained confidence and went galloping over the wide green plain.

We reached the beginning of the pass which divides Russian from Chinese territory. For a long way on the latter side there were plains and low hills covered with beautiful grass. It was ideal country for grazing cattle and sheep and yet it was deserted. We discovered later that the Kirghiz were forbidden to camp within a certain radius of the border. Thinking that the pass might be too conspicuous a place to explore, we rode up a hill-side on the west side of the route. Then leaving the ponies, Eric and I climbed on and worked our way round and up a steep, rocky hill overlooking the pass. It was hard work as the loose rocks slipped at every step. Our efforts to keep quiet were thwarted by a continuous cascade of stones. Finally we climbed on to the top and on Russian territory, looked across into Russia. The same empty country rolled away into the distance as we could see on the Chinese side.

There is always something exciting about a frontier. We were running a rather foolish risk in having crossed this one. The country seemed deserted but should there be a patrol about the men might well act promptly, and ask questions later. That the frontier was guarded efficiently was proved by our discovery of a dug-out, overlooking the pass, with the comparatively fresh butts of Russian cigarettes on the floor. The dug-out covered the exact frontier line, marked by a pole across the top of the pass. On the Chinese side there was the rough hill track. This ended abruptly and an excellent road led away into the Russian distance.

The whole atmosphere of furtiveness and guilt was enhanced by the ominous roll of thunder in the distance. The storms were not yet over and the sky threatened more. We slipped rapidly down the loose scree back into Sinkiang. Although rain was already falling lightly, we decided to eat some lunch before going back. Tethering our ponies widely apart, we had just settled down to cake and dhai when the black horse broke loose and made an attack on his rival. I had never seen horses fight before and it was horrible. Rearing up on their hind legs, striking out with their fore legs, they seemed suddenly to become a quite different species of animal. We dared not approach the wheeling, clashing battle. Finally the milder red horse broke away and fled up the opposite hill-side. Through this pandemonium my smug little mare went on munching the delicious grass as if the quarrel was not her concern. Seizing the black horse we held him while the guide chased the red. He rode the mare as a decoy and finally brought both of them back. I was heartily sick of this passionate love story by now and anxious to see the last of the two wretched rivals.

We rode back faster than we had come, and as we rode the storm broke. Galloping along across the lonely country, with lightning flashing, the thunder shuddering the hills and sharp hail cutting into our faces, it felt like some dramatic ride in a poem. I was desperately cold but a combination of exhilaration and fear predominated. I had never ridden so fast and so far before.

Gradually the storm and our speed died down. Near Toyin we were met by two policemen, a Chinese and a Turki. Apparently news of our travels had reached the garrison commander at Chakmak and he had ordered these two men to look for us. Again we were uncertain whether they were sent to keep an eye upon us or as a compliment to Eric's position. They were very friendly and suggested that we should come to take tea with their Toyin hosts. Later one of the men drew Eric aside and said he realized that we had been up to the frontier; this did not matter to him, but he strongly recommended our keeping quiet about it.

At intervals during this call someone had to run out to deal with the ardent black horse; it was still stampeding and causing havoc all round. I never felt any sympathy for either of our pair again when I saw them loaded with baggage, Kapak and Sali.

That evening the owner of all the sheep round our camp arrived from Artush. We discovered that our host was only a paid employee of the big man. Contentedly tired from our day's expedition, we retired to bed in our little tent, where Gyalgen brought us a delicious dinner of roast chikor. Later we were informed that the rich owner had slaughtered a sheep in our honour. I am afraid I left the civilities to Eric, and after a short visit to the akoi, Eric handed them on to our servants. Gyalgen told us the next morning that they had had to sit up until after midnight to eat the sheep.

A twenty-five mile march brought us to Chakmak. It was a long day and with only an occasional donkey ride to relieve my feet, I was tired. But only pleasantly, physically tired. In the unpredictable way of moods, I had felt content all day. None of the events of the day had jarred on me as sometimes they did. Even more violent storms did not matter but added to the exhilaration I felt. Having been soaked by rain we did not present a very dignified appearance as we entered the Chakmak fort. All day we had been wondering if we could avoid spending the night with the garrison; but there seemed no chance of escape as it lay in our direct path and the escort had heralded our coming. These grim, sordid little outposts were always a problem to us. I do not suppose the officers in charge wanted our company but they felt compelled to invite us in and it was difficult to refuse the invitation. After our own simple camps or the colourful comfort of a Kirghiz akoi, the dilapidated, gloomy rooms, with doubtful-looking beds, and the threat of rats, were a sad contrast. The officers, even the Chinese ones, seemed resigned to living for several years in these lonely forts without any attempt to make themselves comfortable, or their rooms less depressing. Yet they would glibly talk of the "primitive" Kirghiz and apologize for the wretched conditions we had probably found on our journey. How far they were from understanding our own liking for wandering, our affection for the nomads, and the very real comfort and good-living we found among them.

Perhaps the Chinese officer at Chakmak was short of rations. We had no desire to impose upon him. We had plenty of food and were quite independent. But the difference in hospitality between this dominating fort and the humble Kirghiz, was very marked, indeed. We received nothing but a gloomy room.

The next day, however, the officer ordered an escort to go with us and kindly lent us horses to ford the flooded Chakmak river. I was terrified of my large army horse. I decided to let Gyalgen deal with it while I rode pillion behind him. We had to cross the river frequently as it swirled from side to side of the high-walled valley. Sola had a hard time battling against the current and I was always expecting to see her swept away. The donkeys also had a struggle and I was thankful we were not dependent on them to get us across. Riding pillion was a painful process without proper padding underneath. So until we left the river I spent the day clambering on and off the horse—only getting on at the fords.

Our orders to Mir Humza had been that on the sixth day after our departure, he should drive as far towards Chakmak as the lorry would go. Completing a circle we hoped to be met by him after we had left the river and crossed a small pass which led down towards Ishtik Karaul. At the top of this pass the escort said they must return. Once more we were reduced to our own two baggage ponies and the two donkeys. The country was now quite waterless; the storms had abated and it was hot; again the way seemed to me dull and featureless. To prove how scenery can depend on one's mood I found that Eric thought it a fascinating valley—full of interesting geological formations, colourful and exciting. On subsequent trips to the same place I realized what he meant and I, too, found the country attractive in its rather stark, lonely way. But the energy and enjoyment I had felt that morning seemed to have been

sucked away by my thirst and tiredness. We kept seeing
the tracks of tyres and realized that Mir Humza had come
and gone. The extra day spent at Toyin had upset our
arrangements.

At about 6.30 p.m. we sighted poplar trees in the distance,
always the sure signal of an oasis. Half an hour later we
were sitting near a little house while Mir Humza waited on
us with tea. He had come up the valley on the correct day
but returned to this tiny hamlet for water, and had decided
to wait there until we came. It was here that we first made
the acquaintance of Kurban, the Kirghiz.

Sola was as exhausted as I was and towards the end of the
march had so dragged and loitered that we had walked on
ahead. Later in the evening we sent Kapak out on a pony to
find her and he had great difficulty in persuading her onwards.

By making an early start we reached Kashgar at 10.30 in
the morning. The traces of "Ma Chung-ying's road" had
been discernible all the way up the valley to the small pass.
It was not very much help to us. We gave our original
guide his first trip in a motor-car and dropped him at
Ishtik Karaul. Six days of mountain travel, each day so
different and so full, seem much longer than six even days
spent at home. I felt I had known the little man for a long
time, and I was sorry to see him go. But I was, as usual,
as pleased to get back to the comforts of home as I always
was to leave them again after a long period in Kashgar.

CHAPTER X

The Ice Mountain

WHEN ERIC WAS IN KASHGAR from 1940 to 1942, his freedom was restricted. When he returned with me in 1946 the political scene was very different. We were completely free to travel wherever we chose. We were expected to notify the authorities when and where we were going, but we always received permission to go, and any help we might need. Eric had long had a plan to combine an official tour to the Sarikol area with meeting his friend, Mr. W. H. Tilman, who was to come up to Sinkiang after a climbing expedition in Hunza. The plan finally crystallized at the end of July, 1947.

I enjoyed the business of planning and packing for our trips; the tingling feeling of anticipation, the conjectures, arrangements, the whole design ahead of us. When everything was ready and we left the Consulate it reminded me of the start of seaside holidays as a child. Then ordinary rules were relaxed, everyone seemed a little different in their casual clothes, and buckets and spades already heralded the sea and the sand.

We followed the route of the mail runners, only we covered the first sixty-three miles to Ighizyar by lorry. Gyalgen, Rosa Beg and Kapak came with us. The question of transport had been a difficult one. For some reason horses were scarce and in spite of planning well ahead, no one could provide more than three for us. Donkeys were to make up the deficiency. At Ighizyar we were handsomely received by a rich gentleman who, I gathered, was anxious to please Eric. He had prepared food and red bunting archways and he insisted that we should *borrow* two of the horses from him. This necessitated lavish presents in return which cost little less than the hire of the two ponies would have done. Not without difficulty, and the usual attack on Gyalgen's dark treasures, we managed to load our baggage on to six donkeys. Saddle bags and small things were put on to the three riding ponies and we had a man and a boy in charge of the transport.

When we rode Eric adopted a stout little black pony and I had a roan. At first I was rather pleased with my mount, he seemed willing but was easily controlled. By the end of four weeks I had learnt heartily to loathe him. As usual it was probably my inability to handle a horse, but I think everyone found him lazy and morose. If he was behind his friend he would keep up a reasonable pace, but when alone he dragged and loitered and, without constant prodding, would come to a complete standstill. Only once during our trip did he gallop, and that was without my permission.

Sola startled a camel (which was carrying some of our baggage) and, like a horrible version of "The house that Jack built", the camel alarmed my pony. I found myself flying along, unwittingly chased by a camel, which had thrown half its load and was dragging the other half on the ground. The bumping of the boxes added to the camel's terror and there seemed no prospect of ending the awful race. Finally I pulled up in a state of mingled rage and tears and was, as always, soothed by Gyalgen. He ignored my undignified explosions, and led the still quivering pony away. Several of our boxes were broken by the camel and a tin of fat had emptied itself all over the contents of a haversack.

This episode came later in our travels. The seven days' journey to Tashkurghan was uneventful and pleasant. Nearly everything in that first week seemed to me effortless and delightful. Physically I felt well and energetic. The country was not difficult, although there were surprisingly few habitations and we had to rely on our own supplies. Most of the other travellers we met were driving small caravans of donkeys. Presumably these require much less food than ponies and camels, are strong, reliable and cheap. How they manage to cross the swollen rivers in summer, I never understood. On the Karakoram route, in October, we had seen men standing waist-deep in water to help their donkeys across. Going to Tashkurghan our drivers had to do the same at every river crossing. The water was not so cold but it was deep, and I felt guilty as I rode comfortably over on my pony.

The worst river crossing was after Tangita, at the entrance to the narrow valley which later developed into a fierce gorge. We had to reload nearly everything on to the ponies and cross in slow relays. This was a laborious process and I visualized a tedious day if there were many similar crossings to make. But a couple of miles beyond Tangita we were met by a "rescue" party.

In Tashkurghan there was a "Mail Supervisor" called Fati Ali Khan. The Chinese had made several requests that this post and all the mail carriers' shelters along the way, be abolished. Up to that time the Consulate had managed to retain the former but had closed all the latter. The carriers got food and shelter from shepherds and other locals paid to look after them. Fati Ali had now sent his brother, and two servants, to meet us with yaks, to escort us up the gorge. They were all Hunza men, wearing the typical flat, round white hats of their country. The idea of riding a yak rather alarmed me but I found that I had only to sit on the well-padded saddle while a man led the animal by a string through its nose. It was as comfortable as an arm-chair and about as rapid, but it felt secure and solid in the racing, rock-strewn river. It was a striking little gorge. A narrow defile was worn through the rocks by water and our route zigzagged up the river itself. Rock walls rose sharply on either side, the sound of the water echoed loudly between them as it cascaded, eddied and rushed along. At one point a boiling hot spring gushed from the rock.

Altogether we crossed four main passes between Ighizyar and Tashkurghan; two of them over 15,000 ft. There was fine, sweeping country round the Chikchilik Pass and from there we had our first view of Muztagh Ata (24,300 ft.), one of the great mountains of the Pamirs which is not visible from Kashgar.

Dropping gently down from this pass, we reached a place of vivid grass and a clear shallow stream. These sound ordinary enough, but so many of the rivers and streams we came to were mud-coloured, or cloudy, glacier-fed water, and so much of the "grass" was coarse and dun-coloured. Another variety looked green and inviting but proved to be wickedly sharp and prickly if you touched it.

On the high passes Eric chased ram-chikor. I did not join in this but walked on alone. Only on the last day did my golden mood dull a little. There was a very long, very rough descent from the 15,000-ft. pass and in the tantalizing way of that wide country we could see Tashkurghan for many miles before we reached it. It was hotter as we dropped down; I did not want to ride and I did not want to walk; the march seemed interminable. About eight miles from Tashkurghan, Fati Ali himself met us. He was a stout, fine-looking man with magnificent moustaches, like a sergeant-major. Of course, he expected me to ride and promised us the honour of a deputation of officials, a few miles farther on.

My inferior horse and inferior riding decided me against joining this reception, and while Eric and Fati Ali galloped on, I followed slowly with Gyalgen and Fati Ali's brother. The latter soon got exasperated with us and was obviously unwilling to miss all the ceremony and excitement ahead. With a muttered excuse he, too, galloped on, leaving poor Gyalgen to his fate. The last five miles seemed the longest of the entire week's journey. In the wide, green, treeless plain of Tashkurghan we could see the cavalcade in front, going on and on into the distance. The most my roan would do was an uncomfortable trot; every time it dropped into a walk Gyalgen whipped it on again. When eventually we rode down the one street of Tashkurghan bazaar, I felt jolted out of my senses.

But I could drink and eat, and I soon recovered. The unhappy Mussulmans were then observing the fast of Ramazan. They could neither eat nor drink until after sunset. I was thankful when the thirty days of the fast were over, because so often on the journey we had our meals in embarrassing isolation while everyone else watched, unable to join us.

Fati Ali had erected an akoi for us near his house. Even after so placid a journey it was good to rest, to relax and not move on. Bill Tilman arrived the day after we did and almost immediately he and Eric were studying maps and discussing plans. Their final decision was to make an attempt to climb Muztagh Ata.

In the midst of plans, packing and arrangements we had to enter into the social life of Tashkurghan. We were asked to a luncheon given by all the local officials and under pressure from Fati Ali asked all the same people back to dinner. I had not come prepared to entertain, and Fati Ali's establishment was very humble. We finally decided to have dinner in our akoi and a strange collection of chairs, cutlery, mugs and plates was somehow assembled. The evening wind, which I learnt was a permanent feature of that country, began to batter at the tent and no one seemed to have considered how we were to keep alight a flickering candle. People were sent running to borrow a lamp and the usual hole in the akoi roof was draped with carpets, lashed to the ground. In most akois an ingenious pulley system draws a flap over this hole when required, but our bedroom had no such amenity.

Gyalgen and Rosa Beg produced a very edible three-course dinner and a bottle of brandy I had brought for "medicinal" use soothed the party along. At one point I was horrified to see the magistrate take a long drink of brandy from his tin mug, in mistake (I think) for water. It seemed to come as a shock to him, for he emerged visibly suffering. He seized a tea pot, which served as our water jug, and drank hastily from the spout.

Our party was reshuffled at Tashkurghan. Kapak and the pony man took the hired donkeys and the horse back to Ighizyar. From then on we were to be dependent on local transport from day to day. Amir-i-Khan, the boy from Ighizyar, complete with his own donkey, came on with us to tend our two borrowed riding ponies. A new member

of the party was a lame old Hunza, Nyat Shah, who was to
be our interpreter. A complicated mixture of races and
languages meet in the Sarikol area. There are a few Chinese
officials; there are Kirghiz, Tajiks, Wakhis, Turkis and
Hunzas. Nyat Shah could speak to all of these people,
except the Chinese, and also understood Urdu, which was
our only link with him. It proved a rather slender one.

After a delayed start we finally left Tashkurghan on
August 8th. Bill and Eric rode ahead with the inevitable
party of officials come to see us off, while I again followed
in the rear with Gyalgen. This time I walked while he rode.
On sighting the returning cavalcade, Gyalgen insisted that
I mount quickly or I should lose considerable "face". With
great dignity I rode up to the party and received an elaborate
farewell address. When safely past them I walked once more.

The march to Beshkurghan was spoilt by the heavy dust
haze which had been hanging over the country for several
days. A monotonous blanket enveloped the hills and we
only caught tantalizing glimpses of ice peaks ahead.
Heavily escorted as we were by Fati Ali, two policemen
and two guides, there was no hope of a peaceful, simple
camp. We were led to the house of the Beg in Beshkurghan
and installed in his minute guest room. This consisted almost entirely of a raised platform. The remaining strip
of floor led to another room, closed by a heavily padlocked
door. It seemed to be the sole duty of a large, bounding
woman to come in and out to unlock this door, busy herself
inside the room and then elaborately lock it up again.
I suspected that a fascinated inspection of us had some
connection with her many visits. Quite regardless of
whether we were sleeping, eating or attempting to dress,
she burst her way through to the mysterious room at all
hours.

At midnight a dog began to bark immediately outside
and sleep seemed impossible. I never got used to the dogs
of Sinkiang. They were completely unloved; they were
only kept as watch dogs, with the result that they were a
cringing, cowardly race with a noisy show of ferocity. At
night Kashgar was often a bedlam of noise with all the
dogs barking at each other. I got no sympathy from Eric who

remarked that there was nothing to be done about the dog, and I must learn to block my ears to the noise.

Through Fati Ali, Eric had elaborately explained our needs and our plans to our escort. But the more people we had to "help" us the greater became the confusion. At first no transport appeared to take us on the next day and when finally the caravan started we were led in the wrong direction. No one, including Fati Ali, seemed to have understood Fati Ali's final instructions. Now that he had turned back we were dependent upon Nyat Shah. So we began the march with several hot, unnecessary miles and it continued to be rather a weary effort.

There is nothing more depressing than an uphill walk on soft sand. It makes the legs feel weighted with lead and the miles endless. As usual we had to share the horses with Gyalgen and Rosa Beg and it was on such a day that I appreciated to the full, all Eric's views on riding in Asia. If he had wanted to triumph I had nothing to say in reply.

At lunch time the pack ponies passed us. I asked Nyat Shah to make sure that the men knew we were going to Kara Su for the night. They disappeared at a good speed and we followed leisurely. As we passed round the Muztagh Ata Massif it changed shape all the time—from a rounded dome on the south side it developed into three distinct peaks from the west. The main peak resembled a giant slice of iced cake; a slab of ice-covered rock leading in an apparently gentle slope up to 24,300 ft.

At 5.30 p.m. we reached Kara Su—dignified on the map with a name, but in fact marked by nothing but a spring. There was no sign of the caravan. It was obvious that Nyat Shah had not checked with the pony men and they had gone on. How I disliked that poor, crippled old man at that moment. It is only possible to appreciate my feelings if you have been hot, tired, buoyed up with thoughts of the evening camp and cup of tea, and then faced blank emptiness and the prospect of a further march.

A policemen galloped on to stop the transport ponies and the rest of us began the march once more. It became a little cooler, and with the emergency I felt a determination not to be defeated. My energy revived a little and I plodded on in a mood of defiance—defiance to myself, I suppose. Nyat Shah, of course, had to ride. The two guides went on ahead and the remaining five of us shared two horses in relays. Rosa Beg managed to ride pillion with each relay in turn! The second policeman suddenly developed a lame horse, which he had to lead. The situation reminded me of the rhyme of the Ten little Nigger Boys.

So the party crawled on. To complicate matters we had a 15,000 ft. pass to cross. It was a gentle slope up but a long one, and there were several false tops. When finally we reached the real top, one of the unforgettable views that are a complete recompense for all weariness, was spread round us. A scene of space, grandeur and sweeping lines, coloured by the evening light.

Added to the splendour was the welcome sight of our caravan waiting below the pass. Having joined it we all went on to the nearest water and camped at 8.30. We were on a wide, exposed stretch of grass-land and the evening wind swept round us as we struggled to pitch the tents and light a fire. Gyalgen could work miracles with yak dung and soon had a furnace burning and a row of pots bubbling. He always made an ingenious "range" out of stones or clods of earth, and no fuel was too meagre or too wretched for him to produce a good fire. His tea was not so successful, and that evening he made one of his nastiest brews. It tasted glorious at the time. We handed round tea and cigarettes to the pony men and rather unwillingly, to our useless "guides".

The lame horse led by one policeman limped in an hour later while the other policeman we never saw, or heard of, again. I was worried about Amir-i-Khan, who was last seen with a horse, a donkey and Sola, soon after our lunch halt. The Russian border ran close to the track near Kara Su and we began to fear that the little caravan had wandered off across the frontier. However, late at night it reached camp and we gathered that Sola had caused the delay and given the poor boy a lot of trouble. For some time past we had suspected that Sola's eyesight was weak. She stumbled over stones, fell down ditches and did not notice anything held out to her. On the march she would stray off the route

MILKING TIME AT TOYIN-TOBA

AKOIS AT SUBASHI BELOW MUZTAGH ATA

and fail to return. The idea of blindness was so horrible that we kept on hoping we were wrong, and that Sola was merely stupid and clumsy. She appeared to enjoy life in her own ridiculous way. She still chased shadows and enjoyed the splash of stones into water.

Muztagh Ata loomed high above us the next morning but the miserable dust haze only allowed us a blurred view of the mountain. Having, unintentionally, gone so far the day before, we now had only a short march to Yambulak—a small valley below Muztagh Ata. Here we found only one akoi and our party of thirteen descended upon a poor Kirghiz woman and her three children. I thought she would be frightened by this invasion and I hastily produced tea and presents in return for the dhai she served us. But she seemed quite self-possessed and received us with the usual hospitality and good manners of the Kirghiz. Her husband was out, she said, but they were intending to move lower down the valley that day. Having explained to her our plans, and our intention of camping at Yambulak, she very kindly agreed to stay there for a few days and so keep us supplied with milk and cream.

We paid off the pack-pony drivers and had little difficulty in persuading our escort to go, too. They were an unattractive trio; unhelpful, unfriendly, and obviously disliking the whole expedition. They ate our food and also imposed on the Kirghiz. I had watched them ride up to a shepherd boy and calmly demand one of his sheep. Although I tried to find out if the boy had been paid, I gathered that the transaction was considered a form of "tax", and it was not suitable to interfere. If the Chinese can be accused of oppression, the local Turkis, Tajiks and even Kirghiz, in small official positions are equally severe to the people.

The serious part of the expedition began the next day, August 11th. Eric, Bill Tilman and Gyalgen, having taken supplies for about six days hoped to climb Muztagh Ata in considerably less. Following the example of Sven Hedin, the famous Swedish explorer, they hired a yak to carry the loads to their first camp—at about 17,500 ft. Rosa Beg and I accompanied them as far as this. As Eric has already described the whole episode so much better than I can, I shall only sketch it lightly to keep the continuity of the story and to explain my own small share in it.

As Yambulak lay at about 14,000 ft. we had some 3,500 ft. to climb to the first camp. Glaciers flowing down from the mountain forced us to keep low, and to traverse across the hills below them, before we could begin to climb. The mountain itself began as a slope that even I found unalarming. But it was a steady rise and the altitude soon began to affect me. I tried to follow Eric's instructions and maintain a slow, rhythmical pace. As always when climbing steeply, I counted all the time; an occupation which seems to dull my thoughts and help the rhythm of my steps. We tried to train Rosa Beg to climb slowly but he liked to race for a short distance and then take a long rest.

Eric, Bill Tilman and I were well ahead by about 12.30. and the rest of the party nowhere in sight. When Eric and Bill went down to investigate, they found that the yak and its owner had both collapsed. They had both been goaded on by Gyalgen, but had now reached a point where nothing could persuade them farther. There was no alternative but to carry the loads ourselves. Gyalgen had the largest share and, like all Tibetans, took the weight on a head-strap across his forehead. I carried a small load for the first time in my life, and the depleted party climbed on again.

It was disappointing for the climbers to have the extra work of carrying to Camp 1, and my opinion of yaks dropped considerably. Having seen the tents pitched and tea on the boil, Rosa Beg and I turned back. With a lonely feeling I climbed down. I felt full of vague fears and misgivings as I saw Eric standing alone, silhouetted against the sky, waving goodbye.

We took three hours to get back to our camp, running down the loose scree, working our way across below the glaciers again and crossing the icy streams, now grown to small torrents from the melting ice. I crossed the first one in bare feet, but the pain was so acute from the cold and the sharp stones, that I never tried it again, and always walked across in my shoes. I reached the akoi exhausted, and so thirsty that I drank one cup of tea after another in burning gulps. Everyone was very concerned about me and very attentive. Old Nyat Shah insisted on rubbing my feet and the Kirghiz woman pressed food on me that I could not touch. Why we came there to struggle up ice mountains and weary ourselves among the hills, for no apparent gain, must have been a question the Kirghiz never answered.

The next three days I spent clambering about the surrounding country and searching the ice slope above, through a telescope, for any sign of the climbers. I gazed anxiously at the mountain from different vantage points, but I never saw anything except bleak rock and ice. Once Rosa Beg shouted "There they are". I snatched the telescope from him only to find that he had picked out three small, black stones which had already deceived me.

The weather was sparkling and clear but a cold wind blew almost incessantly. I found meals alone in the akoi an embarrassing ritual. The family watched my every mouthful and whispered a running commentary to one another. Nyat Shah sat attentive and useless. He wanted to help, I know, but was unable to think of anything to do but hover near me like a dilapidated hen. I escaped to my own small tent as much as possible, but very often the three children would follow me there, and sit in a whispering bunch while I pretended to read.

The chief of police in Subashi, five miles away, came twice to call and to make sure that all was well. I felt very inadequate on these occasions, conscious that as a mere female I counted for little. On his second visit he asked me for some medicine, for a policeman in a post some thirty miles away. With my poor knowledge of Urdu, and, I suspect, Nyat Shah's poor knowledge of anything, I had great difficulty in diagnosing the case. Either the patient had a headache or a cut head. I finally decided on the latter and sent him some Dettol and a piece of Elastoplast.

Ever since the day Yusuf had torn off a finger-nail, I had travelled with a small first-aid box which I had designed for myself. It was very limited and only intended for our party. But on this expedition I had also brought some simple medicines for the Kirghiz and got the doctor to give me some simple instruction. News of these medicines spread fast and at every camp a large collection of patients, real and imaginary, collected round me. I suppose every traveller among primitive people has been faced with the same requests for help and the same pathetic faith. In my turn I had to solve the problem of how much to delude them with an aspirin, and how much to admit that I could do nothing. There did not appear to be much serious disease among the Kirghiz. In my evening "dispensaries" there were always one or two sad incurables, convinced that I could work miracles; one or two people with sores and festered wounds, which I tried to clean and dress; but the majority complained only of head and stomach aches. I suspect that the mysterious white powders, being free, induced most of these sudden pains. If I put drops into the badly inflamed eye of one man, there would be a sudden outbreak of bad eyes. Men would come and lie down in front of me pointing tragically to a quite healthy-looking eye. I was only a very amateur nurse and I was worried by the cripples and the blind whom I could not help. Even the sketchy, temporary aid I could give sometimes seemed a complete waste of time. But if nothing else, the aspirins and the doses of kaolin gave great pleasure and interest. Perhaps they did some real good sometimes.

My most serious "case" at Yambulak was a wretched boy who, with natural curiosity, had picked up some form of hand-grenade he had found lying on the ground. It must have been an unexploded relic of the 1945 troubles. He had lost the four fingers of one hand and his face was slightly hurt. I tried to persuade his father to bring him to Kashgar to see our doctor, but the old man would not undertake the long journey. I did what I could for him but it was very little.

On my second day alone I took Rosa Beg and Amir-i-Khan with me to explore the glacier which ran down between the two great ridges of Muztagh Ata. I was nervous of our united inexperience among the crevasses and ice-falls. The boys insisted on clambering off on their own and I knew that I could do nothing if they got themselves into difficulties. In the trough between the two ridges a broken river of ice led to the snow-covered col which connected them higher up. Above us, to the south, towered the main ridge. Somewhere up there climbed Eric, Bill and Gyalgen. Occasionally an avalanche broke from the heights above and thundered down; the sound following some time after I had seen the snow fall. I had hoped to reach the col, but without ropes, proper boots and knowledge, I dared not risk the ice any more. We scrambled off the glacier and up a steep scree-filled gully on the northern side. At every step we slipped backwards, and only by clinging to uncertain rock at the side did we manage to crawl up on to the ridge above. We ate a lunch of dhai, bread and raisins and then Rosa Beg agreed to come higher with me. I had no particular aim but to get a better view and also to keep myself occupied. Sitting idly in the camp I brooded and worried and visualized one spectacular disaster after another overtaking the climbers.

Describing scenery is liable to the restrictions of photographs of scenery. Carefully selected words may make beautiful sentences, as a carefully arranged, well lighted photograph may make a beautiful picture. But neither wholly catches the atmosphere, the feeling of space, air, colour and the fullness of the composer's own emotions. I am tempted to avoid describing scenery altogether. Accurate, geographical description is not my sphere, nor can I attempt poetic flourish. But the whole beauty of country, of different kinds and in different moods, is what makes travel worth the doing and so must be some part of a book of travels.

That afternoon on the mountain, at somewhere about 17,000 ft. I had a vividly clear view. To the north lay Kungur and a long line of snow peaks—sharply defined. Immediately to my right was the neighbouring ridge of Muztagh Ata and I looked down on the many glaciers flowing from the mountain. The more distant ones showed only their higher ice pinnacles above the brown hills in between. The startlingly white towers looked curious in that Down-like country; resembling the sails of a boat rising above fields when the canal is invisible. Over to the west the plain, dun hills rolled on into Russian territory.

The distances were immense. I felt triumphantly high up and yet humiliatingly insignificant.

I could not stay long looking at this enormous scene. A cutting wind was blowing and we had to hurry down. Amir-i-Khan was a boy of the plains and had probably never been so high on a mountain before. He was obviously feeling the altitude and we found him asleep lower down. I had developed a headache myself, and was glad to get back to camp and a cup of tea. I was glad to feel tired, to go early to sleep and to forget my unquenchable anxiety.

Except to carry things, I do not like being accompanied on my walks by a servant to whom I cannot speak. It makes me feel self-conscious to be followed everywhere. When Rosa Beg went down to Subashi, after lunch the next day, I was glad of the excuse to go out alone. Nyat Shah protested, but I assured him I would not go far and set off to climb a hill to the north. I had given up taking Sola and she seemed content to stay in the camp. Crossing two streams in my shoes, I had a long, slow climb—first up a rocky gully and then up the open hill-side. As always, I alternated between thinking what a ridiculous waste of energy and how pointless it was to reach the top, and how essential it was, whatever the effort.

I reached the highest point among the hills above the camp and it gave me nearly the same advantage as the ridge of the previous day. A new and spectacular feature of the scene was a brilliant lake lying almost immediately below me. The wind still blew; an eagle circled alarmingly close; the grandeur and the lonely beauty were awe-inspiring. As the sun began to sink I went down the hill.

This was the third day since I had left Eric, although it seemed so many more. All the way back to the camp I reasoned with myself that the climbers could not have returned. Yet I did not quite convince myself. I knew that if I could see four tents again instead of three, they would have come back. But looking down on the camp I counted only three tents and my spirits fell. As I approached I noticed Nyat Shah limping towards me and another figure walking slowly. I began to run as I realized that it was Eric coming up to meet me. I was so delighted to see him; so relieved that all the party was safe; and I felt so freshened and exhilerated from my small climb, that it took me a little time to realize that Eric and Bill were completely exhausted.

Both of them had got a frost-bitten foot, although Bill's was only lightly touched. They were in no mood for my exuberance; I damped down my first delight and began hurriedly to organize tea and food. I found it was later than I had thought and that Eric had sent Amit-i-Khan to look for me. Gyalgen had been left near the foot of the Muztagh Ata slope to guard the loads, while Eric and Bill had come on to the camp to get transport. This explained why I had seen only three tents. Later Gyalgen returned, and for the first time since I had known him, admitted that he was "a little tired". In fact he was too exhausted to eat and even refused a cup of tea.

Gradually I heard the story of the climb. Muztagh Ata had defeated them but only by a few feet. The summit dome was a long, featureless slope of snow. Flogging their way through this, on August 13th, they had had no means of checking their height or how much farther they had to climb. All three were very tired and the biting wind that I had experienced on the lower ridge was, of course, much more severe at a higher altitude. It was not until they returned to their second camp that Eric discovered the condition of his left foot. This obviously prevented another attempt to reach the summit and the party came down the following day—August 14th.

At the time I was so thankful to see them all again that their defeat did not worry me at all. But it had been a disappointing climb for Eric and Bill, and Eric's foot put an end to all their further plans. We now wanted to get back to Kashgar as quickly as possible.

CHAPTER XI

High Horse Pass

ALL THE TOES OF ERIC'S left foot were black and blistered. None of us had much knowledge of the correct treatment for frost-bite and at first we were persuaded to follow the Kirghiz' instructions. They made an evil-looking paste of cheese and ash which they insisted was an infallible cure. But after the first application both Eric and I felt doubtful of this and I put on sulphonamide. The foot gave Eric little pain but Bill had one or two sleepless nights as his feet returned to life. All three climbers had numbed fingers for many days. Eric said that in all his mountain experience he had never suffered such cold and such a penetrating wind.

Having rested one day at Yambulak, we moved down to Subashi, where the Beg and the chief of police were anxious to entertain us. It was a large Kirghiz encampment and the Beg's akoi was the most handsome we had yet seen. The contrast between this clean, colourful, luxurious tent and the depressing, dilapidated police headquarters, was as marked as ever. We only paid a brief call at the latter where we ate steaks of ovis poli. It was delicious meat and the Tajik police officer said he and his men often hunted these animals in the hills.

At Subashi we watched an akoi being dismantled for cleaning. The felts were removed, leaving the skeleton of the tent exposed—a complicated trellis-work of wood, which could be folded up into a compact load. The woven bands, holding the tent together on the inside, showed a natural good taste and sense of colour that is found in the old Kirghiz carpets. It is an artistic sense that I did not notice among the people of Kashgar. They seem to have been seduced by the horrors of modern Chinese production. Although the Kirghiz still weave their tent bands of deep reds and blues, they all agreed that carpets were no longer made among them. I never discovered the reason for this and it seems tragic that the crudely coloured, badly designed, poor quality Chinese carpets should find their way into the Kirghiz akois.

We were handsomely entertained by the Beg of Subashi and the evening meal he gave us was, eventually, a memorable one. But the inevitable slaughtering and preparing of a sheep was a lengthy process. A soup of bones and meat bubbled over the central fire, tantalizing us with delicious smells. Our hostess prepared a complicated flaky pastry under our very noses. Every time we thought it was ready to be cooked, she cut it into another series of strips and patterns, added more butter and cream and began again. We tried to conceal our impatience as the preparations went on all round us. To make matters worse, at about 8 o'clock our host and hostess began to drink soup and gnaw bones with noisy relish. As they had observed the Ramazan fast all day, they deserved some food, and we had no cause to complain. But for some reason we were extremely hungry, and this waiting was a refined torture. Eventually the ceremonial cloth was spread, our hands were washed and the tent began to fill with an expectant crowd of guests.

The meal was worth waiting for and the coils of hot, light pastry the most delicious I have ever eaten. It even surpassed the pastry made by our elderly Kirghiz hostess, on the road to the Kara Teke Pass. The round akoi, dimly lit by a tiny wick floating in butter, was a fascinating picture. A dark scene, with flickering light illuminating the circle of faces, such as Rembrandt loved to paint. The sound of bones being chewed down to the marrow and contented belches, was a satisfactory accompaniment. We ended the meal with salted, creamy tea. This was very different from the heavy Tibetan drink, and I thought it excellent. Tea is valuable to the Kirghiz and used sparingly. It was always a weak infusion, and often flavoured with salt, pepper or spices, to give it interest. Sometimes our hosts had no proper tea at all, and gave us a herbal drink. As long as one forgot the English conception of tea, these variants were good. But the Beg's tea, with cream and salt was the best of them all.

The day at Subashi was an unintentional delay due to Nyat Shah's stupidity. We particularly wanted to camp by the lake lower down the valley, and thinking that the Beg's home was near it, we had accepted his invitation. Discovering our mistake we could not extricate ourselves. I was not sorry to say goodbye to Nyat Shah at Subashi; he returned to Tashkurghan from there.

On August 17th we rode seven or eight miles to the shores of the lake. I remember this place as the culminating point of beauty in all my Sinkiang travels. Again mere description of ice peaks to the north, Muztagh Ata's fine shape towering above us and the indefinable blue of the lake reflecting it, leaves a bald impression—as inadequate as a photograph. It was the combination of clear air, bright green grass, calm water and sunshine, which made up my happiness and the whole enchantment. The smaller, immediate scene was framed by the majestic ice mountains and glaciers in the middle and far distance. From this side Muztagh Ata was a far more impressive mountain. It was more isolated and a more definite shape. The grandeur of the mountains awed me, the lapping of the lake soothed me, the sunshine warmed me, and I felt wrapt round in beauty.

We spent the day lying by the lake, pretending to shoot the flights of duck and geese overhead, but really basking in the splendour of the place.

Before tea I bathed in the lake which was cold and shallow. Having no bathing dress and no privacy, I had to sacrifice a shirt and a pair of knickers. Swimming idly in the clear water the still beauty of the lake and the mountains was more magical than ever. I felt even closer to them, as if I were melting into the scene.

We explored another, smaller lake, towards evening and watched the setting sun dye the mountains pink and then drain them again to a lonely white.

The chief of police had escorted us to our camp and then gone off to shoot geese. He returned in the evening with two, one of which was presented to us. I discovered later that Gyalgen had insisted upon this.

"These Tajiks are very mean," he announced firmly. "You have to take things from them, they will never give you anything." I don't know on what he based this assertion, but we were the richer by one goose. The officer left two policemen to guard us and returned to Subashi. They were a pleasant pair, but as useless as most of our guides and escorts. Having allowed the baggage to get well ahead, the next day, they suddenly announced that we must climb up into the hills to avoid a swollen river. We had a hot, dusty, tedious march along narrow paths high on the hill-side, while one of the policemen chased our transport camels to bring them back to the by-pass.

We reached Bulunkul in the evening. As so often before, we wished that we could avoid the unappetizing fort. But flanked by our escort there was no escape and we rode into the courtyard of the police headquarters. Added to the dreariness of the place was an unusually frigid welcome. We were wondering the cause of this when, with apologies for the poor reception, it was explained that the commanding officer had died the day before. This was the unhappy man to whom I had sent a little Dettol and Elastoplast! We discovered that the bolt of his gun had burst back into his forehead and penetrated his brain. It was extraordinary that he had lived so long. Remembering the miserable help I had sent, my only consolation was that nothing I could have done would have been of any use.

This disaster gave us an excuse for leaving the fort and we camped in the plain below. But an unpleasant atmosphere seemed to attach to Bulunkul; there was none of the friendliness and hospitality we had grown to expect. The few akois were miserable and dirty. The people, and the soldiers from the army garrison, only gathered round us to stare and to demand medicines. I did not like to refuse these requests in case I denied a genuine patient. But I felt that the majority only wanted something free, and to be provided with a little light entertainment while I unpacked my box and took out my medicines. Throughout our stay in Bulunkul, we were haunted by a tough Chinese soldier, with grenades tied to his belt, who wanted me to treat him. As Gyalgen refused to translate his complaint to me, I could do nothing. Whatever this sinister disease may have been, the soldier was completely satisfied with some iodine which I finally gave to him. I can only hope it did him some good. Gyalgen was getting more and more annoyed with my elementary doctoring, as it meant he had always to be near to translate. I think he knew, as well as I did, that half our patients were impostors.

The unpleasantnesss of Bulunkul persevered to the end. The next morning we had the greatest difficulty in getting transport, and all the various officials, civil and military, stood about saying that it was the duty of someone else to organize it. Finally we rode away at 10 o'clock with our baggage on two camels. It was a short march and a fascinating one. We crossed a wide, sandy river bed with snow peaks high above us. Towards the west was a line of hills deeply covered with drifts of white sand. It gave them the effect of being moonlit, it was so white and conspicuous. Then the country changed to a green valley once more. All over this plain were little clusters of akois. We rode up to the first encampment we saw intending to ask for dhai. A strange chanting attracted us. In his usual emphatic way, Gyalgen announced that this was to celebrate the end of Ramazan.

"Rather a mournful celebration," I said, "it sounds more like a funeral."

My half-joking remark proved to be more accurate than Gyalgen's assured guess-work. This encampment was the home of the Bulunkul police officer; friends and relations were mourning his death. We felt we were intruding on sorrow and rode quickly on.

We were now in the Chakragil valley and the south side of that lovely mountain hung above it. It was a very different scene from the pine-covered hills and steep, grassy slopes we had visited in May. In its way it was as delightful. The wide plain was a rich green and there were small lakes dotted about. The ice peaks were clear, the sky was blue, the Kirghiz here were cheerful and friendly. After a leisurely march we found a pleasant camp site; while I held a "surgery hour", Eric went duck shooting on horseback and Bill made bread.

Throughout this journey Bill was our baker. To the astonishment of the locals he began his preparations immediately we pitched camp. In spite of high winds, primitive utensils and a yak dung fire, he always produced scones and loaves as delicious as any made in a civilized kitchen, with electric ovens and other advantages.

After our supper that night we went over to one of the akois to make coffee and to get some milk. There were only women and children in the tent and at first they were shy and retiring. But gradually, with cigarettes, tea and especially the present of toy whistles to the children, the atmosphere began to thaw. One of the girls was unusually attractive and I was fascinated by her elaborate jewellery. Her old mother was a delightful person. By the end of the evening, in spite of our inability to speak to one another, I felt I had had an amusing party among friends. As we emerged from the tent I saw one of those tiny, vivid pictures that are often the best remembered, and are most typical of a country. Two horsemen had just arrived at the tent door and, still in the saddle, were silhouetted against the rising moon. It was like a small, beautiful cameo.

The Beg of this area was agitated because we had not stayed in his akoi. We compromised by calling there, on our way up the valley to Kuntigmes. Just as we were leaving again I was excited to see women in the fascinating, traditional Kirghiz headdress. In all the books about these people I had seen descriptions and photographs of this high, cocoon-like pile of white material. But in spite of my inquiries I had never seen one for myself, and I concluded that even among the Kirghiz there is a change in fashions. Or perhaps the large quantity of material required now makes it too expensive? This was the only place I ever saw the high head-dress and the wearers were dressed for some very particular occasion. One woman allowed me to take her picture with the greatest delight. She arranged herself carefully, with her children, and put on her best "photograph face". It was pleasant, after the false coyness so many people assume immediately one produces a camera.

We had a long march that day, but each of us had a horse and once more I realized the value of riding across such wide, limitless country. Not that I liked my roan any better. He was as lazy and obstinate as ever and I had considerable difficulty in keeping up with the others. Eric and I had different views about these marches. Being a nervous rider I liked to keep up a steady, moderate pace. Eric preferred to gallop over the country for a short time and then take a long rest in some attractive spot. I saw his point of view, but my pony did not and the pony was usually in control.

Kuntigmes seemed to be populated entirely by women and either very old or very young men. Everyone was quite hospitable, however, and our hostess there was most friendly. But no Beg appeared and there was no one willing to organize our transport. The pitching of our tents, and our every movement was, as usual, watched by a fascinated audience. Becoming part of a moving circus, takes a little getting used to. At first I felt annoyed by this constant curiosity and the complete lack of privacy. But it was as much a part of Asian travel as the desert or the dust—something one must accept. I became so accustomed to the interested crowds that I was quite offended if, by chance, people did not gather round to stare; as if our travelling show had had a poor reception. Only at Kuntigmes I lost my temper with one woman. Her curiosity knew no limits and having examined everything I possessed, she began gently poking me; presumably to find out if English women were formed in the same way as Kirghiz women.

On August 21st we set off with the five ponies and two donkeys we had eventually managed to hire. Three young boys were in charge of the pack animals; the rest of the party rode. We were finally free of any escort, as there was no one at Kuntigmes to insist upon one. We had tried to discuss the route with our hosts. Although they all agreed that it was a hard march over the Ulugh Art Pass (High Horse Pass, 16,600 ft.), no one had questioned our being able to cross it in one day.

We began with a long, slow climb through a dull little range of hills. I was thankful not to be walking up. Later in the day I felt so sorry for Sola, stumbling along a stony valley, that I carried her on my pony. But she was very heavy to hold in my arms and spent her time shifting restlessly, and trying to jump off. So I put her down again and she went quite well with the pack ponies.

The path now followed along the hill-side of a severe, rocky valley. We climbed steadily and were soon above a large glacier. Like a petrified sea the waves of ice came down the valley from the south-east and washed away from us to the north-west. As we rode on we could see the pass far ahead—the path rising in a final, sharp zig-zag. We had to cross several glacier streams now swollen by the melting ice. One of these took us nearly an hour to negotiate. Finally after we had beaten and cajoled our ponies in vain, I waded in, dragging my horse through the torrent; luckily Eric's horse followed the lead and so Eric's bad foot was kept dry. We waited to watch the caravan across. The boys successfully hauled each animal over separately, on a rope. This delayed us so much that at about 6 p.m., I suggested camping for the night. But the suggestion was vetoed. The three Kirghiz said they wanted grazing for their animals on the other side of the pass. The caravan was going well.

In places the path was alarmingly narrow as it hung above the glacier; it climbed and dropped steeply and continuously. We were now in a stern region of ice, rock and fierce streams. I preferred to walk along the meagre paths and dragged my pony unwillingly behind me. The final rise of the Ulugh Art came sooner than I had expected. It was very sharp, indeed, but I could not climb slowly and rhythmically because my pony liked to go in short, sharp rushes. If left to himself he did not go at all. This painful progress finally ended when all his saddlery and rugs fell off, owing to the steep angle at which we were climbing. I was unable to lift it all again and sat down to await help. Eric and Bill were above me and the main caravan had reached the foot of the final rise. There it stopped. After useless efforts to spur it on again, shouted from above, Eric suddenly lost his temper and began stumping down the hill—leaving his pony behind. He found that the Kirghiz now wanted to stop for the night, insisting that the animals could go no farther. Why they had changed their minds so suddenly we did not know. I suspect that Gyalgen was partly responsible for the suggestion that it was too late to go on. All my efforts wasted I went down the hill again.

We made a miserable camp among the rocks. At about 16,000 ft. it was extremely cold and the only fuel was such dung as we could find. There was nothing for the animals to eat.

Although we had been disappointed not to cross the pass in one day, we now had only the final 600 ft. or so to complete. There seemed nothing particularly dramatic about the steep path ahead. It was hard on the animals to have no food, but we had seen animals endure greater and more protracted hardship on the Karakoram route. To ease the ponies' work we all decided to walk to the top of the pass. In any case it was an uncomfortable ride, up such a sharp rise. Eric, Bill and I left the camp at 7.30 a.m., and in under an hour had nearly reached the top. At 8.15, we saw our caravan just beginning to wind up the zigzag. We passed several small caravans coming down. Presumably they had started up early, from the other side. The eastern side was steeper and the path rougher than the ascent we had just made, but it seemed to have given these animals no trouble. It was cold on the pass and we started down to avoid the wind—Eric hobbling slowly. We halted several times, to rest Eric's foot and to allow the caravan to catch us up. By 11 a.m. there was no sign of our party. Only once a head had appeared on the skyline and then disappeared again. Even climbing slowly, it was impossible for the caravan to take three hours to reach the top. So having exhausted all our conjectures, it was agreed that Bill should climb up again to investigate the delay.

ERIC AND BILL TILMAN HAVING TEA

THE KIRGHIZ TRADITIONAL HEADDRESS

GYALGEN

LHAKPA

Expecting to be over the pass by breakfast time, we had only had an early cup of tea before starting. We were getting hungry; we were already cold; and sitting still wondering and worrying was an unsatisfactory business. At mid-day Bill returned alone. His news was startling. Eric's stout black pony, brought from Ighizyar, had died. In its fall it had broken his gun. The three Kirghiz thereupon announced that if they went on *all* the ponies would die, so one boy had turned back with the five hired horses. Gyalgen had persuaded the other two to stay with their two donkeys to help us. We still had my roan and Amir-i-Khan's donkey. So the sad little party had began to relay loads up the pass. It was a sudden dramatic turn of events and we could not understand the reason for it. Perhaps the black pony, from the plains, was not as sturdy as it had looked and, unaccustomed to hills, had suffered from the height and the cold? How sick the Kirghiz ponies really were we did not know. Probably the boys were frightened by the death of our horse and had decided to risk nothing.

We three continued down the hill feeling somewhat subdued. We came to a muddy spring and as Bill had brought supplies, we made ourselves some nasty, but welcome tea. As our bread was finished we ate a curious meal of tinned sausages, cheese and raisins. Eric could do nothing but sit still; Bill buried his feelings in bread-making; I spent my time looking for dung, for the fire. I became quite keen on my search—a fine piece of yak dung was a triumph, mere horse dung only tolerated.

The whole of that day was spent relaying the loads over the pass. As the servants straggled in I gave them tea, cheese and cigarettes, but a heavy pall of gloom hung over everyone. The two Kirghiz were a mournful pair, they sat about in huddled misery, making no attempt to help themselves or anyone else. Gyalgen and Rosa Beg struggled alone with heavy loads. In the crisis Gyalgen's best qualities appeared. He remained cheerful, determined, undefeated. Amir-i-Khan was completely broken. It was difficult to believe that he had a real affection for the black horse under his care; I expect he was frightened of the consequences when he returned home. As proof of its death he had promptly skinned the poor horse where it fell, and to my horror produced this sad remains for me to see. He wept, and in sudden sympathy I wept too. My roan was very weak, but it had survived. To complete the events of the day, we discovered that Sola was missing. After all his hard work, Gyalgen volunteered to climb up the pass again, to search for her. He found her curled up asleep on the top!

We now found ourselves in an uninhabited valley, without sufficient transport. The only encouragement was from a passing traveller. There were some Kirghiz in an adjoining valley, some seven miles farther down, he said.

The next day Gyalgen started off alone to find them. We managed to load everything on to the three gallant donkeys, with a light load on the roan horse, and each of us carrying a share of the baggage. It was a mournful march. I walked slowly with Eric, while the haversack and the broken gun I carried, grew heavier and heavier. We kept on hoping to meet Gyalgen bringing transport, but the only sign of him was a page of *Picture Post* with his name scrawled across it, lying in the path. There was still no proper grass for the animals. We bought a melon from a caravan we met and fed the skins to them. Even stray pieces of straw I treasured, and gave to my old enemy the roan horse.

We camped at the junction of our valley with that of Yamen Serai, where the Kirghiz were reported to be. There was excellent firewood, but meagre grazing. In despair we decided to cook our own food for the animals, and set Rosa Beg and Amir-i-Khan to making chapattis. These are round, flat "pan-cakes" made of flour and water, and baked on a hot plate.

There was still no sign of Gyalgen, so I decided to walk up the valley in search of him—and the longed-for transport. A twenty-five minutes' walk brought me to two humble akois. Inside one of these I saw a familiar pair of dark glasses and a tobacco tin. A few minutes later an exhausted Gyalgen walked in. He had been chasing Kirghiz all day. At his approach all the able-bodied men had fled and none of his promises, threats, bribes or pleas had any effect. Apparently it was thought that he was an officer come to commandeer men or animals, and nothing he said would alter this conviction. Now, at 5.30 p.m., he thought he had persuaded a man to hire us some donkeys. But he advised me to go back and he would follow when he had the animals. I found a new crisis had arisen. Both our two Kirghiz were in tears and imploring us to let them go home. Promises of food, money and rich presents seemed to leave them unmoved. All they asked was not to go any farther.

Gyalgen did not return that night. At 6.30 the next morning he appeared with the doleful news that the promised donkeys had not materialized, and some yaks which he had procured had run away as he drove them down. We then decided to try the effect of rice and flour on the timid Kirghiz. It would also help to lighten our baggage. The valiant Gyalgen disappeared up the valley once more. On his second appearance he came in triumphant procession with six yaks and their young. The owner was said to be following. However, it was one thing to drive a carefree yak, but to secure and load it was a more complicated manœuvre. The technique was to creep up to the animal and then, making a dive at its forelegs, tie them together. Gyalgen achieved this, but no sooner were the loads on and the feet *untied*, than the wretched creatures ran amok and baggage was hurled in every direction. After two yaks had given this exhibition, they disappeared into the distance. At last two more co-operative ones were loaded and the Kirghiz reluctantly agreed to drive the herd down to Yolchi-moinak.

Eric now rode the roan horse very carefully, while the rest of us walked. The strange caravan of three little donkeys and a family party of yaks, wound slowly down the valley to the Promised Land, where we expected to find houses and transport in abundance. We found delicious green grass, a clear stream and plenty of firewood. But there was only one small, mud house inhabited by an old man. He told us that there was no transport in Yolchi-moinak. I was so thankful to sit down, to drink tea and to see our animals enjoying the grass that I did not take in the significance of this fresh disappointment. I felt cheerful and contented and looked round for the Kirghiz boys to share in our fine, green camp. They, the yaks and two of the donkeys had completely disappeared! While we had been busying ourselves making tea and pitching camp, the boys had made good their escape. Apparently they preferred to forfeit money and presents (if they had ever believed in our promises) rather than be forced on any farther. It was difficult to understand their morose, miserable attitude. We had fed them well, given them cigarettes and tried to be friendly, but they had never responded and had behaved throughout like unhappy victims of a press-gang. We could only hope they returned the yaks to their owner, for he had never appeared. This desertion left us with one donkey and a sick horse.

Once more Gyalgen went in search of transport. Guided by the old man he found some Kirghiz in the hills, but they treated him with the same obstinate fear as the previous group. We never discovered why the Kirghiz in this area were so nervous and unfriendly. Perhaps they had suffered in the 1945 rebellions, like the people of Bostanterek? To them Gyalgen looked strange and so was suspect. He told us later that at Yolchi-moinak he had decided to intimidate rather than cajole the Kirghiz. Threatening to beat one man, shaking off the weeping mother of another, he finally collected two camels. It made a good story and, whatever the truth of Gyalgen's tactics, transport did appear.

This time he brought animals and owners to the camp and made them stay there overnight. The men looked far from friendly. Anxious to pacify them we entertained them to supper and paid over half the money they demanded. We did not want to earn a reputation for not paying. Already our name was jeopardized by the desertion of the two boys without their money. We all sat round the camp fire and gradually the tension eased.

Soothed, and relieved of immediate anxiety, we went to bed. But near our tent were the camels. One of these was a young mother. Having been compelled to leave her child behind, she cried all night—a cry of unutterable despair, like a sad and powerful fog horn. To my surprise I did eventually go to sleep.

August 25th was the last day of our trek with animal transport. An efficient and early start promised well. The fact that we had any transport at all was such a relief, that I had not thought about the thirty-mile walk ahead of us. At Yolchi-moinak the hills melted down gradually into the flat, open desert. We had a long, hot march to the oasis of Opal. One kind feature of that dreadful day was a cloudy haze which dulled the strength of the sun. For about four hours I walked briskly and well. Eric rode the one horse, which was still weak. To give me a rest, he decided to try sitting on a camel, while I had a turn on the pony. But I was soon exasperated by the poor creeping creature and I walked again. Then I too tried riding on a camel. It was my first experience and I do not recommend it as a form of transport. With the camel on its knees I climbed up on to the pile of baggage and was borne upwards in a series of alarming lurches. Then began a back-breaking motion which allowed no rest. Moving slowly across the grey desert, with no landmarks of any sort to break the monotony, it seemed as if we were stationary. But I suppose one would become used to travelling on a camel, and would readjust one's whole conception of time, speed and distance. Rosa Beg, clinging on precariously on the "back seat" of my mount, slept quite happily nearly all the way.

Alternating between the exhaustion of walking, the irritation of riding and the back-ache of sitting on a camel, I covered the slow miles. Throughout the march Bill walked, and during the morning kept well ahead. After our short halt to change mounts, at about 11.30, Eric and I had noticed that Sola was missing. We thought she must either be with the main caravan or in front with Bill. I asked a man we passed if he had seen, "a sahib and a small dog". He replied that he had. At about 1 o'clock we found Bill sitting waiting for us, but Sola was not with him. Nor was she with the caravan.

Looking back it seems as if we took this loss very casually. I have felt guilty and unhappy about it ever since. But we had covered roughly half the march and if we had turned back we could not have reached Opal that day. The camel men would certainly not have agreed either to

return or to wait for a dog. They would probably have
refused to transport us a second time. The horse was too
weak to do any extra miles. There seemed to be no solution
and we went on. Later we offered a large reward for Sola
and asked the Opal officials to help in the search. But from
that day we heard nothing and have never known what
happened to the poor little dog. I do not know what we
could have done at the time, but I have a gnawing feeling
that we should have done something.

The loss of Sola tipped the scales still more heavily
down on the gloomy side. There seemed to be an evil
genie haunting the journey—delighting in small torments.
When we reached the oasis I thought things would improve.
Except for the refreshing melons we bought straight from
a field, they did not. The camel men were determined to
reach Opal bazaar; if we camped anywhere on the way they
announced that they would leave us. This forced us on
until 7.30, when I begged Eric to stop. Bill also seemed
willing to camp. We had just decided to risk getting transport the next day, and had selected a dreary field of stubble
for our tents, when two Chinese soldiers rode by. On
inquiring who we were they were extremely shocked at the
idea of our spending the night in "the open". Eric also
had misgivings about our collapsing just outside Opal
in this undignified way. Everyone in chorus assured us
that the bazaar was "near". The soldiers agreed to ride
ahead with Eric to warn the Beg of our coming.

Wearily resigned I trudged off once more. I walked for
another hour and a half; on and on along the dusty country
roads in the gathering darkness. Whenever I asked the
way people repeated the dreadful word "near". All the
time I thought of the Beg's house where we had been entertained on our way to Bostanterek in March. I thought, as
usual, of tea, of melons and food, of somewhere to lie
down and sleep.

At last I saw the tiny dancing lights of the bazaar and
heard the steady rhythm of a drum beating at some celebration. I climbed the little hill to the familiar house we
had visited before and found—nothing. The place was
in darkness, there was no sign of Eric or of anyone

else. Tiredness, acute disappointment, and an under-
lying misery about Sola, combined to reduce me to tears.
In the dark I sat on a step and cried; a form of indulgence
which I decided I had earned. A man eventually appeared
and told us that the Beg was in Kashgar. He had not
seen Eric. The caravan turned dismally away and we went
down to the bazaar. There we were rescued by a guide
who led us to the house of another rich Turki. In a high,
dim room, we found Eric and a large collection of officials.
The man originally sent to direct us to our new host, had
missed us on the way.

It was 9 o'clock when we reached this house. We had
been on the road since 7.15 a.m., with hardly any halts.
I was asleep long before the evening meal was ready and
had to be woken at midnight to eat it. Eric struggled
valiantly to talk to the officials. Among other things they
promised to send a messenger immediately to Kashgar, to
summon our lorry. He would ride all night, they said.
Full of trust we went to bed.

When making arrangements in the East it is a mistake
to think in terms of the West. If one calculates time and
distance, works out a neat time-table and expects it to be
followed, one is doomed to disappointment. We had so
confidently pictured Mir Humza receiving our message at
about 7.30 a.m., and setting off at once, to reach Opal in three
or four hours. We eventually discovered that the messenger
sent "at once" on a "fast horse", had actually left at about
mid-day on a donkey. So we formed a new plan: to send
Gyalgen in on a good horse. Again everything was
promised with extreme promptness. At 9 o'clock that
evening Gyalgen left in a cart. It was impossible to trace
the complications and intricacies of these delays. Perhaps
each official hoped that someone else would arrange everything.

It was good not to have to move and our hosts were
kind. But waiting all day for the sound of a lorry was
unsettling. We were so near home that this final small
torment of the genie was difficult to bear. I tried to read
and relax but the flies were like a new plague of Egypt—a
thick, black, buzzing mass. I occupied myself with Eric's

foot, which I had dressed every day; with attending to a burnt knee our hostess asked me to look at; and trying to treat a bad sore on the roan horse's back. Going out into the yard, the dreadful, sweet smell of the dead horse's skin, overpowered me. Amir-i-Khan had treasured it all the way and now the heat of the plains had developed the smell. I hope he did not get into trouble when he returned home. We paid well for the black horse and treated my roan to good food and nursing in Kashgar, before Amir-i-Khan took it back to Ighizyar.

The slow day came to an end and no lorry had arrived. We planned to ride to Kashgar on the following day, rather than spend another in fly-blown idleness in Opal. At 12.30 that night we were woken by the distant roar of an engine. The whole household rose with cries of "machina." The faithful Mir Humza had not received our message until 7.30 p.m., but nevertheless he had started out immediately. In the desert before Opal he had lost the way, but he made no comment or complaint.

We drove back to Kashgar the following morning. There was an impressive welcome awaiting us, with garlands thrown round our necks and everyone out to receive us. It seemed much more than twenty-nine days since we had left the Consulate. The expedition had been an uneven sequence of delight and depression.

Eric's bad foot tied him to the house for a couple of months and completely spoilt his plans for small trips with Bill, during the latter's short stay in Kashgar, before he returned to England.

CHAPTER XII

To the Capital

FOR VARIOUS REASONS ERIC'S
official tour to Urumchi was continually being postponed.
But he wanted to visit the capital before the winter and we
finally arranged to leave towards the end of October. It
was rather late in the year for the journey, and going
north it would be colder than in Kashgar. Urumchi suffers
a much more severe winter than the southern part of the
province. But we were prepared for this and did not
expect to find it too harsh in October and November. I
was delighted with a cumbersome pair of Chinese army
felt boots. In these I lumbered about, clumsy but warm.
We prepared elaborate fur and felt bootees for Eric's
bad foot. He was still using crutches although he gave them
up on the way.

This journey was a new experience for me. So far most
of my Central Asian travels had been with animal transport.
But Sir Eric Teichman had created a precedent when he
drove from Peking to Kashgar in 1935. Since then several
British Consuls-General, including Eric in 1942, had made
the journey as far as Urumchi, by lorry. It would take about
eight weeks to cover the 980 miles with a caravan. In some
ways I should prefer it. The "main road" is still too rough
to make motoring a pleasure, or even the negative process
of getting quickly from one place to another. Nevertheless,
with a reasonable truck the journey can be done in under

eight days instead of eight weeks, and it would be a little precious to insist upon the latter. As if one were to ride from London to Scotland on horseback, now that there are trains and motor cars. However much one may regret the coming of motor transport to primitive places, once it has come it seems an affectation, a stunt, not to use it.

To make a road across Central Asia is a huge undertaking and it is not fair to compare such a road with an English or European one. When I saw the relentless miles of desert which we crossed on the way to Urumchi, I was amazed that a road existed at all. I thought of the men forced to labour in the strong heat and sharp cold of those dry wastes. When with much hardship the road had been made it is understandable that the Government forbade the carts to use it. It may seem a pointless tyranny to drive the local people back on to their old tracks; but otherwise the hard cart wheels would soon ruin the surface and so begin the labour all over again.

One of the most irritating features of the road, in parts, was the ditches cutting across it every few hundred yards. These were the only form of drainage and they varied a great deal in depth and danger. Sometimes there was a gentle dip, paved with stones, sometimes a sharp drop into a rough water-course. It was impossible to tell the type until nearly into the ditch. So for each one we had to slow down and lose our hard-won speed. This dipping, bobbing process was extraordinarily annoying. The road stretched ahead, straight, and so deceptively good, yet we were continuously checked. I almost preferred the bad bits which were consistently bad and raised no false hopes of speed.

In his book "Journey to Turkistan", Sir Eric Teichman says, ". . . one cannot beat the Ford V.8 truck for expedition work but it is foolish to trust to anything but new machinery for a journey of this kind". His lorry certainly confirmed the first half of his statement, but disproved the second. Although it was nearing the end of its hard life when we took it once more on the road to Urumchi, and it did eventually let us down, it had given twelve years of good service under severe conditions. Undoubtedly Mir Humza's loving care had prolonged its life, but its record was a fine one.

At 6 o'clock on a dark October morning a party of nine left the Consulate in the old Ford. We were taking Mr. Robertson and his fiancée back to Urumchi; Mr. Yang accompanied us as interpreter and the Assistant Chief of Police was alleged to be our escort. It was more probable that he wanted a free and comfortable lift to the capital. Gyalgen, Mir Humza and a new assistant mechanic, whom I had last seen as a gardener, completed the party. The Consulate personnel seemed to be very adaptable. I found that a gatekeeper was Eric's barber; Mr. Khan's cook became our head gardener; the tailor was a watchman, and, as I have said, Mir Humza was the best cook in the place. I liked the gardener-mechanic and he took his place meekly as the victim of Mir Humza's cuffings and curses.

We favoured early starts and liked to be on the road before dawn. The miles covered in those first hours were soon forgotten, and by the time it was light nearly twenty miles of the day's schedule were finished. It was attractive to watch the sky gradually lighten and the sun flood over the country. The darkness before dawn seemed so much less bleak and forbidding than the darkness after sunset, when we were tired and approaching an unknown place for the night.

Shelter for the night was a vexed question. With the exception of the first one, spent in the uninhabited, water-less desert, there were towns and villages all the way to Urumchi. For sensible travellers there was no reason to camp in the open. It was easy to understand the dis-approval and resentment of Mr. Yang and the police officer when we elected to spend the night out. To them it was inconceivable that anyone should prefer the sky overhead, the rapid, simple meal round a camp fire, followed by an early bed. They yearned for the security of four walls, for a long Chinese meal and all the etiquette due to honoured visitors.

This split in the party tended to spoil the journey to Urumchi. We allowed ourselves four, out of the seven, nights in the open; but a heavy atmosphere of martyrdom

hung over these camps. Mr. Yang even went on a hunger
strike, to prove his extreme sensitivity, and inability to
eat our barbaric food. A breakdown, and the need for
petrol, forced us to spend three nights in official Yamens.
Then I became the martyr and with an ill-grace suffered
the delays, the tedium and elaborate politeness of Chinese
hospitality. I certainly exaggerated my feelings, in irritated
reaction to the uncompromising attitude of our companions.
But after a weary day spent rattling and bumping along the
rough road, official entertainment seemed exasperating.
The host's "face" was of more importance than the guest's
comfort. So the latter must wait hour after hour on a hard,
narrow chair while a complicated meal was prepared, and
conferences were held about accommodation. It is difficult
to be polite, and to make meaningless conversation
when one is dusty, tired and hungry. My first experience of this was at Aksu. We had to stop there for petrol
and although we reached the place at 2.30 p.m. we were
compelled to stay for the night. We sipped tea for two hours
while our hosts discussed meals and rooms for our entertainment. There was a keen rivalry for our bodies, between
the civil and military officials. By 5 p.m. it began to look
as if we should get neither dinner nor beds, or have to
eat two dinners. Having asked for somewhere to rest my
aching head I was taken to the women's quarters and had a
disturbed hour's "sleep", amidst an interested audience.
I found Eric still sitting on the small, wooden chair where
I had left him, and our fate undecided. Finally we settled
the hideous problems for ourselves. We accepted an
invitation to dine with the local general and selected our
own rooms in the Yamen. When we returned to them after
dinner, they were just ready for our use. If we had left
the decisions to our hosts I think we would still be sitting
on those unspeakable chairs. This was, perhaps, an extreme
case of elaborate delay. But we did spend many weary
hours waiting for involved preparations which we did
not want.

On the way back we resigned ourselves completely to
nights in the Yamens. In late November it was cold for
the servants to sleep out and we only had three small tents

between a party of nine. So Mr. Yang had a comparatively contented journey.

He startled us one day by remarking how informal the Chinese were compared with the English. It seemed unbelievable that he really thought so. We tried to explain our point of view about the delays and complications, the emphasis on "face" which leads to so much discomfort for weary guests. Mr. Yang admitted that a certain amount of preparation was inevitable. No host could allow himself to offer a camp bed and a simple supper, however hungry or tired his guests might be.

But he also pointed out that at a Chinese party a guest was free to leave with no excuse; guests and host could get up from the table without explanation; everyone helped themselves and stretched across to the various dishes without elaborate serving; if anyone felt inclined to belch he could do so. He saw nothing odd in a woman feeding her baby at a dinner table. One of our Chinese acquaintances in Kashgar brought her infant to all the parties. In a striking magenta plush jockey cap, the baby suckled happily while his mother acknowledged toasts, smiled and chatted. This certainly seemed to me extreme informality. It all helps to prove that one's own manners and customs are so taken for granted that they are unnoticed. For a foreigner they may add up to a complicated, and in his opinion unnecessary, series of restrictions.

My criticisms sound remarkably ungrateful. Ordinarily I enjoyed Chinese food and I was prepared to accept their manner of entertaining. But on a journey, when tired and aching, hungry, and a little dazed, I was less tolerant and not at all appreciative of complicated etiquette.

In 980 miles we crossed very varied country, but for most of the way the road kept to the open desert. There was nothing of the modern "autobahn" about the Urumchi road. But by local standards, it was a remarkable one. It had been enormously improved since Eric's previous trip. There were bridges where there used only to be ferries; new alignments avoided the complicated country roads through the oases, and new well-graded sections climbed the more severe hills. But the endless miles of barren, lonely country were almost frightening when one is accustomed to the neat, colourful, small scale of the English countryside.

We crossed high plateaus of grey gravel, where there was not a single living plant to be seen; it was rare, even in the many deserts we had crossed, not to find some form of scrub growing among the stones. However, in October, this severity was relieved by the spectacular glory of the autumn colours—wherever there *was* any growth. In the oases the poplars were on fire with orange leaves; in the desert the tamarisk blazed with every shade of red, crimson, yellow, rust and brown. It was like an artist's palette, a blurred confusion of colour. On the return journey the palette had been cleaned and all the colour drained from the now bare trees and bushes.

We had several passes to cross—the highest only 5,800 ft.—but up a rough track these were hard work for the Ford. On the third day of our journey to Urumchi, it was apparent that the valiant old lorry was weakening. Our progress became slower and slower and all the time we were waiting for the final collapse. The knocks and noises became increasingly sinister. On the sixth day there was a loud bang when a spring broke. With his usual resource and energy Mir Humza proceeded to mend it and we hobbled onwards. He had already warned us that one of those mysterious things, a big end, was in danger of "going". So far he had persuaded the lorry along and hoped, with Eric's careful driving, to get us to Urumchi. Going up the passes he sat on a front mud-guard ready to make a dive into the engine if necessary. We noticed him offer up a quick prayer of thanks as we crawled to the top of one particularly steep, rough pass—lifting his hands and stroking his beard with reverence. All his opinions about the lorry, the road and our progress were prefaced with, "Insha Allah",—"If God is Willing".

Soon after the long delay over the spring, the big end decided to struggle no more. We came to a standstill in the open desert. Again Mir Humza began immediately to repair the damage. He promised nothing, but, "Insha Allah", he could patch it up sufficiently to complete the journey. At that moment a Chinese army convoy of three trucks came by; one of them contained a rotund, cheerful little man we had met in Kashgar. Seeing our plight he offered to take us all in to the next small town of Ushak Tal. I crushed in between the driver of the second truck and our friend, but Eric and Mr. Yang had to climb high on to the top of the loads. Over a particularly bad stretch of road we raced at a dreadful speed; dashing up to the uncertain ditches we either stopped dead or hurtled across them. We were both blinded and suffocated from the dust of the leading lorry, but only once did the driver stop to let the fog clear away. I sat inside with my eyes shut, visualizing the horror of the drive for Eric and Mr. Yang, uncertain whether they would manage to stay on at all. At Ushak Tal two completely white, dust-covered figures climbed down. They were battered, bruised, shaken and had only clung on with difficulty.

Faced with a day in the dreary little town, and even more dreary confines of the magistrate's office, Eric and I asked for horses and went out in search of some shooting. Starting with my usual apprehension, I found I had one of those rare creatures, a horse which I liked. It was as fat, white and comfortable as a rocking horse, but very willing to move. After quite useless guiding by the guide allotted to us, we were turning back when I heard the familiar call of chikor. Among the low scrub of the desert we found many coveys of the little partridge and chased them until it was too dark to see. We returned to the town to find our lorry waiting in the main street. Mir Humza, Gyalgen and the gardener had worked all day, by the road-side, without proper food or any drink, and had finally triumphed.

In spite of breakdowns we completed the journey in eight days. Although it was tiring, driving over the rough road, we were not hard pressed. We often stopped to shoot chikor or gazelle near the road; to enjoy a picnic meal, or a lunch in a Chinese restaurant. By local standards our journey was considered a fast one. The Chinese army lorries and the commercial lorries are usually heavily overloaded and hopelessly maintained. The result is that they break down

continuously. About forty miles from Kashgar we had
overtaken a perilously loaded lorry creeping noisily along.
Later it stopped near us, during one of our halts. A long-
suffering passenger asked Gyalgen how many days ago we
had left Kashgar. I do not suppose he believed the answer
of a few hours. They had left four days ago said the man.
The new machines must sometimes seem a poor substitute
for the old carts or a reliable horse.

Confined inside the cab of the lorry, smelling petrol, the
sound of the engine always in my ears, I felt divorced from
the country we were passing through. It was difficult to
realize the limitless space and desolation of the desert;
to appreciate the height and grandeur of the narrow gorges
we drove through; even the significance of dropping
below sea level, into the Turfan Depression, was a little
dulled. The lorry seemed to cut us off from the exciting
geography; to make us simply a self-contained, rather
noisy, bad smelling, little unit, hurrying along as fast as
possible to finish each day's allotted schedule. Central
Asia, the Tien Shan or Celestial Mountains, The Turfan
Depression are names full of romance. The realities tended
to be tarnished by the very unromantic truck. To be honest,
I was glad not to have to spend eight weeks crossing that
stern country on a horse. I am quite certain I should shed
much vague romanticism on such a journey. But still a
slight regret lingered in me as we ground along. A long
train of camels moving with dignified silent steps, made
me dissatisfied with our noise. I felt we were something
alien and out of place.

As we drove north the Chinese influence grew stronger.
The roofs of the houses often tilted upwards at the corners;
there were many more Chinese in the streets of the towns;
veiled women were nowhere to be seen. Near Urumchi,
the country itself was very different, more lonely and treeless. The poplars and irrigated fields of Kashgar were
gone. The city lay among gentle hills, a sudden, ugly
blot of buildings, distinguished by factory chimneys.

As we drove into the outskirts of the capital on a bluster-
ing October day, I thought it a miserable place. The three
weeks I stayed there, in early winter, did nothing to alter

my first impression. It had all the depressing characteristics of a semi-westernized town, none of the charm of a frankly native one. The main street was flanked by solid, two-storied buildings. There were shops with counters; there were pavements, and policemen on point duty. But all this seemed an uncertain, pathetic façade. The essential primitiveness showed through the veneer all the time. Poor Chinese struck me as much more dirty and dilapidated than poor Turkis. The sight of White Russians, reduced to a humble misery, was startling. There are none in the south as far as I know. The tragedy behind the exile of these people haunted me. Immediately outside the main gates of the town an ugly, tumbledown, haphazard bazaar broke out like a rash. The main impression was one of dirt; an impression I never had of Kashgar, in spite of its mud houses, poky little shops and dust. Perhaps knowledge of evil things done in this town, of political intrigue and murder, coloured my feelings. People said it was easier to get into Urumchi than to get out of it. No sooner had we arrived than I began planning to leave.

During a second visit to Urumchi, on my way home to England in 1948, I had time to explore a part of the country immediately outside the city. In early spring I changed my earlier opinions of the countryside. With more rain to clear the air than Kashgar gets, the views of snow mountains were often vivid and fine. The low hills became softly green, there were a few little copses of natural trees which were pleasant after the uniform poplars and willows of the irrigated oases. And there were the wild flowers. Wandering alone among the hills and occasional little lakes, the scene was often strangely familiar to me. I would find myself in the tangled untidiness of a copse with flowers under my feet and the smell of wet earth to remind me of England. Then climbing again into open country I was dramatically in Central Asia once more—huge expanses rolled away to the snow mountains, blue-white, sharply defined or with clouds winding among them. A camel caravan or a party of loaded donkeys, their bells ringing, crossed the scene and added to its fascinating but foreign charm. But I persistently disliked the ugly city itself and

13

the depressing conglomeration of nationalities in the streets, frankly ragged or aggressively slick.

However, there was nothing unpleasant about our welcome when we arrived in October, 1947. The American Consul and his wife, Mr. and Mrs. Paxton, entertained us to all meals and did everything in their power to make our visit comfortable. The British and United States Consulates were then side by side on the edge of the town. After the lavish establishment at Kashgar the British Consulate in Urumchi was a very humble place. It had been unoccupied for eight months; the tiny, mud house was badly in need of paint and repair; the courtyard was a tangle of dead weeds and an atmosphere of sad neglect hung over everything. We slept in one of the five small rooms but there was no bathroom and we had a cold walk to the outside lavatory—the usual hole in the floor. I had been thoroughly spoilt by my queenly state in Kashgar.

We were soon whirled into a series of dinners and lunches in our honour. Urumchi society was more sophisticated than that of Kashgar. Many of the Chinese we met could speak English or French. The Chinese ladies were smarter and more accomplished. Conversation was not the same halting effort I was used to and it was a delight to be able to talk without an interpreter.

We met a French journalist (who later visited Kashgar); a charming and vivacious Polish lady, married to a Chinese official; and cultured Turkis who could speak English or French; while we were there a United States aeroplane came in for one night, and suddenly the Paxtons' sitting-room was filled with seven Americans. We even met two Englishmen. They had undertaken to drive up a new lorry from Central China, for the British Consulate in Urumchi. I began to feel I was in touch with the great outer world once more. After the isolation of Kashgar the sudden arrival and departure by air, the cosmopolitan atmosphere of society, seemed exciting and gay. The Paxtons, having considered themselves in a lonely outpost, were surprised to find that we thought of Urumchi as the beginning of civilization. Even switching on the electric light was quite an event for us.

During Eric's previous visit he had made a trip up into the mountains to see the Heavenly Pool—a lake sheltering among pine-covered hills about sixty odd miles from Urumchi. In November it was a little late for mountain holidays but Eric was anxious for me to see the place. Also we wanted to escape from the social whirl. Everyone warned us against the cold, the snow and the discomfort, but nevertheless we got permission to go.

The first fifty miles or so can be covered by motor-car. The long-suffering Ford was said to be repaired and ready, and we started off. It got us along with difficulty, and when the road finally faded out, we camped among low hills near a collection of Kazak tents.

I was interested to see these nomads, so closely akin to the Kirghiz in their way of life. In the short time I spent with them it is impossible to pretend to any real knowledge of them. To a casual observer, however, there seemed few differences between the two tribes. They struck me as rather more forceful. Our police escort seemed to have a healthy respect for them and were unwilling to offend them in any way. But they received us with friendly hospitality and insisted on slaughtering the customary sheep. Now that it was cold and dark outside, the complete process of butchery, preparation and cooking was done inside the akoi where we sat. There was not a moment's delay between the presentation of the victim to us, a muttered prayer and the immediate death of the animal. I had to sit gazing at the floor while it was skinned, gutted and cut up, to avoid the sight of blood, raw meat and entrails all round me. Having always disliked even a well-ordered English butcher's shop, it was an ordeal. I am afraid this delicacy sounds affected. I did try to suppress it. I certainly enjoyed the meal when it was finally ready—delicious soup and unexpectedly tender meat.

The next day we rode up the valley towards the lake. It must be an enchanting place in the summer. Even in November it was attractive. A sparkling stream ran through tangled woods; miniature gorges made a dark, exciting scene, a place set for a fairy tale. Gradually we climbed up into the pine country where snow lay deep on the ground. On the way Eric and Mir Humza stopped at intervals to chase chikor which were calling everywhere. Not until the very end of our march did we see the lake. Then riding through the dark trees we saw it, smooth and peaceful, cupped among the forest-clad mountains. After the deserts and the barren hills we had crossed on our journey from Kashgar; after the rolling, open hills round Urumchi, this scene was a remarkable contrast. I felt as if we had been suddenly spirited out of Central Asia and put down in Switzerland.

Above the shores of the lake there was an unoccupied T'aoist monastery. Since the Heavenly Pool had become something of a summer resort for Urumchi society, this building had been adapted for visitors. On either side of the main courtyard were rooms furnished with beds and rough stools. But opposite the entrance gate was the shrine of the monastery, to remind us that the place was not a mere hotel.

Here in a dark room, in three separate partitions, sat large, crude idols. Each idol had his two smaller attendants and one of the three was a ferocious black. None of them had the peaceful, passive expression of Buddha, they reminded me more of the grotesque images of the Hindu temples. I thought perhaps Gyalgen might feel on holy ground and so made no comment, but he did not regard the place with any reverence. Mir Humza looked at it all in a humorous, patronizing way, smiling at us to share his condescension.

It was a long time before we could unearth the care-taker. He lived in a Kazak encampment near the lake and, rather naturally, had not expected visitors in mid-November. As the rooms contained no fire-places and were made entirely of wood, we made our kitchen in the courtyard and built another fire of pine wood to keep us warm. On the hard little stools, we sat in the snow round the fire, the night clear and bright, the invisible idols dominating the atmosphere of their own monastery. The slightly eerie feeling was accentuated through the night by the sounds of snuffling, scratching, and padding feet, all round the buildings. I do not know what animals were about in

search of food. Gyalgen said they were "wild dogs".
Mir Humza said he had heard that there were wild pigs in
the hills. I did not get out of bed to investigate.

We spent one complete day among the hills. On horses
we climbed up above the monastery to a pass. Looking
one way we saw the pine-covered hills protecting the still
blue of the Heavenly Pool, far below us. Bogdo Ola, the
main peak of the little range, was just visible above its
surrounding mountains. On his previous visit Eric had
climbed one of these, but had had no equipment for a serious
attempt on Bogdo itself. Now it was too late in the year
and his frost-bitten foot prevented him. Turning the other
way, on our pass, the hills lost height and the pines disappeared; we saw the distant plains washing away from the
range like a dim, grey sea.

On the fourth day of our little expedition we went down
the hill again to our Kazak friends, and back to Urumchi on
the fifth day. Driving across the open country once more
we passed parties of Kazaks on the move. The men, on
horseback, in their magnificent high hats of fur and brocade, drove their flocks of sheep and cattle before them;
the women, in their white cotton headdresses worn like a
wimple, often rode with a cradle held in front of them on
the saddle; the folded akois and all the household necessities, were loaded on ponies or camels. I am told that the
Kazaks depend on horses more than their Kirghiz cousins.
They eat, converse and spend endless hours in the saddle.
It is a custom inherited from remote ancestors. Some
historians allege that the conception of taming the horse
for riding came from Central Asia; that this led to the
introduction of trousers where hitherto only skirts had
been worn. Certainly the invincible conquerors who
swept out of Central Asia into China, India and Europe,
relied entirely on swift cavalry tactics. Seeing the mounted
Kazak caravans moving to new pastures, history seemed
to melt away and I was watching the nomads of an ancient
time.

On our return to Urumchi, Eric accepted the invitation
of the Soviet doctor to amputate the most obstinate of his
frost-bitten toes, at the first joint. All except one were now

healed, but this first toe remained black and dead. After the operation we waited a few days for the pain to subside, and then began preparations for our return. I was beginning to get restive and Urumchi was beginning to get cold.

On the homeward journey we were still a party of nine but a different party. The police "escort" had never been seen again; we were informed that he had "resigned" his position in Kashgar and was not returning. In his place we were giving a lift to one of the Indian traders from Kashgar who had been to Central China on business. He was a tiny, bird-like Hindu; always elaborately polite and twisted up with flowery speeches in incomprehensible English. Instead of our two guests we had a destitute Turki woman who had pleaded with me to take her and her son back to Kashgar. She wept every time I looked in her direction, and haunted the British Consulate until I made Eric agree to the plan.

On the day of our departure the first serious snow-fall began, and we drove away in a rapidly increasing blizzard. We soon discovered that the Ford had no windscreen wiper. The only solution was for someone to stand on the running-board and wipe the glass continuously. As we left the comparative shelter of the Urumchi hollow the wind raced across the open country and howled dismally round us. All traces of a road were rapidly disappearing. The telegraph poles were a deceptive guide as they wandered far to the left and right of the route; soon there were few other indications that any road existed. In spite of the cold Mir Humza insisted on sitting in his favourite seat on the mudguard, near the radiator. From there he could pick up faint signs of a track, or jump off to search the ground. Eric decided to open the windscreen to save the men and it was severely cold as the wind and snow whirled in. I began to feel there could be no solution to our problem. If we lost the road completely we might drive for miles into the empty desert. It was as difficult to find the way back as to find the road ahead. But if we waited for the storm to die down the tracks would only be more deeply buried. There was nothing to be done but to crawl on, searching for the road. Sometimes Mir Humza ran before us, waving us to the right or the left as he saw half-buried wheel marks. Eric told me to watch for the elusive telegraph poles—at least they indicated the right direction to keep. But they were frequently swallowed up in the mist and snow as they veered away from our path.

The situation seemed dramatic at the time. Mir Humza, bearded, muffled in his sheepskin coat and balaclava, going ahead into the bleak, snow-filled scene, reminded me suddenly of a picture of Captain Oates, which as a child I had hated. But I romanticized our predicament. When reluctant gleams of sun began to pierce the gloom, I felt foolish. Soon the snow fell more lightly and then it stopped altogether. We were now about fifty miles from Urumchi and quite suddenly there was no trace of storm or snow. The past few hours seemed a fantasy.

In the little village of Tapan Cheng we stopped to have lunch in a Chinese restaurant. At first I had been nervous of these places. I brought with me exaggerated ideas of hygiene. But hunger, and interest, began to cure me. I was never consistent about my ideas on cleanliness. In our own house I tried to supervise the boiling of milk and water, a degree of cleaning and scrubbing in the kitchen, but only Gyalgen knows how often the instructions were faithfully carried out. One must take some risks and gradually I took more. It seemed to me that while travelling about I must either stop fussing altogether, or fuss all the time. Eric knew of an American who set off on an Himalayan expedition with all his drinking water. That was logical if he wanted to be one of the whole-time fussers. With only occasional attempts to safeguard Eric and myself against disease, I stopped worrying unduly. I found the Chinese restaurants comparatively clean. As I never mastered the use of chopsticks properly, I used my own spoon which saved me from the uncertainties of Chinese washing-up. But usually I was too hungry to worry about anything else.

Our meal of rice and excellent Chinese cabbage over, we drove on to Toksun, in the Turfan Depression. Following our decision to sleep indoors, we went to the magistrate's Yamen. The magistrate was a pleasant but rather awkward Turki—he seemed worried by the alarming influx of people, until we assured him we only wanted a room for the night. He gave us his office, complete with active rats in the roof.

We sampled the local restaurant for supper. At separate tables sat parties of Chinese soldiers, a large Chinese family and groups of passengers from the commercial lorries. They were all drinking tea or shovelling rice into their mouths, with the little bowls held close and the chopsticks flicking fast. Dim lamps lit the room and the air was heavy with cigarette smoke and the smell of food. At intervals a loud, staccato order was called back to the kitchen and acknowledged equally loudly. It was all oddly familiar; like a third-rate cafe somewhere in England—only somehow distorted like a looking-glass scene.

We made an early start the next day and began the long climb out of the Depression. The Ford seemed to me no worse than usual; it laboured heavily in low gear. At one of our periodical halts for oil and water Mir Humza buried his head in the engine. He emerged looking more harassed than I had ever seen him. He began to shout at the gardener with unusual venom. Then he announced the discovery of a crack in the cylinder head. It was as if he had diagnosed cancer in a dear friend. Dismally we turned back to Toksun, and reluctantly we drove up to the Yamen once more.

After holding a conference it was decided that Mir Humza and the local blacksmith should make an attempt to repair the damage. In the afternoon we drove off once more but we only covered eight miles before the solder melted and all Mir Humza's work was wasted. Highly embarrassed, we returned for the second time to the long-suffering magistrate.

"We will ring up the Paxtons," we decided gaily. But there was no telephone connection between Toksun and Urumchi. There were more deliberations. Finally Mir Humza was sent into Urumchi on a commercial lorry, with a request to the two Englishmen to hand over the new Chevrolet belonging to the British Consulate.

We resigned ourselves to an indefinite wait.

Eric soon began to make inquiries about the possibilities of shooting. The first day of our stay in Toksun we borrowed ponies and rode out to look for duck in a nearby river. We only saw one, far-distant, flight. The country was dusty and dull; the fields empty for the winter; the desert all round seemed anxious to swallow up the meagre cultivated ground as soon as it had the chance.

Clouds of dust and shouts attracted our attention as we rode on, unhopeful now of any duck. Joining the crowd we found the celebrated game of "baiga" in progress. It has been so often and so carefully described that I will only explain it briefly as a fierce contest, on horseback, for the decapitated, degutted carcass of a sheep. This is thrown down amidst the mêlée; as soon as someone has secured it he tucks it under one leg and rides off while the "field" follows in an attempt to drag it from him. In this case the object was to hurl the carcass over a wall and gain a small prize of money. We took up a dangerous stand on the wall, and, amidst a fog of dust, watched the racing, wheeling, struggling horsemen. At intervals the whole field would charge towards the wall and crush up against it, nearly knocking us off. Then with a triumphant shout a man would heave the heavy, limp carcass over the top and the game began afresh.

We found that all this was to celebrate a circumcision. As the celebration dinner was just ready we were invited to join the party. We followed the host to his house feeling self-conscious intruders. There Eric and I were separated. From ineffectual duck shooting I suddenly found myself transferred into the middle of a room full of women. We could not say much to each other but naturally I was eyed with curiosity. I began to feel remarkably untidy and dilapidated among all the ladies in their party clothes. I sipped tea, pecked at pilau with chopsticks, and did what I could with smiles and my few words of Turki. As usual any Turki words were received with astonished delight. In these gatherings there was, as a rule, one woman more quick-witted than the rest. She could follow my strange accent and could "translate" to the others. "*She* says, how many children have you", and then everyone would nod and buzz and repeat the question to one another.

It was a delightfully friendly gesture to ask us in, and we tried to make a small return by offering more prizes in the baiga game. Standing on the wall Eric and Gyalgen constituted themselves as goal posts, and the sheep had to be thrown between them. The contest became more heated; the dust was suffocating; the abuse and advice of the spectators rose to a high pitch; one player had lost his hat and blood trickled from a small cut on his forehead; it was all enormously exciting. I found myself joining in the shouts with vigour and jumping up and down on the wall.

Two more days we spent in Toksun. Expecting the lorry at any moment we did not like to go far afield. I began to loathe our dark, rat-inhabited room. As in many Turki houses the ceiling of the room was merely thin paper pasted across the rafters. I could not convince myself that the scratching rats would not work their way through this and fall down into the room—probably on to my bed. On our second night I insisted on sleeping in a tent in the garden.

On the fifth evening of our stay I walked several miles out on the Urumchi road hoping to meet our new lorry. Eric's toe still did not enable him to walk far. Whenever an engine droned towards me my hopes rose. Each time I was disappointed and finally I wandered back to Toksun again. I had hardly entered our room when excited shouts announced that Mir Humza had arrived after all.

We decided we must garage the Ford in Toksun until we could rescue it with a new cylinder head. The magistrate gave us an empty out-house, and having squeezed the lorry in, with only inches to spare, the place was bricked up. It felt like the burial (half alive) of a friend, and I turned almost with resentment to the unknown Chevrolet. It was a cumbersome machine, heavy and yet small. Its engine was pushed in between the driver's and passenger's seat and behind these there was little space for all our party and baggage. I was afraid we might have to jettison someone; but had not the courage to turn away the Turki woman and her son, who really had the least claim on us. When finally everyone, except Mir Humza, was packed uncomfortably in, I gave him my place and lodged myself on the iron casing of the wheel—which rose immediately in front of the passenger's seat. Like carrying a suit-case the discomfort of this seat seemed negligible at first but grew steadily worse. After seven days my own seat was sore and bruised, my legs cramped and weary and I hated that Chevrolet. I am convinced that it bucked and rolled more uncontrollably than our Ford.

On the return journey I felt more remote from the country than ever. We were all so uncomfortable it was difficult to think of anything but the end of each day, when we could get out of the lorry. In spite of a new machine we were not free from engine troubles—chiefly due to the appalling Chinese petrol. Perhaps the old Ford was hardened to this diet, but the Chevrolet disliked it. Twice during the night time the well-watered petrol froze in the pipes. We waited tedious hours while Mir Humza worked under the lorry with a primus stove.

The day we left Aksu we could only limp a few hundred yards at a time before dirt clogged the flow of petrol. It was exasperating and delayed us badly. When finally Mir Humza cleaned out the tank and strained the filthy-looking petrol, we managed to make better time. We pressed on and on, not even stopping to eat. Then the men saw some gazelle and wasted over an hour chasing them. By now we had collected four bodies on the roof. When the first of these was shot we saw the thin little Hindu merchant heading the race to the kill. Like all good Hindus he was a vegetarian and not allowed to take life. But the excitement of the sport must have affected him, for he flew first across the desert to the fallen gazelle.

Having tied the animal on to the lorry we went on into the darkness. Since the middle of the afternoon a wind-storm had been increasing in violence. Gradually the dust blocked out the hills and the desert, and clouds of it hurtled towards us in a smothering fog. It would have been diffi-cult to pitch tents, impossible to light a fire. So we headed for a small, wayside shelter which we knew lay

about 143 miles from Kashgar. This two-roomed mud hut
had no door but a generous supply of firewood. At 8
o'clock at night we all huddled inside, and while Gyalgen
made tea and a pilau, Eric and I dozed on the floor. Mr.
Yang and the Hindu then suggested that as conditions
indoors and out, were so unpleasant we should cut short
the agony and drive all night. Weakly, we agreed to this.

The Chevrolet was again disapproving of the Chinese
petrol. It was running badly, and half-way through the
night the lights fused. So our progress was again slow.
Hour after weary hour we crawled along. I tried lying in
the back among the baggage and the bodies, but at every
severe bump something descended on my head. Eric left
Mir Humza to drive and succeeded in sleeping soundly,
in spite of the strange bulges and sharp corners underneath,
and the thunderbolts from above.

At last light began to creep into the sky. The wind had
abated and to our delight the Pamirs were clear. The
mountains we had grown to know so well, welcomed us
back to Kashgar—a shining view we did not have again
for over six weeks.

A boy was selling hard-boiled eggs by the roadside near
Artush, and we stopped for breakfast at his home. In
another two hours we drove into the outskirts of the
Kashgar oasis. Even in its winter austerity I felt little
shivers of excitement and delight to see it again. The nearer
we got to the Consulate the more excited I felt. After the
unfamiliar North, South Sinkiang seemed like home. We
were back in a country of trees, of women peeping out from
behind their veils, a strongly Turki country. I had grown
so attached to it; the British Consulate had become so
much my home, that our return felt like a modified version
of a return to England after being abroad.

CHAPTER XIII

The Mongols' Tomb

"I HAVE DISCOVERED SOME-
thing very interesting!" M. Salvarelli the French journalist,
announced excitedly.

At the office of the Administrative Superintendent (the
most senior official in Kashgar and a position then held
by a Turki with a Chinese Assistant) he had heard a remarkable story. Some Mongols of the Karashahr area had long
known of the existence of an ancient Mongolian grave near
Kashgar. It was said that they even had a chart of the place.
Through a trader they had recently petitioned the local
authorities to carry out some excavations for them, and,
above all, to find a certain valued bowl which they claimed
was in the grave. This was all they asked from the
treasure trove which might lie buried. The story seemed
fantastic, but in spite of encroaching Western "civilization", Central Asia is still a land of fantasy. Even the senior
officials hesitated to mock, or was there perhaps a faint
hope of profit to be gained from this particular fairy tale?
We were cynics enough to doubt whether officialdom would
trouble itself to humour distant Mongols for nothing, or
that pure and unadulterated interest in archæology led the
Administrative Superintendent to arrange an expedition

into the desert. It is not the habit of elderly Turkis and
dapper Chinese to go digging in lonely places in the
interests of history.

But the Administrative Superintendent *had* arranged an
expedition to the tomb although he had no idea of its
whereabouts. M. Salvarelli had been invited to go and
Eric, the doctor and I invited ourselves. We asked
Mr. Yang to join the party to interpret for us and to my
surprise Mrs. Yang decided to come too. As requested by
our hosts the five of us reached the Yamen at 7 o'clock one
cold, dark February morning. We found the house was also
dark and everyone was fast asleep! Ruthlessly Mr. Yang
roused the Assistant Administrative Superintendent, a
charming man called Mr. Chu, and he gradually got the
machinery of the house rotating. Lamps were lit; we were
offered sickly sweet cocoa; we waited an hour or two while
the party assembled. M. Salvarelli arrived breathless and
unbreakfasted from the New City; the Administrative
Superintendent appeared calm and dignified two hours
late. Eventually everyone was ready.

We were to go in the official lorry but still we had no
idea *where* we were going. Even the general direction was
doubtful. "But the driver knows," we were told brightly.
So we clambered into the back of the open truck (a very
dilapidated Russian model) where narrow benches had
been arranged and a sheep, two cocks and three Turkis
were already waiting. One of the three was a venerable,
white-turbaned man who looked far too frail for such an
expedition.

Eric and I were intrigued to see which road we would
take out of the town—north, south, east or west. We
started on the road to Urumchi. It was cuttingly cold and
I soon abandoned the waving bench for the floor. I nestled
there with Mr. Chu and the Administrative Superintendent.
Hitherto I had only met the latter at official functions. He was
a stout, pleasant-looking Turki who always seemed a little
bewildered by his position; I had often noticed Mr. Chu giving
him a surreptitious nudge or whispered advice. He seemed
shy and somewhat inattentive but undoubtedly dignified.
On this expedition he revealed unknown characteristics.

As we approached the familiar turn-off to Ishtik Karaul Eric and I began nodding knowingly to one another. The expedition into the unknown was following for us a very well-worn path, as we headed for Ishtik and beyond. As usual we tried to work out an estimate of distance and tried to juggle "potais" and Chinese "li" into good solid miles. We were not very successful because none of the official party was concerned with time or distance—a general direction was now known and that was sufficient. "Well, we must be back by four o'clock," M. Salvarelli announced firmly, "I have an engagement to dine with Mrs. Chao before I leave for Urumchi to-morrow." We thought him optimistic but said nothing and no one else took any interest at all.

We drove on along "Ma's road", every ditch, corner and bump so well known to us; we ground successfully up the most severe of the small passes and sped recklessly down the steep hills. M. Salvarelli had travelled in the lorry before and assured us that it had no brakes. However, we reached Ishtik Karaul where we all got out for lunch. Where do we go from here, Eric and I wondered. At this point the valley forked—to the left lay Kurban's home and the faint continuation of Ma's road; to the right lay the route we had followed when we went, with donkeys, towards the Kara Teke Pass. There is no motor road that way, we said confidently. The driver was undismayed. He was a good driver, he handled his battered truck fiercely and firmly but he was not particular about roads. So we headed for open country and went at it like a determined rider at a difficult fence. The benches rocked and occasionally hurled passengers on top of one another; the cocks and sheep were continuously trodden on and protested loudly. The dignity of the Administrative Superintendent was fading; he alternately whooped and cat-called like a Bank Holiday reveller or screamed at the driver to stop. The driver ignored him. We were seeing the Administrative Superintendent in a new light. He became a small boy either frightened as we crawled at a hideous angle along a hill-side, or hilariously amused at the rolling lurching progress. Sometimes he feigned fear to mock poor Mr. Yang who sat mute and enduring throughout the journey. Whatever his mood Mr. Chu and the Turki attendants smiled indulgently upon him. It was difficult to realize that he was their chief.

Then came the most precipitous hill we had yet encountered—it dropped steeply from a firm gravel plateau into a valley and the last few yards were thick with ice. I was convinced that the driver would flinch at this, but although everyone, except the Administrative Superintendent and the doctor, got out in anxious haste he remained calmly at the wheel. These three stayed in the truck and off it went—rolling and slipping. The rest of us walked down, crossed the valley and climbed up the other side. As we waited on the opposite plateau we watched the truck attack the rise bravely. Standing up in the back, oblivious of the peril, the Administrative Superintendent and the doctor were happily dicing with a couple of knuckle bones salvaged from lunch. But the lorry stuck half-way up the hill. This time, I thought, we are defeated.

We wandered aimlessly on across the grey, empty table-land, more to occupy ourselves than to get anywhere. As far as we, by elaborate questioning and involved translation could gather, we had six more miles to go. But how difficult those six miles would be no one knew, and already it was the middle of the afternoon. M. Salveralli, keenly conscious of his dinner engagement was getting more and more agitated. But even should we turn back now, we could not possibly reach Kashgar by 4 o'clock, we told him. There was nothing to be done, and sympathetic as we felt, with our agitating Western sense of punctuality, no one else was in the least concerned, and we were helpless.

We strolled about, we ate melons; the Administrative Superintendent entertained us with a "parlour trick". Squatting on the ground, in the bleak desert, he placed small stones in two rows and offered to tell me which one I had selected. With great solemnity he worked out his little problem and triumphantly handed me the correct stone. He appeared to be quite unconcerned about our situation and it seemed ill-mannered to fuss in the face of such child-like inconsequence.

Finally we returned to the abandoned lorry and found it

exactly where we had left it. Apparently no one had been
doing anything but smoke and eat melons. So the driver
had admitted defeat after all. But the Administrative
Superintendent had not. Once more he startled us. The
humoured child was gone and in his place was a strong-
willed leader of expeditions. There was no question of
asking us our wishes, no listening to the wails of M.
Salvarelli, we must go *on* said the Administrative Superintendent. It was not a mere whim, it was a serious
matter of religion. If the expedition turned back now it
would be an inauspicious omen, the entire project would
be in danger of failure.

We now learnt that there was more involved in this
expedition than an amateur archæological interest—or
anyone's desire to please obscure Mongols. Chart or no
chart a tomb had already been discovered and digging
begun under the direction of a rich Turki. Whatever their
reasons the officials had sanctioned and assisted the enterprise and we were part of a religious mission bringing holy
blessings, and a supply unit bringing food, for the workers.
The frail old man was a priest; the cocks were to be
sacrificed; the sheep slaughtered for meat. As curious
interlopers, taken out of kindness, we were in no position
to influence the plans of the leaders.

Realizing that the Administrative Superintendent was
determined to go on, we set ourselves to get the lorry up the
slope. It was not a severe one, but the wheels could not
easily grip on the loose stones. By backing down, and trying
a new line, carefully prepared, the driver eventually roared
to the top. We were off again—into empty grey desert.
The surrounding hills were low and unimpressive; there
was no sign of water and very little firewood. Convinced
by now that we would not be returning to Kashgar that
day, I visualized, with some gloom, an exceedingly cold
night in the open with nothing to eat but the mangled
remains of lunch, and no bed-clothes at all. Our hosts
seemed quite unperturbed as we crawled onwards, and the
whole expedition had such an air of light-hearted comedy,
that my fears somehow evaporated.

We rolled, banged, slithered, jolted and lurched with

14

stout perseverance. Only now and again we all got out as the driver negotiated some particularly hair-raising climb or descent. But it had to be very severe before he agreed to let us dismount. If he did not choose to hear anxious cries from the back, we were helpless. I shut my eyes and prayed as we crept down one defile—steep, narrow and rock-strewn. The Administrative Superintendent screamed and shouted more loudly than before. It was incredible that we did not tip forward or strike a stone and crash over sideways.

When not unhappily occupied with such treacherous places, the way seemed long. To amuse ourselves Eric and I taught M. Salvarelli the game of "Twenty Questions". Eric was really too interested in the country to take more than an intermittent part, but M. Salvarelli took a sudden intense interest in the game and he laboured earnestly to track down the answers or to think up an intricate problem for us to solve. Ignoring the drunken progress, unaware of rolling off his seat from time to time, he persevered doggedly. Often Eric and I had forgotten the game when a worried voice would inquire "Is it made of wood?" "Is it visible?" and we would be jerked back to the really serious problem of the day.

It must have been about 5 o'clock when a cloud over the sun and the evening chill were making me once more aware of a cold night ahead, that we turned abruptly into a narrow ravine. We headed down it and above us loomed an impressive rock face pitted with caves. "There is the place" announced one of the Turkis, pointing to a hole about three-quarters of the way up the mountain. We turned round a corner of rock in the defile and to our complete surprise, saw two akois. Quite suddenly we had reached our goal, and here was shelter for the night. We began to feel a little foolish with our time-tables and agitated estimates of distance. The attitude of our hosts seemed eminently sensible. They arranged an expedition to a place in placid indifference to where the place might be. They persisted in their journey, trusting to their driver and attendants, and now here we were. I suppose one or more of the attendants had already visited the place on horseback—

the way *was* known but not surveyed for a lorry. We should have reached it much more quickly on horses. I wish I could cultivate a little more of this passive attitude. My travelling is so often marred by useless anxiety, by harassed anticipation of disasters and dangers which never materialize.

Everyone at the camp was very pleased to see us—the men working on the excavations and the Kirghiz who owned the akois. A smiling woman seized Mrs. Yang and me by the hand, leading us into her tent she insisted upon removing my boots with little coos of welcome.

We all decided to visit the diggings at once and a long string of people started up the rough little track. Eric, the doctor, M. Salvarelli and I were soon in the lead—it was only a short steep climb to the mouth of the cave. Below me I watched the Yang family struggling valiantly, on what was probably the first climb they had ever attempted. Groaning and puffing, the Administrative Superintendent followed them, assisted by Mr. Chu and various attendants. For all of them it must have been a new and energetic experience. Not waiting for everyone to arrive we plunged into the tomb. We had to crawl on our hands and knees into a dark tunnel which dropped almost immediately into unknown depths. I knew I should dislike the restricted darkness, and as a panic of claustrophobia seized me I crawled out backwards into daylight. According to Eric the first drop brought them to a narrow ledge and a hole leading farther into the earth. They explored as far as possible but there was little to be seen. Outside the cave we were shown a small, worn, wooden bowl and a few tattered pieces of material—the only "finds" to date. I did not think the Mongols would be content with that little bowl. However, the diggers were still optimistic and the priest and the cocks having been dragged up the hill, all was ready for the sacrifice which would bless and favour their work.

Finding the tomb and the "treasure" something of an anti-climax, we decided to explore the fascinating country round us. Eric and I, with M. Salvarelli and the doctor went climbing on up the mountain in search of other, if less sensational caves. It was good, hard rock; with Eric's help I followed where he led and we came to a vast, natural cave, thick with pigeons' droppings. It was a high, wide opening, not leading very deeply into the hill. Having clambered about for a time the doctor and I went down for tea while Eric and M. Salvarelli returned to the tomb once more.

As well as the sad little discoveries we had seen, they were shown two human skulls dug from the tomb. I wish some of us had had sufficient knowledge to be able to date the discoveries, even roughly. They might well be interesting material for the experts. But they were very inadequate and it was increasingly obvious that the unusual enterprise had only been undertaken in the naïve hope of finding "treasure". The sacrifice at the cave entrance; the talk of visions seen by a small girl, all added to the fascination of our expedition, but solid facts were melting away. I must admit I was becoming somewhat flippant about the expedition as far as serious discoveries were concerned, but nevertheless it was good to feel that little girls still see visions in which grown-up men solemnly believe; that elderly officials are willing to plunge into unknown country to hunt for hidden gold and that the blood of a cock gives them confidence in their success. Perhaps I sound patronizing. I had no right to be and one remarkable fact still remained unexplained, to lend accuracy to the original story. How had the excavators discovered this particular burial place in this remote cave? Perhaps there really was an ancient chart after all?

Sitting in the akoi drinking tea and eating painfully hot kababs off a skewer, put caves and buried treasure out of my mind. Small pieces of mutton (from the freshly slaughtered sheep) were roasted over the fire to a delicious, crisp brown. Having eaten myself full and covered myself with fat, I discovered that the kababs were only an appetizer and that supper was yet to come! To recover from this Eric and I went for a short walk in the greyness of evening. The sun had gone, it was cold and, beyond the akois, startlingly lonely. The mountain of many caves hung above us and in that rocky, treeless country it was very quiet.

Back in the akoi sheep's bones bubbled in the central

cauldron and we all sat in a circle waiting for supper. The little seer came in to tell her story once more. But translated from Turki to Chinese, from Chinese to English, the significance seemed to evaporate; we were left with a pitiful jumble of nonsense. Then we attacked the sheep again; ate chunks of mutton, dipped bread into bowls of broth and forgot all about our previous hearty meal of kababs. Mr. Yang abhorred mutton in every form; he disliked the taste, the smell, the very thought of it. So he nibbled bread sadly and with resignation. The whole expedition was an ordeal for him. The terrors of the drive, the exhaustion of the climb, the barbarity of a night in an akoi and finally, the mutton. He endured it all with stoic calm. His wife entered into the adventure with unexpected enthusiasm and vigour. Chinese ladies do not venture out into the wilds as a rule. M. Salvarelli was still worrying about his broken engagement and his distress had run like a theme song throughout the day.

At last we were filled and the remains were handed out to the excavators, the Administrative Superintendent's staff and the Kirghiz. Shortly afterwards the Administrative Superintendent prepared for bed. Once more like a little boy, his men tenderly tucked him up in blankets, and with the ease of a tired child he fell asleep. The rest of us sat round the dying fire until it was decided that we should all go to bed. The wall of quilts and rugs behind us was broken and a soft bed for seven was prepared. In a curving row, M. Salvarelli, the doctor, the Yangs, Mr. Chu, Eric and I lay down. I do not know what happened to the owners of the akoi. A chattering and a clattering, long after we had retired, suggested that they were arranging a temporary shelter in the lorry.

It was cold at first, and the mountain of heavy covers made it difficult to sleep. The Administrative Superintendent snored rhythmically and the three Chinese talked for a long time. I never learnt to like the sound of the staccato monosyllables of their language. M. Salvarelli suddenly revived his interest in Twenty Questions, and through a haze of sleep I struggled to ask intelligent ones. Neither Eric nor I made any headway, and what hope had we when M. Salvarelli had thought of "the iron in spinach"?

Woken occasionally by the bark of a watch dog or a selection of snores, on the whole I slept well. About 7 a.m. Eric suggested that we all get up, although our hosts seemed content to linger indefinitely. Gradually, dishevelled bodies rose from the communal bed; a candle flickered, the fire was lit, and the day began. We had tea and were offered some mutton. As we had brought a small picnic basket with us we still had some remnants of bread, butter and jam to save us from congealed meat in the early morning. The Western custom of serving certain specified foods and dishes for each meal is not strictly followed in the East. Roughly the same menu is eaten for every meal, and Eric was once even offered sea slugs at 5 a.m. by a generous Chinese host.

We left at about 9.30 waving a friendly farewell to the Kirghiz and the excavators. Having come unprepared to meet any Kirghiz I had little to give the kind woman who had greeted us. I offered her the hand-mirror from my bag which seemed to be a success. Blessed and encouraged I hope the workers had new vigour for their digging. What they found we have never heard.

The return journey was comparatively quick. We took a slightly different route and avoided some of the more difficult climbs by bumping down a dry river bed. Once or twice we stopped and at each halt we ate melons—very often expertly cut in the correct Turki way, by the Administrative Superintendent himself. We saw two eagles, motionless and proud on a crag, which Mr. Chu was keen to shoot. He was keen to shoot anything and during one of the halts suddenly lay down for a little target practice. Gazelle in the distance caused excitement, and Eric tried to aim as we rattled along in the back of the lorry. Just as he had them sighted, and was about to fire, for some unknown reason the driver opened his door and the view was blocked.

Wistful and silent the old priest bumped and rolled without a murmur. But suddenly he broke into a chant-like song and was transformed into quite a different person. The quiet old man became a forceful performer holding the

stage. His face reddened, his veins stood up with the effort
of his tremendous song which was very long, melancholy
and loud. Although he quavered on the higher notes, he
sang passionately and undaunted with a strength that was
astonishing. I thought it was a deeply religious hymn but
we were told that it was a song about a mother. It seemed
incongruous in the noisy lorry but the weird noise suited the
bare scenery of Central Asia and the fantasy of our sudden,
unplanned expedition. The four Europeans then sang a
chorus—loudly and far less appealingly. We knew that
Mr. Yang was an enthusiast of Chinese opera so persuaded
him to sing us an operatic song—strange wavering music
even less understandable than the Turki chant.

M. Salvarelli, the doctor, Eric and I then played another
childish game which lasted until we reached Kashgar.
Choosing a letter of the alphabet, we had in turn to supply
a town, country, river or mountain, anywhere in the world,
which began with that letter. By now we had all abandoned
the benches and were rolling like marbles in the empty
lorry. This did not interfere with the seriousness of our
game and if ever we showed signs of flagging, M. Salvarelli
goaded us on again. He never by any chance won, his
geography was weak, but his enthusiasm was inexhaustible
and he attacked each new letter with vigour. Even as we
drove into the Consulate, he was supplying yet another
river beginning with S.

We got back in time for lunch to the great relief of the
staff. Lhakpa and Gyalgen assured us that they had been
up nearly all night—keeping dinner hot, worrying about
our lack of food and bedding, imagining every sort of
accident and catastrophe. At 5 a.m. they had got up and
had been hoping for our arrival, or at any rate for some
news of us, ever since.

It had proved a comedy expedition rather than a dramatic
discovery of hidden treasure or ancient remains. But, however abortive our search for serious archæological "finds",
we had been rewarded with much laughter, some interesting
country and a little fantasy.

Epilogue

WHEN WRITING THIS BOOK in the peaceful isolation of Kashgar, I had intended to finish it with a chapter about my return journey to England, having always planned to leave before Eric. The quickest route home is through Russia—a route Lady Macartney and her children had always followed and one I was interested to see. I duly applied for a visa. Without any explanation this was refused. I then decided to return via the Gilgit road, and as all communication with Srinagar was cut, owing to the troubles which had broken out in October 1947, I planned to travel from Gilgit, through Chitral and Peshawar. I should be in Mussulman country all the way, but even the Pakistan Government had little control over the roaming tribesmen of the border hills. Once again there was the harassing uncertainty of a road menaced by men on the watch for loot, and men with little respect for nationality or diplomatic etiquette. I decided to risk these dangers and to leave in early May when the passes should be open.

Then in March, Mr. and Mrs. Paxton came to Kashgar on their official tour of South Sinkiang. They came with a suggestion that I return to Urumchi with them and from there get a free and secure lift to Shanghai in an American aeroplane, due shortly to make a flight up to the capital. I had never flown and had always refused to consider returning via China. But this kind offer of quick transport, with all my luggage, as opposed to the long and perhaps dangerous journey to India, overcame my prejudices. Still hesitating, very reluctant and with a variety of emotions pulling me in opposite directions, I finally left Kashgar in April 1948.

For the third time I bumped along the Urumchi road. Only this time, with American love of speed, we completed the thousand miles in six and a half days. I waited three weeks in Urumchi and there was no sign of the American aeroplane. Finally my patience evaporated and I booked a seat on one of the aeroplanes of the Chinese line, which used to run a fortnightly service from Shanghai. It was not a comfortable experience, flying for two days in a roughly equipped Dakota, one's back to a tiny round window, the luggage (and we were only allowed 30 lb. per person) strapped down the middle of the plane and a number of very ill Chinese travelling companions. It was relieved by visits to the pilot's cabin where at intervals I was invited by the friendly American pilot. From there I had a magnificent view of the vast, lonely country below as we crossed deserts and mountains, or of the checkered green cultivation of China. I gazed down with interested awe on to Communist-held territory—it looked exactly the same as the rest of the country.

I do not think I shall learn to like flying—and in contrast to my journey *to* Kashgar, my return felt depressingly detached from reality. Even the comforts of the better air lines I travelled by later, were small compensation for this feeling of artificiality. Dropping rapidly down to a place after six or eight hours of idle emptiness, much of the value and significance one feels after the slow approach of a twenty-milem arch is lost. I was glad to have the opportunity to see Shanghai, Hong Kong and later Bangkok, but I should still prefer to reach them more slowly, travelling by land or sea. The return to civilization was too sudden to be anything but very confusing. I like savouring first one excitement and then another as one comes gradually back to simple luxuries one has missed, such as electric light, a proper bathroom, a daily post. By air the transitions are altogether too abrupt.

The number of people who now travel by air, and the familiarity of the places I saw, make an account of my flight home a very ordinary story. For me there was novelty, anxiety, small personal problems to solve and loneliness. But as a journey to record it lacks originality and interest. I had to wait four days in Shanghai for a passage to Hong Kong, two days in Hong Kong for a passage to Bangkok, and eventually came home to England on the normal B.O.A.C. route. Only the charm of Hong Kong island with its rich flowers and vegetation, the delight of seeing the sea again, the brilliant sugar cake temples and massive bronze Buddhas of Bangkok, the golden finger of Rangoon's great pagoda are a valued memory. Except for the final delight of landing on Southampton Water, the journey is a grey haze of feeling very sick. My travels of many hundreds of miles from Central Asia, across so many countries, ended in comic anti-climax. I finished the final forty miles to my home in a local bus. My ears and head still throbbing from the aeroplane, I listened to the country people placidly discussing the weather and the crops, saw the fresh green of English fields and trees, and a mist of tears confused me as I returned home.

Now England is familiar once more. I again want grey desolation, vast emptiness, lonely ice mountains, and now they are more remote than ever. So many of the places we knew and loved are now places of battle and distress. Kashmir is clutched by war. Even in Ladakh there is fighting and to Leh has come the noise and ugliness of aeroplanes. Above all others Ladakh seemed to me a remote land of peaceful contentment. But everywhere there is discord; more and more frontiers are closing and the future looks bleak for travel.

This book, begun in a place where time was unrestricted, has had to be finished in the harassing domestic routine of a child and a house. It is difficult to think of two existences more different. How often I long to see Rosa Beg's cheerful face and to hear Gyalgen explaining with elaborate reason why he has used up the week's butter ration.

But one must go forward to new experiences, only looking back in deep appreciation of the interest, the fun, the beauty, the novelty and the hazard one has had in a past experience. The story of Kashgar is finished.

THE END

Some other Oxford Paperbacks for readers interested in Central Asia, China and South-east Asia, past and present

CAMBODIA

GEORGE COEDÈS
Angkor

MALCOLM MacDONALD
Ankor and the Khmers*

CENTRAL ASIA

PETER FLEMING
Bayonets to Lhasa

ANDRÉ GUIBAUT
Tibetan Venture

LADY MACARTNEY
An English Lady in
Chinese Turkestan

DIANA SHIPTON
The Antique Land

C. P. SKRINE AND
PAMELA NIGHTINGALE
Macartney at Kashgar*

ALBERT VON LE COQ
Buried Treasures of
Chinese Turkestan

AITCHEN K. WU
Turkistan Tumult

CHINA

All About Shanghai:
A Standard Guide

HAROLD ACTON
Peonies and Ponies

VICKI BAUM
Shanghai '37

ERNEST BRAMAH
Kai Lung's Golden
Hours*

ERNEST BRAMAH
The Wallet of Kai Lung*

ANN BRIDGE
The Ginger Griffin

CHANG HSIN-HAI
The Fabulous Concubine*

CARL CROW
Handbook for China

PETER FLEMING
The Siege at Peking

MARY HOOKER
Behind the Scenes in Peking

CORRINNE LAMB
The Chinese Festive Board

W. SOMERSET MAUGHAM
On a Chinese Screen*

G. E. MORRISON
An Australian in China

DESMOND NEILL
Elegant Flower

PETER QUENNELL
A Superficial Journey
through Tokyo and Peking

OSBERT SITWELL
Escape with Me! An Oriental
Sketch-book

J. A. TURNER
Kwang Tung or Five Years in
South China

HONG KONG AND MACAU

AUSTIN COATES
City of Broken Promises

AUSTIN COATES
A Macao Narrative

AUSTIN COATES
Myself a Mandarin

AUSTIN COATES
The Road

The Hong Kong Guide 1893

INDONESIA

S. TAKDIR ALISJAHBANA
Indonesia: Social and
Cultural Revolution

DAVID ATTENBOROUGH
Zoo Quest for a Dragon*

VICKI BAUM
A Tale from Bali*

'BENGAL CIVILIAN'
Rambles in Java and the
Straits in 1852

MIGUEL COVARRUBIAS
Island of Bali*

BERYL DE ZOETE AND
WALTER SPIES
Dance and Drama in Bali

AUGUSTA DE WIT
Java: Facts and Fancies

JACQUES DUMARÇAY
Borobudur

JACQUES DUMARÇAY
The Temples of Java

ANNA FORBES
Unbeaten Tracks in Islands of
the Far East

GEOFFREY GORER
Bali and Angkor

JENNIFER LINDSAY
Javanese Gamelan

EDWIN M. LOEB
Sumatra: Its History and
People

MOCHTAR LUBIS
The Outlaw and Other Stories

MOCHTAR LUBIS
Twilight in Djakarta

MADELON H. LULOFS
Coolie*

MADELON H. LULOFS
Rubber

COLIN McPHEE
A House in Bali*

ERIC MJOBERG
Forest Life and Adventures in
the Malay Archipelago

HICKMAN POWELL
The Last Paradise

E. R. SCIDMORE
Java, Garden of the East

MICHAEL SMITHIES
Yogyakarta: Cultural
Heart of Indonesia

LADISLAO SZÉKELY
Tropic Fever: The Adventures
of a Planter in Sumatra

EDWARD C. VAN NESS AND
SHITA PRAWIROHARDJO
Javanese Wayang Kulit

MALAYSIA

ISABELLA L. BIRD
The Golden Chersonese:
Travels in Malaya in 1879

MARGARET BROOKE
THE RANEE OF SARAWAK
My Life in Sarawak

HENRI FAUCONNIER
The Soul of Malaya

W. R. GEDDES
Nine Dayak Nights

A. G. GLENISTER
The Birds of the Malay

Peninsula, Singapore and
Penang

C. W. HARRISON
Illustrated Guide to the
Federated Malay States
(1923)

BARBARA HARRISSON
Orang-Utan

TOM HARRISSON
World Within: A Borneo
Story

CHARLES HOSE
The Field-Book of a
Jungle-Wallah

EMILY INNES
The Chersonese with the
Gilding Off

W. SOMERSET MAUGHAM
Ah King and Other Stories*

W. SOMERSET MAUGHAM
The Casuarina Tree*

MARY McMINNIES
The Flying Fox*

ROBERT PAYNE
The White Rajahs of Sarawak

OWEN RUTTER
The Pirate Wind

ROBERT W. SHELFORD
A Naturalist in Borneo

CARVETH WELLS
Six Years in the Malay Jungle

SINGAPORE

RUSSELL GRENFELL
Main Fleet to Singapore

R. W. E. HARPER AND HARRY
MILLER
Singapore Mutiny

JANET LIM
Sold for Silver

G. M. REITH
Handbook to Singapore
(1907)

C. E. WURTZBURG
Raffles of the Eastern Isles

THAILAND

CARL BOCK
Temples and Elephants

REGINALD CAMPBELL
Teak-Wallah

MALCOLM SMITH
A Physician at the Court of
Siam

ERNEST YOUNG
The Kingdom of the Yellow
Robe

Titles marked with an asterisk have restricted rights.

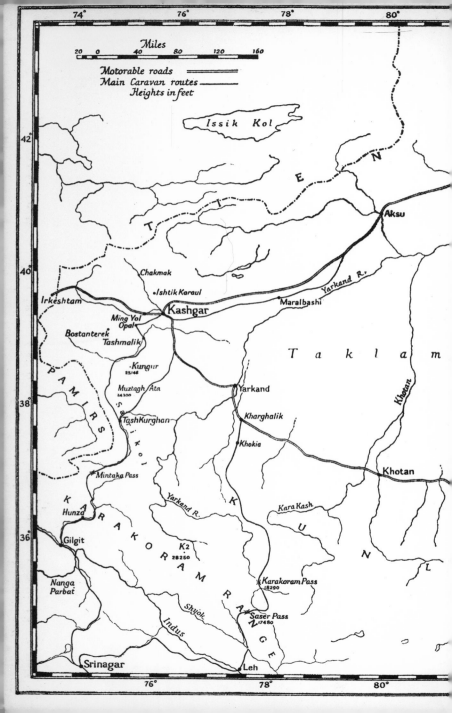